SOCIOLOGICAL THEORY AND THE QUESTION OF RELIGION

Religion lies near the heart of the classical sociological tradition, yet it no longer occupies the same place within the contemporary sociological enterprise. This relative absence has left sociology under-prepared for thinking about religion's continuing importance in new issues, movements, and events in the twenty-first century. This book seeks to address this lacunae by offering a variety of theoretical perspectives on the study of religion that bridge the gap between mainstream concerns of sociologists and the sociology of religion.

Following an assessment of the current state of the field, the authors develop an emerging critical perspective within the sociology of religion with particular focus on the importance of historical background. Re-assessing the themes of aesthetics, listening and different degrees of spiritual self-discipline, the authors draw on ethnographic studies of religious involvement in Norway and the UK. They highlight the importance of power in the sociology of religion with help from Pierre Bourdieu, Marx and Critical Discourse Analysis. This book points to emerging currents in the field and offers a productive and lively way forward, not just for sociological theory of religion, but for the sociology of religion more generally.

THEOLOGY AND RELIGION IN INTERDISCIPLINARY PERSPECTIVE
SERIES IN ASSOCIATION WITH THE
BSA SOCIOLOGY OF RELIGION STUDY GROUP

BSA Sociology of Religion Study Group Series editor:
Pink Dandelion and the publications committee

Theology and Religion in Interdisciplinary Perspective Series editors:
Douglas Davies and Richard Fenn

The British Sociological Association Sociology of Religion Study Group began in 1975 and provides the primary forum in Britain for scholarship in the sociology of religion. The nature of religion remains of key academic interest and this series draws on the latest worldwide scholarship in compelling and coherent collections on critical themes. Secularisation and the future of religion; gender; the negotiation and presentation of religious identities, beliefs and values; and the interplay between group and individual in religious settings are some of the areas addressed. Ultimately, these books reflect not just on religious life but on how wider society is affected by the enduring religious framing of human relationships, morality and the nature of society itself.

Other titles published in the BSA Sociology of Religion Study Group series

Christianity in the Modern World
Changes and Controversies
Edited by Giselle Vincett and Elijah Obinna with Elizabeth Olson and Afe Adogame

Religion and Knowledge
Edited by Sylvia Collins-Mayo and Pink Dandelion

Religion and Youth
Edited by Sylvia Collins-Mayo and Pink Dandelion

Exploring Religion and the Sacred in a Media Age
Edited by Christopher Deacy and Elisabeth Arweck

Religion and the Individual
Belief, Practice, Identity
Edited by Abby Day

Sociological Theory and the Question of Religion

Edited by

ANDREW MCKINNON and MARTA TRZEBIATOWSKA
University of Aberdeen, UK

ASHGATE

© Andrew McKinnon and Marta Trzebiatowska 2014

All rights reserved. No part of this publication may be reproduced, stored in a retrieval system or transmitted in any form or by any means, electronic, mechanical, photocopying, recording or otherwise without the prior permission of the publisher.

Andrew McKinnon and Marta Trzebiatowska have asserted their right under the Copyright, Designs and Patents Act, 1988, to be identified as the editors of this work.

Published by
Ashgate Publishing Limited
Wey Court East
Union Road
Farnham
Surrey, GU9 7PT
England

Ashgate Publishing Company
110 Cherry Street
Suite 3-1
Burlington, VT 05401-3818
USA

www.ashgate.com

British Library Cataloguing in Publication Data
A catalogue record for this book is available from the British Library

The Library of Congress has cataloged the printed edition as follows:
Sociological theory and the question of religion / edited by Andrew McKinnon and Marta Trzebiatowska.
    pages cm. -- (Theology and religion in interdisciplinary perspective series in association with the BSA Sociology of Religion Study Group)
  Includes index.
  ISBN 978-1-4094-6551-5 (hardcover) -- ISBN 978-1-4094-6552-2 (ebook) -- ISBN 978-1-4094-6553-9 (epub) 1. Religion and sociology. I. McKinnon, Andrew, editor.

BL60.S6255 2014
306.6--dc23

2014016695

ISBN 9781409465515 (hbk)
ISBN 9781409465522 (ebk – PDF)
ISBN 9781409465539 (ebk – ePUB)

Printed in the United Kingdom by Henry Ling Limited, at the Dorset Press, Dorchester, DT1 1HD

Contents

List of Contributors   *vii*

Introduction: Thinking Theoretically in the Sociology of Religion   1
   Andrew McKinnon and Marta Trzebiatowska

PART I: THE STATE OF THE ART AND SCIENCE OF THE SOCIOLOGY OF RELIGION

1   Thinking Sociologically about Religion: A Step Change in the Debate?   19
     Grace Davie

2   What Sort of Social Theory Would Benefit the Sociology of Religion?   33
     Steve Bruce

PART II: HISTORY AND RELIGION

3   The Axial Age Religions: The Debate and its Legacy for Contemporary Sociology   51
     Bryan S. Turner

4   Hope and Religion   75
     David Lehmann

5   The Sacramental Mechanism: Religion and the Civilizing Process in Christian Western Europe with Particular Reference to the Peace of God Movement and its Aftermath   105
     Andrew McKinnon

PART III: RELIGION AND MODERNITY

6   Religion and Monetary Culture in the Sociology of
    Georg Simmel   129
    Dominika Motak

7   Putting Baby Back in the Bath: Theorising Modernity for the
    Contemporary Sociology of Religion   151
    Andrew Dawson

PART IV: ETHNOGRAPHIES OF LISTENING TO CHURCHES: AESTHETICS AND RATIONALITY

8   Playing the Sensual Card in Churches: Studying the
    Aestheticization of Religion   179
    Anne Margit Løvland and Pål Repstad

9   Listening Subjects, Rationality and Modernity   199
    Anna Strhan

PART V: POWER, GENDER AND DISCOURSE

10 Critical Discourse Analysis and Critical Sociology of Religion 223
    Titus Hjelm

11 Beyond Habitus: Researching Gender and Religion through the
    Ontology of Social Relations   243
    Marta Trzebiatowska

Index   261

List of Contributors

Steve Bruce was born in Edinburgh in 1954 and educated at the Queen Victoria School, Dunblane, Perthshire. He studied sociology and religious studies at the University of Stirling. He taught at the Queen's University, Belfast, from 1978 to 1991 when he became Professor of Sociology at the University of Aberdeen. In 2003 he was elected a Fellow of the British Academy and in 2005 he was elected a Fellow of the Royal Society of Edinburgh. He has published some 140 articles in journals and edited collections. His 24 books include *God Save Ulster: The Religion and Politics of Paisleyism* (Oxford 1986); *Religion in the Modern World: From Cathedrals to Cults* (Oxford 1996); *Conservative Protestant Politics* (Oxford 1998); *Choice and Religion: A Critique of Rational Choice Theory* (Oxford 2000); *Fundamentalism* (Polity 2001); *God is Dead: Secularization in the West* (Blackwell 2002); *Politics and Religion* (Polity 2003); *Paisley* (Oxford 2007), *The Theory of Secularization* (Oxford 2010) and *Scottish Gods* (Edinburgh 2014).

Grace Davie is Professor Emeritus in the Sociology of Religion at the University of Exeter UK and a senior adviser to the Impact of Religion Research Programme at Uppsala University. She is a past-president of the American Association for the Sociology of Religion (2003) and of the Research Committee 22 (Sociology of Religion) of the International Sociological Association (2002–6). In 2000–1 she was the Kerstin-Hesselgren Professor at Uppsala, where she returned for extended visits in 2006–7, 2010 and 2012. In January 2008, she received an honorary degree from Uppsala. She has also held visiting appointments at the Ecole Pratique des Hautes Etudes (1996) and at the Ecole des Hautes Etudes en Sciences Sociales (1998 and 2003), both in Paris. In addition to numerous chapters and articles, she is the author of *Religion in Britain since 1945* (Blackwell 1994), *Religion in Modern Europe* (Oxford University Press 2000), *Europe: The Exceptional Case* (DLT 2002) and *The Sociology of Religion* (Sage 2007/2013); she is the co-author of *Religious America, Secular Europe* (Ashgate 2008), and co-editor of *Predicting Religion* (Ashgate 2003) and *Welfare and Religion in 21st Century Europe* (2 vols) (Ashgate 2010 and 2011).

Andrew Dawson is Senior Lecturer in the Department of Politics, Philosophy and Religion at Lancaster University, UK. He obtained his doctorate at Oxford University and has degrees in social science and religious studies from US and other UK institutions. His principal research interest concerns the interface of religion and late-modern society. Among his more recent publications are: *Sociology of Religion* (2011), *Santo Daime: A New World Religion* (2013), (as editor) *Summoning the Spirits* (2011) and *The Politics and Practice of Religious Diversity* (forthcoming), and (as co-editor) *Religion, Migration and Mobility: The Brazilian Experience* (forthcoming).

Titus Hjelm is Lecturer in Finnish Society and Culture at University College London, UK. His publications include *Social Constructionisms* (Palgrave 2014), *Religion and Social Problems* (ed., Routledge 2011), *Studying Religion and Society: Sociological Self-Portraits* (ed. with Phil Zuckerman, Routledge 2013). In addition, he has published several books in Finnish and articles in journals such as *Critical Sociology*, *Social Compass*, *Religion* and *Journal of Contemporary Religion*. He is the co-editor of the *Journal of Religion in Europe* (published by Brill) and the founding chair of the American Academy of Religion's Sociology of Religion Group.

David Lehmann is Emeritus Reader in Social Science at the University of Cambridge. His main works are *Democracy and Development in Latin America: Economics, Politics and Religion in the Post War Period* (1990), *Struggle for the Spirit: Popular Culture and Religious Transformation in Brazil and Latin America* (1996) and (with Batia Siebzehner) *Remaking Israeli Judaism* (2006). In 2007 he began to work on multiculturalism and affirmative action policies in Brazil, Mexico and Peru, while also working on secularism. His new research is on Judaism in the Pentecostal imaginary, based on a study of Brazilian Pentecostals and on messianic Jews in Brazil, Israel and London.

Anne Margit Løvland, dr. art., is Associate Professor at the Department of Nordic and Media Studies, University of Agder, Norway. She has published several social semiotic studies in Norwegian on multimodality, especially in schools and religious settings, for instance Christmas concerts in churches. Her publications in English include 'Social Meaning in Multimodal Student Texts', in Maj Asplund Carlsson, Anne Løvland and Gun Malmgren (eds), *Multimodality: Text, Culture and Use. Proceedings from the 2nd International Conference on Multimodality* (2005).

Andrew McKinnon is Senior Lecturer in Sociology and Director of Postgraduate Studies in the School of Social Science at the University of Aberdeen. His research interests include: classical sociological theory, historical sociology and the sociology of religion, and he has done empirical research on conflicts in the Anglican Communion (with Christopher Brittain). His publications include contributions to: *Sociological Theory*, *Sociology of Religion*, *The Journal for the Scientific Study of Religion*, *Sociology* and *The Journal of Contemporary Religion*.

Dominika Motak is Associate Professor at the Institute for the Study of Religions of the Jagiellonian University in Kraków. She has published two books dealing with the sociology of religion: *Modernity and Fundamentalism* (2002) and *Between Transcendence and Immanence: Religion in Georg Simmel's Thought* (2013). She has also co-edited (with Ralph W. Hood) *Ritual: New Approaches and Practice Today* (2011) and translated books of Max Weber and Niklas Luhmann. She is a member of editorial board of *Religion in Austria* and former vice-editor of *Studia Religiologica*. She is focusing on the classic conceptualisations of religion and its modern transformations.

Pål Repstad, dr. philos., Professor in Sociology of Religion at University of Agder, Norway. He has published extensively in Norwegian on changes in mainstream religion in the Nordic countries, on relations between theology and sociology and on qualitative methods. His publications in English include articles and reviews in *Journal of Contemporary Religion*, the edited book *Religion and Modernity – Modes of Co-Existence* (1996) and *An Introduction to the Sociology of Religion* (2006, with Inger Furseth). He is editor of the *Nordic Journal of Religion and Society*, and is an honorary doctor at Uppsala University, Sweden.

Anna Strhan is a Leverhulme Early Career Fellow in the Department of Religious Studies at the University of Kent. She has conducted ethnographic fieldwork on evangelical Christianity in London, and is currently working on a three-year project examining the significance of childhood and parenting in British evangelicalism in different contexts ranging from everyday family and church life, formal and informal educational contexts, to wider public debates about childhood and education concerned with the place of religion and secularity in contemporary society. She is the author of *Levinas, Subjectivity, Education: Towards an Ethics of Radical Responsibility* (2012).

Marta Trzebiatowska is Lecturer in Sociology at the University of Aberdeen. She studied sociology at the University of Exeter. Her doctorate (2007) investigated the social construction of femininities in contemporary Catholic convents in Poland. Her research interests include religion, gender and sexuality, migration, and social theory. She has published in the *Journal of Contemporary Religion*, *European Journal of Women's Studies*, *Sociology*, *Feminist Theology*, and *Fieldwork in Religion*. Her first book, *Why Are Women More Religious Than Men?* (Oxford 2012, co-written with Steve Bruce) critiques competing theories of women's greater religiosity.

Bryan S. Turner is the Presidential Professor of Sociology and the Director of the Committee on Religion at the Graduate Center at the City University of New York, and concurrently Director of the Centre for Society and Religion at the Australian Catholic University (Melbourne). He was the Alona Evans Distinguished Visiting Professor of Sociology at Wellesley College (2009–10). His publications in the sociology of religion include *Weber and Islam* (1974), *Religion and Social Theory* (1983), (with Kamaludeen and Pereira) *Muslims in Singapore* (2010), *Religion and Modern Society* (2011) and *The Religious and the Political* (2013). He edited the *New Blackwell Companion to the Sociology of Religion* (2010).

Introduction
Thinking Theoretically in the Sociology of Religion

Andrew McKinnon and Marta Trzebiatowska

In the classical sociological tradition, the analysis of religion lies – if not at the very heart of the entire enterprise, as it does in Weber and in the late Durkheim – then as the fundamental starting point, as it is in Marx. The recent 'post-secular turn' in social theory notwithstanding, religion no longer occupies the same privileged location within the sociological enterprise (though it is undoubtedly more marginal in Britain compared to North America). While this development is not entirely inexplicable, the gaps that have been left behind has left the discipline as a whole under-prepared for thinking about religion in the wake of new issues, movements and events that have reminded us that religion is far from a spent force in the world (Chapter 1, this volume).

If religion has been marginalised within the mainstream of the discipline, we have often found ourselves distressed by the limited engagement on the part of sociologists of religion with fundamental issues of sociological theory, many colleagues seeming to prefer studying religion as a phenomenon that demands attention, but which can be studied without being overly concerned about reflection on other aspects of social life or indeed with the social whole in which religion is located. In short, the sociology of religion often seems bereft of sociological theory. The increasing disengagement of sociology of religion from the 'mainstream' of the discipline (again, a phenomenon much more marked in the English-speaking world in Britain than in North America) seemed to us intellectually disastrous for the sub-discipline, and was the major impetus for both the conference from which these chapters stem, and the present volume in equal measure.

In this introduction we locate religion at the heart of the classical sociological enterprise, turning our attention in particular to the work of Marx, Weber and Durkheim. While we would not want this to be treated as the sum total of sociology's classical inheritance, even on the question of religion, we find this a good place to begin. We then discuss the challenge which provided the impetus to the theme of the conference from which this volume derives. Sociology of religion in Britain, in moving from an endeavour largely located in social science departments to one that is now based primarily in theology and religious studies departments, has benefitted from this move, but also faces a significant challenge in terms of both theory and methods. While we do not find ourselves in wholesale agreement with Bruce's provocative diagnosis of the problem in this volume, we do nevertheless recognise that it is a problem that needs to be addressed. We conclude the chapter with a brief overview of the contributions in the chapters of this volume to putting sociology of religion on a firm footing.

Religion in Sociology's Core Classics

In retrospect, it is somewhat difficult to see why those figures, whose work has come to define the classical tradition in sociology, placed the understanding of religion, its sources, operation and consequences, at the centre of their respective intellectual projects, though it is notable that this is much more true of the writers working in non-English-speaking contexts. By contrast, in the United States, the core problematic was more likely to be shaped by concerns over the disorder of urban modernity (Connell 1997), even if the discipline was markedly shaped by Christians, and was a travelling companion of the reforming spirit of liberal theology. Britain's greatest contribution to classical sociological thought in the nineteenth century, Herbert Spencer was not particularly interested in the question of religion; here the discipline as a whole has been much more shaped by its post-war expansion, when social inequality in the context of an expanding welfare state came to form its overriding questions, even if the collapse of the empire lies not far in the background (Turner 2006).

Marx's work has been much less influential in the sociology of religion than it has been in most of the rest of the discipline, even if there are important attempts to develop his insights for the enterprise today (see Chapter 10, this volume). Nonetheless, for Marx, the 'criticism of religion is the presupposition of all criticism' (1977: 64); in his early work – particularly 'Towards a Critique of Hegel's Philosophy of Right' – there are important starting points for understanding the contradictory nature of religion as both a support of, and always a potential threat to, the relations of domination in any given social order (McKinnon 2005). Even if he didn't write much about religion after the 1840s, Marx's analysis of religion, especially what he learned in critical dialogue with the great atheist theologians Ludwig Feuerbach and Bruno Bauer, continued to shape his analysis of otherwise non-religious phenomena. This is perhaps best exemplified by his analysis of commodity fetishism. There, in an analysis drawn out from the Hebrew prophetic critique of idolatry, the commodity, like a god created by human hands, takes on a life of its own and starts demanding obedience. Understood in these terms, capitalism itself becomes a kind of religion, as Walter Benjamin recognised (see Chapter 6, this volume).

Unfortunately, Marx's legacy has yet to be capitalised upon for the sociology of religion, having been largely ignored, with few, notable exceptions (Maduro 1977; Beckford 1989; Turner 1991; Billings 1990), though there is a rich deposit which sociologists have yet to mine, including the work of not only Marx but also Engels (Boer 2011), not to mention the work of Antonio Gramsci (1971) and the Frankfurt School (Mendieta 2004). Although it may be that the political centre of gravity in the sociology of religion lies further to the right than in most of the rest of the discipline, this does not entirely explain why the intellectual promise of these resources suggest avenues that still need to be developed.

Max Weber makes a clearer case for the centrality of religion in classical sociology of religion. Weber's *Protestant Ethic and the Spirit of Capitalism* is known to most sociologists of religion (though sadly sometimes only as a caricature). While this is undoubtedly Weber's best known and most read book, it was by no means his last word about religion, nor, some would say, is it necessarily his most important (O'Toole 1984). In the period following the publication of the Protestant Ethic essays in 1905–6, Weber spent the next 14 years working away on a massive project on the comparative economic ethics of the world religions, completing volumes on the religions of China ([1915] 1951), India ([1916–17] 1958) and Ancient Judaism ([1917–20] 1956) before his death, leaving undone projected volumes on Medieval Christianity and Islam (and much speculation on what those would have entailed). He did nonetheless bring this project to a provisional close, publishing these volumes together with an introduction ('The Social Psychology of the World Religions', [1915] 1946a, and 'Intermediate Reflections' ('The Religious Rejections of the World and Their Directions', [1915] 1946b). Also important is the section on religion in Weber's posthumously published *Economy and Society* (1978: 399–634), though some (cf. Tenbruck 1980) have challenged the claim that this volume should be seen as 'the sum of Max Weber's scholarly vision of society' (Roth, in Weber 1978: xxxiii).

Unlike Durkheim, Weber drew no sharp distinction between religion and magic; rather magic forms the core of his analysis of primitive religion, and an ongoing, important component of popular religion. Whereas in prayer, people beg the gods for something that they need, in magic, they compel the gods to act on their behalf (1978: 422ff.). In practice, the distinction between asking and compelling is a thin one, especially when set rituals for supplication or sacrifice are involved. For Durkheim, it was this practical purpose of magic, 'the technical, utilitarian ends' he called it (2005: 58), as much as its purported non-collective nature, that made magic so different from religion. On the other hand, for Weber the most elementary religion is thoroughly practical, oriented not to the 'hereafter', but to this world. Thus:

> Religion is man's continuous effort to deal rationally with the irrationalities of life. Religion arises out of the Not [poverty, hardship] of existence, its ambiguities and conflicts, and gives the necessary *Begeisterung* [spirit, enthusiasm] to live. It makes life's precariousness acceptable, gives life preciousness and prescribes a way of life that makes living worthwhile. (Steeman 1964: 56)

Religion gives meaning in the face of the difficulties of life, and the ubiquity of hardship, suffering and death. Religion starts, for Weber, not with the experience of collective effervescence, but rather with the problems of embodied existence (Turner 1991), thus, even in societies where religious beliefs and institutions are not as important as they once were, Weber's sociology of religion does not thereby become irrelevant.

Religion is, thus:

> heavily concerned with the basic needs and routines of mundane existence while offering the opportunity of transcending them in the search for meaning and the good life ... [religion may therefore] be the means by which human beings adjust to their natural, social, economic, political and intellectual environments, it may also, a fortiori, be the means by which these are transcended or changed. (O'Toole 1984: 140–141)

Thus, Weber's project was concerned with the tendency in particular religious traditions towards adjustment to the world. Thus: Confucianism 'reduced tension with the world to an absolute minimum ... The world was the best of all possible worlds' (Weber 1951: 227). Confucianism thereby promoted an ethic for living a good life, on learning to adjust to the natural and social world, and this made Confucianism popular with many rulers in East Asia (including in Japan where state-Shinto is a form of neo-Confucianism), who promoted it for its contributions to social harmony and integration.

The 'salvation religions' (*Erlösungsreligionen*), exist in (and promote) tension with 'the world'. In Weber's view, Christianity, Islam, Judaism, Buddhism and

Jainism are all religions of salvation, although within these traditions there are different ways of responding to this tension. Mystics, which exist in all of the major salvation religions, attempt to merge their soul with the divine reality, escaping all 'worldly' distractions in order to do so (early Buddhism is the clearest type for Weber). In contrast to mysticism, 'other-worldly asceticism' involves self-mastery in the interests of devotion, but does not involve the mystical flight from the world, but a physical flight from the world into religious communities. Here Weber seems to have the medieval European monasticism foremost in his mind – monks could devote themselves to saying the mass and living in exclusive service to the divine, unencumbered by the demands of daily living outside the monastery. What Weber calls 'inner-worldly asceticism' (*innerweltlich askese*) has been less common historically, but it plays a vital role in the development of western rationalism. (Although it may have been better if the first generation of translators had opted for the less literal rendition 'this-worldly' asceticism, 'inner worldly' has become the standard technical term.) The puritans, who are the heroes of *The Protestant Ethic* are the archetype of inner-worldly ascetics. They have eschewed the mystic's union with God, and the other-worldly ascetic's escape from the world to the monastery. The remaining route for dealing with the tensions between the world of sin and the demands of God is to change the world in accordance with God's precepts. If the mystic tries to be the vessel of God, the ascetic, especially the ascetic of the inner-worldly type, tries to be God's tool for transforming the world. It is for this reason that he devotes himself to his calling in the world with such devotion. He is called upon to be God's tool in that occupation, doing God's work in the world. This, as in the case of ascetic Protestants, giving birth to modern capitalism as they lived their calling in the world; their faith provided a major impetus for social change, even if the change was inadvertent, unintentional and developed in ways nobody could have expected.

Although the difference between Protestants and Catholics features in the argument of *Suicide* ([1897] 2002), Durkheim's project for the development of a sociological science is not manifestly preoccupied with the question of religion until after his move to the Sorbonne in 1902, and culminating in his masterpiece, *The Elementary Forms of the Religious Life* (2001). In that book, religion becomes the very heart of the social, even as the social becomes the soul of religion. Ostensibly writing about Australian Aborigines but in reality providing an analysis of religion in Europe, Durkheim makes several arguments about the fundamentals of social order that locate the institutions we have come to understand as 'religion' at its very heart. For Durkheim, religious rituals that bring the society together serve to produce the collective effervescence that lies at the heart of social attachments, create shared identities in collectively worshipped (proto-) gods, and create, maintain and successfully negotiate the boundaries that distinguish sacred from profane.

The Elementary Forms is not, and probably never has been, a state-of-the-art discussion of aboriginal totemism – the concept of totemism having already begun to fall from grace in the anthropological literature, even as Durkheim wrote his treatise. As an empirical study of the 'religious' life of the Aborigines, very little that Durkheim wrote is worth much today (Jones 1986). On the other hand, as an analysis of religion in 'our' (contemporary western) societies, Durkheim's analysis is still one of the greatest contributions to the sociological study of religion. Although it is nearly a hundred years old, it continues to challenge readers and to provide new insights into the study of religion; for this reason, it is rightly seen as a 'classic' in the sociology of religion (O'Toole 2001).

Durkheim's explicit argument for why we should examine the 'religion' of the Aborigines in order to understand contemporary religion is undoubtedly evolutionary. Thus, he argues, with more than a hint of tautology, 'All are equally religions, just as all living beings are equally alive from the humblest unicellular organism to man' (Durkheim 2001: 5). If we can accept that all religions are instances of the same thing, then why privilege the study of the 'humblest unicellular organism' for the study of life? Durkheim provides a garden-variety socio-evolutionary argument at this point: totemic religion, like the unicellular organism, is the subject under the microscope in its purest form. By understanding that purest, simplest, earliest form – its 'elementary form', it casts new light on the more recent advanced forms of the same phenomenon. The complexity of later religion, Durkheim argues, makes it more difficult to distinguish primary and secondary elements. Further, the division of labour in religious practice makes it difficult to see the religion as a whole but for the parts: priests, prophets, laity, etc.

In practice, Durkheim shows little interest in 'religion in general' [Introduction, I]; rather, he confesses, 'like all positive science, [his] goal is first and foremost to explain a current reality, something close to us and consequently capable of affecting our beliefs and actions. The reality is man, more specifically, man today' (Durkheim 2001: 1). Indeed, Durkheim does not seem particularly distracted by the evolution of particular religions, 'religion in general', or even in comparisons between religions in different social contexts. For Durkheim, Australian totemism is important because it helps us to understand contemporary French religion.

Durkheim uses numerous metaphors to describe Australian totemism, and all of these serve to bring into association the world of the Aboriginals and our world into association – they are the basic means by which the two societies are compared. He says that the totem is 'not simply a name; it is an emblem, a true coat of arms, and its resemblance to the heraldic coat of arms has often been commented upon' ([Book 2, 1, II] Durkheim 1995: 111). In making this comparison, we understand perfectly well the relationship between the symbol and the group, through an example that is part of 'our' history. Elsewhere, Durkheim says that the totem is the clan's flag [Book 2, 7, III]. Given the upsurge in nationalism in the years leading up to the First World War, this better indicates the emotional intensity with which a totemic symbol can be invested, and the absolute seriousness with which totems are regarded.

Of course, unlike Muslims, Jews and Christians, the beliefs and practices of the Aborigines are not really concerned with a God, gods, or even spirits. The totemic principal, Durkheim informs us, is not a god, but a 'force' or 'energy' (an idea that may derive from Sylvain Lévi's researches on Brahman sacrifice (1898)). There is nonetheless, Durkheim claims, something 'godlike' about the totemic principle, and in fact, he tells us, it is the precursor to the idea of the gods. The totemic principle is a 'semi-divine entity' (2001: 141). It is incarnate in every totemic species, and in particular in those 'holy' things that are set apart by ritual prohibitions. This allows Durkheim to make the connection between the totemic principle as object of worship and representative of the group, with the gods of later religious traditions:

> the totemic god – to use the metaphor we have just adopted – is in them, just as it is in the totemic species and in the people of the clan. Since it is the soul of such different beings, we can see how it differs from those beings in whom it resides. (Durkheim 2001: 141)

Although sometimes underplayed in discussions of *The Elementary Forms*, ritual lies at the very heart of Durkheim's discussion. Positive rites affirm the sacredness of the symbol, and negative rites keep the symbol separate from all that might profane it. Both bring the social group together, where their connection with each other and the sacred, and the shared prohibition of infringement on the sacred, animates (in the literal sense of 'giving soul' to) the group.

Recent Developments in British Sociology of Religion

In the UK, a vibrant sociology of religion stems from the 1960s, and Socrel, now a section of the British Sociological Association, dates from 1975, where it developed around a core of interests, particularly secularisation and new religious movements. Although always a broad tent, sociology of religion was nonetheless firmly at home in sociology as a discipline, and its practitioners primarily housed in sociology departments, even if colleagues in those departments were on occasion somewhat bemused by the interest in what may have sometimes seemed like obscurantist interests. Nonetheless, the sociological interest in religion could be readily justified by reference to the classics (or at least the rendition of them provided by Peter Berger (1967)).

While religion is having something of a comeback in contemporary theory (with the exception of Ulrich Beck, most of it outside sociology) we would contend that these developments are somewhat limited compared with the legacy of the classics for two reasons. First, because a discipline's classic texts form the context of all subsequent sociological conversations (Alexander 1987); they provide a great deal of our most important vocabulary, the inspiration for many of our methods, and the starting point for most of our conversations about the social world – even if their world is occasionally very different from ours. An understanding of their texts is a cost of admission into the field of sociological research (Bourdieu 1990: 30). Second, classics are by definition works that contemporary communities continue to find important and useful, and – somewhat paradoxically – act as sources of innovation. Classic texts are not simply collections of sociological rules to be mastered, nor compilations of hypotheses to be tested. Rather, they 'inspire imitation, invite elaboration and provoke discussion ... [A] surplus of sociological signification ... is the most indelible mark of a genuine disciplinary or sub-disciplinary classic. From this point of view, classics are not terminal destinations but rather points of embarkation for departure on future intellectual journeys' (O'Toole 2001: 140–141). For this reason, every generation reads and interprets the classics in new ways – posing its own questions and challenges to the ancestors, finding new ancestors to add to the pantheon, and (at least temporarily) shelving others. The classics have important challenges for us, as well. Marx, Weber and Durkheim set a very high bar for scholarship with their innovative ways of understanding religion, but also with the breadth and depth of their historical, comparative and philosophical knowledge – not to mention the scope of their research questions.

The canonical texts of classical sociological theory are important, not only for the ideas that they contain, but also for the model of research that they uphold. While we certainly see no reason to disparage the 'pure theory', in examining these canonical classic texts we find that the authors set the task of thinking theoretically in relation to a particular empirical problem, or they are spurred on to their theoretical thinking by the need to solve concrete research problems.

For reasons that still demand a sociological explanation, it is no longer the case that sociology of religion in the UK lives in sociology departments (Chapter 2, this volume): sociologists of religion have largely packed up and moved into theology and religious studies, or increasingly, have been born and grow up there. While this undoubtedly has the advantage of collegial relations with others interested in the topic of religion and opening up the sociological study of religion to other disciplines, and provided an infusion of new ideas and energy, moving home is always expensive. The primary costs, it seems to us, are as follows. First, as the training in sociology of religion, at least in this country, is now happening almost exclusively outside of sociology departments, new generations of sociologists of religion are at risk of missing out on fundamental methods training, but even more vitally, the core theory (classical and contemporary) that makes the enterprise recognisable to other sociologists. While the more 'interdisciplinary' training in theory which undergraduates and increasingly postgraduates explore tends to focus on those theories, theorists and texts that are in the first place interested in religion itself, this is often to the neglect of the 'big picture' or the attempt to connect it with other social processes and phenomena (something that is certainly not true of the classics). Many of the areas of study to which sociology undergraduates are introduced have obvious (though particularly in the UK, largely underexploited) connections to the sociology of religion: the sociology of organisations, crime and deviance, political economy, arts and culture, education, science, family, media and social movements, just to name a few obvious ones, each long-standing lines and topics of inquiry with substantial literatures.

Meanwhile, it is hardly the case that all is well in the old neighbourhood. Judged against the classics, much of contemporary sociological theorising seems rather thin indeed. From our point of view, and the purposes of this chapter, these weaknesses are twofold. First, while every sub-discipline almost inevitably seems to feel that it is ignored and marginalised by the 'mainstream' of the discipline, we do think that sociology has much to learn, not only from the classics, but from contemporary sociologists of religion. Religion, despite the fact that it has returned to the public agenda (including where it is connected to questions of immigration and multiculturalism; conflict, violence, peace-making and terrorism), does seem to be largely ignored in sociology departments (as far as we know, sociology of religion is at present only taught as a core module in undergraduate sociology at Aberdeen). Where important figures in the discipline have begun once again to address religion, one often has the feeling that they are hard at work reinventing the wheel without being fully apprised of the important work of specialists in the field. Thus, Ulrich Beck's (2010) contention that religion has become increasingly individualised will not be experienced as a major revelation by contemporary sociologists of religion. While Jose Casanova, Grace Davie, Steve Bruce and Paul Heelas are all referenced in the bibliography, they are kept out of the discussion itself.

More broadly, and sub-disciplinary special pleading aside, one could argue that even a generation ago sociology, even when it was concerned with contemporary matters, was all the same a firmly historical-comparative discipline (Abrams 1982). While the concept of modernity has come to be questioned in contemporary debates (see Chapter 7, this volume), even those who might reject the notion out of hand will readily accept that the notion of modernity always demanded thinking comparatively, of locating any sociological analysis in a particular present which is different from the past.

Today we are often reminded of the classic distinction, often made by undergraduate students on exams, and which used to result in winks, nudges and third class degrees: 'in olden times ... but in modern times'. By this they inevitably mean within the timeframe of their own lived experience. Unfortunately this is increasingly risking becoming the disciplinary norm for thinking about the present, whether this is conceived as 'post-traditional', 'reflexive', 'liquid' or a hundred other terms for the contemporary social world. When this caricature of 'modernity' becomes the sum total of what sociologists study, without comparative reference over space and time, the whole project is in peril (Elias 1987).

We hope that sociology of religion's recent move into religious studies will in the long-run help to foster healthy cross-cultural comparison, and therefore more sophisticated theorising, due to that discipline's long-standing concern with comparative religions, even if these benefits are not yet particularly apparent. The historical sensibilities of the sociology of religion seem in much greater trouble. Until recently the preoccupation with the study of secularisation in British and European sociology of religion has kept sociology of religion's historical imagination alive, even if the timeframe within which the literature on secularisation concerns itself has made it less conducive to engaging in analysis of the *longue durée* (but see Martin 1978 for an important exception). While the heated debates and disagreements over the conceptions, and adequacy of, secularisation theory are a healthy aspect of the discipline (especially insofar as they begin to incorporate a comparative dimension and recover a sense of the *longue durée*), the current risk is that the apparent waning of interest in sociology of secularisation has begun to diminish the sub-discipline's historical capacities. The historical sociology of religion is by no means synonymous with secularisation, however, and there are other helpful starting places for the development of sociology of religion's historical imagination (Woodhead 2004; Wuthnow 1989, 2009; Gorski 2003, 2013; Bellah 2011; Casanova 1994), and we have included work by others we think may be helpful for this development in this volume.

The Current Volume

This book cannot be taken as a transcription of the events and discussions at Socrel 2011, the conference on which it is based, though it is representative of the general shift in direction we hope we have discerned there, as well as embodying a healthy diversity of views. While there were many excellent papers given at that conference, we were not able to include them all, and most of the authors included here either radically revised their arguments or indeed gave us another contribution entirely. Other participants who were there were unable to contribute to this volume because of other commitments. The volume would have been much richer if it had been able to include others, and in particular representative work by Gordon Lynch (2012) and Jim Beckford (2003); the discerning reader may be able to trace the influences of both of them in individual chapters here, including this Introduction.

Grace Davie's and Steve Bruce's chapters here (chapters 1 and 2) are, if not transcriptions, nonetheless versions of their respective keynote addresses at Socrel 2011, both of which stimulated much discussion and debate. The chapters contain their very different views on the current state of sociology of religion (primarily in Britain) and its prospects with respect to theoretically informed and informative empirical research. Both chapters, though they contain very different diagnoses of the current state of the discipline, make important contributions to our self-examination as sociologists of religion, emphasising in particular that theory cannot be conceived apart from the methods and institutional arrangements of our field of expertise.

The following three chapters address quite different topics, but nonetheless approach their respective problems in terms of what might be called either sociology of 'big history' or '*la longue durée*'. Turner's chapter (Chapter 3) makes a compelling case, following Weber, Karl Jaspers and Robert Bellah, for a historical sociology of religion that begins with the axial age. Only then, he asserts, will we be able to fully grasp the significance and logic of the current 'spiritualities' in North America and Europe, or the religious resurgence in the rest of the world. David Lehmann (Chapter 4) likewise shows how the dialectical relationship between popular and official religious traditions has recently been sundered and reconfigured, with particular reference to Latin American Pentecostalism. While his argument is primarily based on ethnographic research, the change can only be seen when held up against a historical background. McKinnon's chapter (Chapter 5) deals with the omission of religion in Norbert Elias's *Civilizing Process*, a view to which most of Elias's contemporary followers seem wedded – in the argument of that chapter, they omit the sacred to their detriment. With its focus on the 'Peace of God' movement (tenth and eleventh centuries), the chapter makes a case that, even from the very beginning of Elias's story, religious institutions were significant.

The chapters in the following section come the closest of any in this volume to what might be characterised as 'pure theory', but even here, with the focus on 'modernity' as the sociologists' central category, there are empirical or experiential questions that lie in the immediate background. In Chapter 6, Dominika Motak provides an important gift to the sociology of religion by broadening its canonical foundations to include the work of Georg Simmel. Simmel's work has become increasingly important in closely related areas of sociological research, but has yet to have much impact within the sociology of religion. Motak shows clearly that Simmel's sociology of religion is not a late, eccentric offshoot of his theoretical programme. Rather, Simmel's conception of money, God, society and modernity are closely interconnected, and homologous in their logic. This refocused line of inquiry promises to open up new theoretical avenues for sociology of religion, possibly in a much more critical dimension with closer affinities to those Marxists on whom Simmel was so influential (Walter Benjamin and Georg Lukacs). Andrew Dawson (Chapter 7) throws down his gauntlet in response to those who, following a strong version of multiple modernities theory, make comparative research effectively impossible. Recognising some of the difficulties with the old conception of modernity, Dawson tries to chart a path that allows transnational comparison without succumbing to the ethnocentric assumptions of old.

The chapters in Part IV share a focus on listening, Løvland and Repstad on the aesthetic turn in contemporary religion that they have noted in the Norwegian Bible Belt (Chapter 8), and Strhan's chapter on the disciplines of listening in a conservative evangelical church in London (Chapter 9). By means of ethnographic research, particularly at Christmas concerts, Løvland and Repstad argue that the dogmatic aspects of Christianity are giving way to a softer, more aesthetic form. Strhan's Reformed Londoners, are quite different, and perhaps even opposed to the aestheticizing Norwegians, making an art of self-disciplined listening. The comparison is very interesting and potentially instructive. One wonders, for example, if there might be similarities as well as differences brought out in close comparison between the cases, including the possibility that the appreciation of softer aesthetic forms of Christianity in fact requires training and self-discipline, and that in the end there might be a sort of aesthetics to the reformed rationality Strhan describes. These are questions for what we hope might be a productive ongoing conversation.

The final section of the book highlights the understudied importance of power in the sociology of religion, with help from Pierre Bourdieu, Marx and Critical Discourse Analysis. Pierre Bourdieu's sociology has been widely influential in sub-disciplines beyond the sociology of religion, but not much within it, undoubtedly to our detriment. In Chapter 11, Trzebiatowska shows how Bourdieu's sociology might be put to good use in the study of gender within the sociology of religion. While we have some misgivings about the contemporary use of (Critical) Discourse Analysis, one has to recognise that it has also been very influential in other areas of sociology, but virtually ignored in sociology of religion. Titus Hjelm's chapter (Chapter 10), with its strong Marxian inflection, is not at all characteristic of the weaknesses we usually see in Discourse Analytic arguments, quite on the contrary, he makes a rather compelling claim for its utility for sociology of religion, as well as for the need to develop a critical tradition in the sociology of religion.

We are excited about the offerings in this book and are convinced that they offer a productive and lively way forward, not just for sociological theory of religion, but for the sociology of religion more generally. We hope you will gain from reading them as much as we have benefitted from working with the authors whose work is here assembled. We are grateful for all of their contributions and look forward to working with them again in the future.

References

Abrams, P. (1982). *Historical Sociology*. Ithaca: Cornell University Press.
Alexander, J. (1987). The Centrality of the Classics, in *Social Theory Today*, ed. A. Giddens and J. Turner. Stanford: Stanford University Press, pp. 11–57.
Beck, U. (2010). *A God of One's Own: Religion's Capacity for Peace and Potential for Violence*. Cambridge: Polity.
Beckford, J.A. (1989). *Religion and Advanced Industrial Society*. London: Unwin Hyman.
Beckford, J.A. (2003). *Social Theory and Religion*. Cambridge: Cambridge University Press.

Bellah, R.N. (2011). *Religion in Human Evolution: From the Paleolithic to the Axial Age*. Cambridge, MA: Harvard University Press.

Berger, P.L. (1967). *The Sacred Canopy: Elements of a Sociological Theory of Religion*. New York: Amchor Books.

Billings, D.B. (1990). Religion as Opposition: A Gramscian Analysis. *American Journal of Sociology*, 1–31.

Boer, R. (2011). Opium, Idols and Revolution: Marx and Engels on Religion. *Religion Compass*, 5(11), 698–707.

Bourdieu, P. (1990). *In Other Words: Essays Towards a Reflexive Sociology*. Stanford: Stanford University Press.

Casanova, J. (1994). *Public Religions in the Modern World*. Chicago: University of Chicago Press.

Connell, R.W. (1997). Why Is Classical Theory Classical? *The American Journal of Sociology*, 102(6). 1511–57.

Durkheim, É. (1995 [1912]). *The Elementary Forms of Religious Life*, trans. K. Fields. New York: Free Press.

Durkheim, É. (2001 [1912]). *The Elementary Forms of the Religious Life*, trans. C. Cosman. Oxford: Oxford University Press.

Durkheim, É. (2002). *Suicide: A Study in Sociology*. London: Routledge.

Durkheim, É. (2005 [1912]). *Les formes élémentaires de la vie religieuse*, 5th edn. Paris: Quadrige/PUF.

Elias, N. (1987). The Retreat of Sociologists into the Present. *Theory, Culture & Society*, 4(2), 223–47.

Gorski, P.S. (2003). *The Disciplinary Revolution: Calvinism and the Rise of the State in Early Modern Europe*. Chicago: University of Chicago Press.

Gorski, P.S. (2013). *The Protestant Ethic Revisited*. Philadelphia: Temple University Press.

Gramsci, A. (1971). *Selections from the Prison Notebooks of Antonio Gramsci: Ed. and Transl. by Quintin Hoare and Geoffrey Nowell Smith*. New York: International Publishers.

Jones, R.A. (1986). Durkheim, Fraser and Smith: The Role of Analogies and Exemplars in the Development of Durkheim's Sociology of Religion. *The American Sociological Review*, 92(2), 596–627.

Lévi, S. (1898). *La doctrine du sacrifice dans les brâhmanas*. Paris: Ernest Leroux.

Lynch, G. (2012). *The Sacred in the Modern World: A Cultural Sociological Approach*. Oxford: Oxford University Press.

McKinnon, A.M. (2005). Reading Opium of the People: Expression, Protest and the Dialectics of Religion. *Critical Sociology*, 31(1–2), 15–38.

Maduro, O. (1977). New Marxist Approaches to the Relative Autonomy of Religion. *Sociology of Religion*, 38(4), 359–67.

Martin, D. (1978). *A General Theory of Secularization*. Oxford: Blackwell.

Marx, Karl (1977 [1844]). Towards a Critique of Hegel's Philosophy of Right: Introduction, in *Karl Marx: Selected Writings*, ed. David McLellan. Oxford: Oxford University Press, pp. 63–74.

Mendieta, E. (ed.) (2004). *The Frankfurt School on Religion: Key Writings by the Major Thinkers*. New York: Routledge.

O'Toole, R. (1984). *Religion: Classic Sociological Approaches*. Toronto: McGraw-Hill Ryerson.

O'Toole, R. (2001). Classics in the Sociology of Religion: An Ambiguous Legacy, in *The Blackwell Companion to Sociology of Religion*, ed. Richard K. Fenn. Oxford: Blackwell, pp. 133–60.

Steeman, T.M. (1964). Max Weber's Sociology of Religion. *Sociological Analysis*, 25(1), 50–58.

Tenbruck, F. (1980). The Problem of Thematic Unity in Max Weber's Sociology of Religion. *British Journal of Sociology*, 31, 316–51.

Turner, Bryan S. (1991). *Religion and Social Theory*, 2nd edn. London: Sage.

Turner, Bryan S. (2006). British Sociology and Public Intellectuals: Consumer Society and Imperial Decline. *The British Journal of Sociology*, 57(2), 169–88.

Weber, M. (1946a). The Social Psychology of World Religions, in *From Max Weber: Essays in Sociology*, ed. H. Gerth and C.W. Mills. New York: Oxford University Press, pp. 267–301.

Weber, M. (1946b). Religious Rejections of the World and their Directions, in *From Max Weber: Essays in Sociology*, ed. H. Gerth and C.W. Mills. New York: Oxford University Press, pp. 323–359.

Weber, M. (1951). *The Religion of China*. New York: Free Press.

Weber, M. (1956). *Ancient Judaism*, trans. H.H. Gerth and D. Martindale. New York: Free Press.

Weber, M. (1958). *The Religion of India*, trans. H.H. Gerth and D. Martndale. New York: Free Press.

Weber, M. (1978). *Economy and Society*, ed. G. Roth and C. Wittich. Berkley: University of California Press.

Woodhead, L. (2004). *An Introduction to Christianity*. Cambridge: Cambridge University Press.

Wuthnow, R. (1989). *The Restructuring of American Religion: Society and Faith Since World War*. Princeton: Princeton University Press.

Wuthnow, R. (2009). *Communities of Discourse: Ideology and Social Structure in the Reformation, the Enlightenment, and European Socialism.* Cambridge, MA: Harvard University Press.

PART I
The State of the Art and Science of the Sociology of Religion

Chapter 1

Thinking Sociologically about Religion: A Step Change in the Debate?[1]

Grace Davie

More than once in the last two decades, I have been invited to write a chapter or an article about the current state of the sociology of religion. Two of these stand out in my mind. The first took the form of a contribution to an encyclopaedia on religion and society (Davie 1998). A dominant theme in this article concerned the different trajectories of religion in different parts of the world and the effect that these had on academic reflection. The contrast between the relative secularity of Europe and the continuing religious activity in large parts of the United States was central to this discussion. Very different approaches to the discipline have emerged as a result: in Europe, secularization has remained a (if not the) leading theory; in the United States, this is much less the case. In the latter, rational choice is the preferred paradigm for many scholars. Nothing has changed in this respect. It is abundantly clear that the sociology of religion reflects the context in which it finds itself. It is also conditioned by widely differing cultural and academic traditions, not to mention the institutional settings (universities, government agencies, pastoral institutes, etc.) in which it is conducted.

The second piece was published in 2007. This was a book-length treatment of the sociology of religion, commissioned by Sage as part of their New Horizons in Sociology series (Davie 2007). The opening pages of this volume introduce the thread that runs through the book: the notion of a 'critical' agenda, understanding 'critical' in two ways. The agenda in the sociology of religion is 'critical' in that we need to get it right; religion is a crucially important issue in the modern world about which students (and indeed others) need to be properly informed. But I was critical in the sense that I was not at all sure

---

[1] A different version of this chapter was published originally as part ARDA Guiding Paper Series. State College, PA: The Association of Religion Data Archives at The Pennsylvania State University, at http://www.thearda.com/rrh/papers/guidingpapers.asp.

that the profession – those who call themselves sociologists of religion – were responding to this challenge as well as they should. I argued as follows:

> I do not want to sound negative: a great deal of excellent work is being done in this field. There remains, however, a deep seated resistance to the notion that it is entirely normal in most parts of the world, to be both fully modern and fully religious. To overturn this resistance, both in the sociology of religion and in the social sciences more generally, is the principal aim of this book. (Davie 2007: ix)

It is interesting to reflect on this claim some five to six years later.[2] Is the implied critique still justified? In the pages that follow, I will argue that there has been something of a step change in the debate: there has been a real attempt in the sub-discipline to confront the realities of religion in the modern world. What, then, has happened to justify this claim? Where and how has this change taken place? And why has it occurred? These are the questions that frame the argument of this chapter. Two things will become clear in the discussion: both that a great deal of work has been accomplished, but that this in turn is generating new and urgent questions. It is these questions that constitute the concluding section of this chapter.

Evidence of Change

In terms of the topic itself (the visibility of religion in the modern world) it is generally agreed that the final decades of the twentieth century mark a turning point. Three pivotal events encapsulate this shift. These were the Iranian revolution of 1979, the fall of the Berlin Wall in 1989 and the attack on the Twin Towers in 2001. All of them raised questions – unexpected ones – about religion. Why was it, for example, that a pro-Western, relatively secularized Shah was obliged to flee before an Iranian Ayatollah clearly motivated by conservative readings of Islam? Such a scenario had not been anticipated. And why was it that an aggressively secular ideology, not a religious one, collapsed so comprehensively throughout the Soviet bloc – a part of the world that has seen subsequently a marked, if uneven, renaissance of both Christianity and Islam? And why, finally, did the terrifying events of 9/11 come as such a bolt from the blue? Quite simply the unimaginable had happened, requiring – amongst many

---

[2] A revised edition of this book appeared in 2013. A number of the ideas contained in this chapter can be found in the Preface to the new edition.

other things – a radical rethinking of the paradigms that are supposed to explain, indeed to predict, the events of the modern world.

Gilles Kepel, a distinguished French scholar writing in the 1990s, was one of the first to take note of this shift. He describes the evolving situation as follows:

> Around 1975 the whole process [of secularization] went into reverse. A new religious approach took shape, aimed not only at adapting to secular values but at recovering a sacred foundation for the organization of society – by changing society if necessary. Expressed in a multitude of ways, this approach advocated moving on from a modernism that had failed, attributing its setbacks and dead ends to separation from God. The theme was no longer *aggiornamento* but a 'second evangelization of Europe': the aim was no longer to modernize Islam but to 'Islamize modernity'. Since that date this phenomenon has spread throughout the world. (Kepel 1994: 2)

Assuming for the time being that Kepel's analysis was correct, how were Western scholars to deal with this shift, given that their work was very largely premised not only on the understanding that modern societies would be secular societies, but that 'being secular' was, in itself, a good thing?

In terms of scholarship, one of the first things to emerge was a substantial body of work on both sides of the Atlantic concerned with 'fundamentalism' – a term that was widely, if not always wisely, used in public debate. Such an approach is nicely exemplified by an American example, which became known as the 'Fundamentalism Project' established at the University of Chicago in the late 1980s. The project gathered a distinguished team of scholars from many different parts of the world, brought together to document and to explain the rapid and unexpected growth of distinctive forms of religious life in almost every global region. The details of the team, their working methods and the impressive series of publications that emanated from the meetings are easily documented.[3] Even more important, however, are the motivations that lay behind this work and the finance made available to execute the task. Clearly this hugely expensive endeavor was indicative of concern on the part of American academia, and the foundations that resource them, about the forms of religion that were increasingly visible on a global scale. Something had to be done. In this sense the 'Fundamentalism Project' is as much part of the sociological story

---

[3] See for example the introductory material contained in the first volume that appeared (Marty and Appleby 1991). In the end, five volumes were published in the original series; a further volume appeared in 2003, which drew on the material of the project as a whole (Almond et al. 2003).

as it is a body of knowledge about fundamentalism itself. Peter Berger (1999) is even more provocative in his comments: the assumption that we need both to document and to understand the nature of fundamentalism by means of a research project of this stature tells us as much about American academics as it does about fundamentalism itself.[4] Their European equivalents were, if anything, even more perplexed.

Simplifying a necessarily complex story, the situation can be summarized as follows: by this stage, religion (in all its diversity) was no longer invisible to the academic community; it was, however, increasingly constructed as a 'problem'. The problem moreover was more and more present in Western societies, not least in Europe – brought there by immigration. And if it was one thing to acknowledge changes taking place on the other side of the world, it was quite another to admit that they were there on the doorstep. A related point follows from this: these very evident trends were initially seen in terms of ethnicity rather than religion. In other words, the consequences of immigration were acknowledged in some respects, but not in others. Racial or ethnic differences, moreover, were easier for social scientists to deal with within their existing paradigms than their religious equivalents. Bit by bit, however, the mismatch between the perceptions of Western scholars, and the preferred identities of the incoming communities that were establishing themselves, had to be acknowledged, a debate in which the presence of Islam was central. However unexpected, religion and religious differences became increasingly present in the public agendas of European societies. What followed was a delayed reaction. Denial gradually gave way to alarm, generating an impressive array of publicly-funded research programmes, a wide variety of government initiatives, and a flood of publications. A selection of these will be outlined in the following section.

Before embarking on this list, two interconnected issues require attention. The first relates to the difference between reality and perception. Is it the case that religion has 'returned' to a world from which it was absent for most of the twentieth century? Or is this primarily a question of perception? Western social scientists are now obliged to take notice of something that they had ignored for several decades. Or is it a combination of both these things? My own view is that

---

[4] The following quotation sums up Berger's argument: 'The concern that must have led to this Project was based on an upside-down perception of the world, according to which "fundamentalism" ... is a rare, hard-to-explain thing. But a look either at history or at the contemporary world reveals that what is rare is not the phenomenon itself but knowledge of it. The difficult-to-understand phenomenon is not Iranian mullahs but American university professors – it might be worth a multi-million dollar project to try to explain that!' (Berger 1999: 2).

the third alternative comes closest to the truth: religion has been continually present in almost every part of the world, but it is currently asserting itself in innovative and very visible ways. This shift is nicely captured by looking at the evolution of the World Council of Churches (WCC) – a global organization that, by definition, has always paid attention to religion.

Officially founded in 1948, the WCC became the channel through which the varied streams of ecumenical life that already existed in the churches were brought together. At the same time, it was a movement that reflected a whole series of initiatives aimed at establishing and maintaining world peace. In its early years, the WCC was deeply influenced by the Cold War and its consequences for church life. It looked for ways to overcome the divisions between East and West, especially in Europe – encouraging, as far as this was possible, contacts with the churches in Central and East Europe. Post-1989, however, the context has altered radically. The Cold War has given way to a very different reading of international affairs, within which religion emerges as a highly significant variable. And to the surprise of many – not only the advocates of the ecumenical movement – it was the conservative, even reactionary forms of religion (both Christian and non-Christian) that were growing fastest in the final decades of the twentieth century.

Hence the dilemma for an organization founded on two assumptions: first that the world would become an increasingly secular place, and second, that the best way forward in this situation was for the churches most open to change and most attentive to the modern world (notably the liberal Protestants) to group together in order to sustain each other in a necessarily hostile environment. The churches that resisted 'the world' would automatically consign themselves to the past. Both assumptions were incorrect. The world is not 'an increasingly secular place'; it is full of very different forms of religious life, many of which are expanding rather than contracting. It is, moreover, the forms of religion least interested in ecumenism that are developing with the greatest confidence. Coming to terms with such shifts constitutes a major challenge to the WCC.

Social scientists are similarly discomfited. Not only must they acknowledge the renewed significance of religion in the modern world order, but they are obliged to accept the forms that it currently takes – whether or not they find these congenial. Such a statement brings us necessarily to the second issue. Is it possible for scholars of religion to move on from their present position? Is it possible in other words for religion, in all its inherent diversity, to cease to be a problem and to become instead an entirely 'normal' feature of the late modern world? In my own work I have tried to encourage this shift by arguing that it is as modern to draw from the religious to critique the secular, as it is to draw from the secular to critique the religious. *It is the quality of the argument that counts* (Davie 2002).

New Initiatives

Whatever the motivation, an unprecedented amount of work is now in progress. The following examples are selective but they are sufficient to indicate the kind of thing that is happening. For the most part they draw from the European case in that the shift in perspective is even more striking here than in other parts of the world. Not only is Europe regarded as a relatively secular global region, it is European (specifically French) understandings of the Enlightenment that lie behind the paradigms that are predicated on the assumption that to be modern means to be secular. How, then, are European scholars, and those who fund their research, responding to the current situation?

It is important first of all to differentiate between projects and programmes. There have always been research *projects* relating to religion, many of which have yielded significant data, not to mention new ways of thinking. These have been valuable initiatives. In the last half decade, however, something rather different has appeared: that is a series of research *programmes*, which are designed to gather together a wide variety of projects and to ensure that the latter add up to more than the sum of their parts. It is the systematic approach to the study of religion which is new. This development, together with the strikingly generous funding that supports it, is growing in momentum.

Given that I am a British sociologist of religion, I will start with the British case. The 'Religion and Society Research Programme', funded jointly by the Arts and Humanities Research Council and the Economic and Social Research Council, exemplifies the trend perfectly.[5] This £12 million initiative, which ran from 2007 to 2012, was without precedent in the UK. It was designed to stimulate collaborative research across the arts, humanities and social sciences and has done precisely that – the range of projects contained in the programme is impressive. The work, moreover, has been innovative: the researchers engaged in this initiative have been asking new things in new ways, and have discovered creative methodologies to achieve their goals. The purpose of the programme was unequivocal: it existed 'to inform public debate and advance understanding

---

[5] See www.religionandsociety.org.uk/ for more details about the Religion and Society Programme itself and the very varied projects that contributed to this [accessed: 7 March 2013].

about religion in a complex world'. Specifically it aimed to further both research and research capacity in the field of religion (with a strong emphasis on training), to facilitate knowledge exchange between the academic community and a wide variety of stakeholders (including the religious communities themselves), and to make links with similar ventures in different parts of the world. Two such ventures can be noted at this point: the remarkably similar 'Religions, State and Society Programme' funded by the Swiss National Science Foundation,[6] and the 'Religion and Diversity Project', based at the University of Ottawa, which despite the term 'project' in the title is a major collaborative research initiative (MCRI) funded by the Canadian Social Sciences and Humanities Research Council.[7] There are many others, both in Europe and beyond.[8]

A parallel set of activities exists at the European, as opposed to national, level. Excellent examples can be found in the emphasis on religion found in the Sixth and Seventh Framework Programmes of the European Commission, both of which have supported a series of projects relating to the growing diversity of Europe and its consequences for economic, political and social life.[9] There is a strong, top-down emphasis in both programmes on policy-making, revealed amongst other things in the close attention paid to social cohesion. Indeed the subtext, indicative perhaps of anxiety, is clear: is the growing religious diversity of Europe damaging to social cohesion, and if so, what is to be done? The projects themselves interrogate these questions in a wide variety of fields (politics, democracy, law, education, welfare), in which key values (tolerance, acceptance, respect, rights, responsibilities, inclusion, exclusion) are thoroughly explored. Many of these programmes foreground the presence and aspiration of minorities in Europe and the reactions of host societies to these groups. Identities can no longer be taken for granted in a part of the world where movement and migration are commonplace, including the movement of significant numbers of people from one part of Europe to another.

A third way of working can be found in university-wide programmes, which draw from the range of interests, skills and training found in one institution, in order to foster imaginative and above all inter-disciplinary work on a common theme. One such, 'Religion in the 21st Century', was located in the University

---

[6] See www.nfp58.ch/e_index.cfm [accessed: 7 March 2013].
[7] See www.religionanddiversity.ca/ [accessed: 7 March 2013].
[8] Particularly interesting in this respect are the systematic attempts to document the religious situation in China. See, for example, the work of the Center on Religion and Chinese Society at Purdue University, IN, www.purdue.edu/crcs/ [accessed: 7 March 2013].
[9] See http://cordis.europa.eu/home_en.html for details of the Framework Programmes [accessed: 7 March 2013].

of Copenhagen from 2003 to 2007 – it was one of four Research Priority Areas established by the university. In this capacity, it 'housed' more than 70 initiatives of various kinds, including a strong emphasis on the training of doctoral students.[10] Somewhat similar is a Linnaeus Centre of Excellence hosted by the Faculty of Theology at Uppsala University. The programme initiated by this Centre is entitled 'The Impact of Religion: Challenges for Society, Law and Democracy' and is jointly funded by the Swedish Research Council and the university itself. It brings together more than 40 researchers from six different faculties, including the hard sciences, and will run for 10 years (2008–18).[11]

The fact that so many initiatives have occurred at more or less the same time is, I contend, evidence of a step change in activity in the study of religion. The numbers of scholars involved in these programmes, their individual and joint publications, the conferences that they both host and attend and the impact that their work will have outside as well as inside the academy will undoubtedly make a difference. New knowledge will be generated in abundance, a new generation of scholars will be trained, and new possibilities for collaboration will emerge. Quite apart from this, new fields of study are becoming apparent almost by the day.

Three of these will be taken as examples: the growing significance of religion for law and law-making, new initiatives in medical practice, and the renewed attention to religion in connection with welfare. All three require the input of very different groups of scholars and have come about at much the same time. It is no coincidence, for instance, that the inaugural meeting of the International Consortium for Law and Religion Studies (ICLARS) took place in 2009. The emphasis of this meeting was on state–church, or more accurately state–religion, relations and brought together constitutional lawyers from all over the world. Clearly the presence of new forms of religion and the aspirations of very different religious actors (both individuals and groups) are straining current arrangements – tensions displayed in both the case studies and the more thematic papers presented at the meeting. A selection of these can be found in Ferrari and Cristofori (2010).[12]

---

[10] See www.ku.dk/priority/Religion/index.asp for more details of the 'Religion in the 21st Century' Research Priority Area and the publications emerging from this [accessed: 7 March 2013].

[11] See www.crs.uu.se/Impact_of_religion/ for the content and structure of this initiative [accessed: 7 March 2013].

[12] Equally relevant is a new journal in this field entitled *Law and Religion*. See http://ojlr.oxfordjournals.org/ for more details [accessed: 7 March 2013].

Human rights lawyers are similarly engaged, recognizing that rights and freedoms often collide with each other. Freedom of expression (in the form of legitimate critique or satire), for example, is not always easy to distinguish from unwarranted criticism of religion, and legislation to outlaw discrimination on the grounds of sexual orientation is likely to conflict with the rights of those who espouse more traditional forms of belief. There are no easy answers to these clashes of interest. Family lawyers, thirdly, are facing new issues – not least the very definition of a family. The beginnings and ends of life are increasingly imprecise as medical technologies advance, and as the unimaginable becomes not only possible but commonplace: a foetus can exist outside the womb, single-sex couples procreate, living wills are increasingly common and assisted suicide is legal in some parts of Europe. These, moreover, are all questions on which religious groups have strong and not always compatible views.

Reactions to the re-emergence of religion in late modern societies are markedly contradictory – a tendency well illustrated by two medical examples. It is clear, on the one hand, that religious or spiritual issues are taken far more seriously that they used to be in certain branches of modern medicine. Clinical psychiatry is a case in point. John Cox, for instance, advocates an approach that takes account of the whole person, acknowledging that more and more patients (notably those who come from overseas) present with 'religious' symptoms. Such an approach draws very directly on the ideas and beliefs of Paul Tournier. Applied systematically, Tournier's 'medicine of the person' (a turning away from the bio-medical model) could have far-reaching effects in many areas of health care (Cox et al. 2006). At the same time, however, certain forms of religious display are more consciously outlawed from the medical environment than used to be the case. In the spring of 2010, an English nurse refused either to remove or to hide a cross while working, and was consequently moved to a desk job. She took her case to an industrial tribunal, which found against her.[13]

In terms of the argument of this chapter, the two medical examples are doubly interesting in that the first regards religion, and even more so spirituality, as a resource in good medical practice, but the second quite clearly sees it a 'problem' – as something that should be literally hidden from view. Such contradictions are not only commonplace in late modern societies but are likely to continue. An important reason both for the inconsistencies themselves and for the intractability of the underlying issues lies in the fact that they hover on the edge

---

[13] This was one of four British cases taken to the European Court of Human Rights in 2012. In all four, the judgments raise interesting issues about the place of religion in the workplace. Balancing the rights of religious people against the right of same-sex people to equality under the law is never easy. The point is clearly made in Rozenberg (2013).

of the public and the private. Simply deeming religion to be a private matter – the 'traditional' European answer – is no longer an adequate solution, but what is? Serious attempts to resolve these questions drive a great deal of the current research agenda, in which many disciplines have a role to play. Reconciling both the rights and responsibilities of different groups of people requires insight from diverse bodies of knowledge.

A rather different point brings this section to a close. For a whole range of reasons (some internal and some external), late modern societies find themselves in serious difficulty regarding the provision of welfare. Demand is rising, but resources are scarce and in the present economic climate are likely to become more so. The focus of the debate varies from place to place, but the underlying themes are the same: the imbalance in the working and non-working sections of the population (especially the growth in the number of elderly people) and a growing awareness that the state can no longer provide from the cradle to the grave – a realization that leads in turn to a search for alternative providers. All that said, it is important to make a distinction between the developed welfare states of many European societies and the very different ways of dealing with these issues in the United States. In the latter, faith-based welfare has always been the norm rather than the exception, but even in Europe, policy-makers are looking again at faith communities as possible providers. In this sense, though sometimes grudgingly, religion is once again seen as a resource for the wider society (Bäckström et al. 2010, 2011).

New Questions

For all these reasons, religion is rising in the public agenda, prompting renewed attention to the topic, expressed among other things in a vigorous research sector. As we have seen, much of this activity is policy-oriented and driven by the changing nature of society. It prompts, however, new questions for the sociology of religion. Three of these will be addressed as a conclusion to this chapter: the notion of the post-secular; the degree to which theoretical approaches (both old and new) can be generalized; and the need to engage the mainstreams of social science in the study of religion. The discussion is brief, deliberately provocative and recalls my earlier writing in this field.

The term 'post-secular' is widely used, but to mean very different things. For a start, it raises once again the possibility that perception may be more important than reality: the world is deemed post-secular because we have chosen to take notice of religion rather than to ignore it. The religious situation itself has not changed that much. Post-secular, secondly, is rarely a neutral term. The increasing visibility of religion is welcome or less welcome depending on who you are, what you do and where you are situated in society. Religion, thirdly, 'returns' in many different ways – some of these are easier to accommodate than others, as indeed are the reactions they provoke. What has become known as the 'new atheism', for example, is largely a response – a vehement one at that – to the re-emergence of religion in the *public* sphere. New atheists are much less concerned about private belief.

My own view is the following. I welcome the current debate concerning the post-secular and the growing body of literature that surrounds it (see for example Molendijk et al. 2010; Baker and Beaumont 2011). Both are signs that religion is taken seriously – that is a good thing. The notion of the post-secular needs, however, considerable refinement. In Europe, for example, two rather different things are happening at once. It is true that religion has re-entered the public square in new and unexpected ways, and is demanding a response. It is equally true that the process of secularization is continuing – remorselessly so in many places. As a result, large sections of the European population have lost the concepts, knowledge and vocabulary that are necessary to talk about religion just when they need them most. It is for this reason that the standard of debate in many parts of Europe is so poor – an evidently worrying feature. A second strand of thinking draws on the work of David Martin: the post-secular, if it exists at all, is unlikely to be a single or unitary thing. It will be as patterned as its predecessor. Indeed, for precisely this reason, Martin (2011) is highly suspicious of the term. The interactions of the religious and secular should rather be seen in the long-term. 'Religious thrusts' and 'secular recoils' have happened for centuries rather than decades and – crucially for Martin – *they work themselves out differently in different places*. The shorthand of 'God is back'[14] cannot do justice to this necessarily complex agenda.

Martin's more nuanced approach builds very directly on to his *General Theory of Secularization* (1978), a book which interrogates the varied pathways of secularization in different parts of the world. This, in turn, underpins the approach of Hans Joas, who distinguishes up to seven different meanings of the term 'secular' (Joas 2002; Joas and Wiegandt 2009). Such complexities must be squarely faced; it is in working through them that a better understanding of late modern society will emerge, not in an exaggerated contrast between

---

[14] This was the title of a much discussed book authored by two senior journalists at *The Economist* (Micklethwait and Wooldridge 2009).

unitary, and thus distorting, understandings of secular and post-secular.[15] Such thinking echoes very clearly the point made in my 1998 article. Many of the difficulties that have arisen in the sociology of religion have their roots in the notion that 'one size fits all'. It was too frequently assumed that secularization was a necessary feature of modernization and that both processes will occur in the rest of the world as they have done in Europe. This is not the case – a shift accepted by increasing numbers of people, both in the academy and outside. The point to stress here is that approaches to the *post*-secular must be equally subtle and varied; it too must be understood in the context in which it occurs.

In 2007 I considered the agenda of the sociology of religion to be critical – in two senses. It was vital that we understood the place of religion in the twenty-first century and its continuing role in the lives of countless individuals and the societies of which they are part. I, however, was critical of a sub-discipline that did not always rise to this challenge. It is my firm belief that the sociology of religion – indeed the study of religion in general – is now in better shape. I welcome this shift unreservedly, but remain sceptical about the motivations for much of the work being done. By and large, religion is still perceived as a 'problem' – and in order to be better managed, it must be thoroughly researched. The emphasis therefore lies on control.

Such a statement requires immediate qualification. It is more applicable in some places than in others, to some disciplines than to others, and to some researchers than to others. Broadly speaking the potential of religion to become a positive resource is most easily appreciated by those who know it best. Specifically, American scholars find it easier than their European equivalents and those who work in the developing world find it easier still – notably anthropologists and development workers. Right from the start, the former were less affected by the secular turn than their sociological cousins. The latter are practical people driven by the circumstances in which they find themselves – very often they work in places where religious networks are both more intact and more reliable than their secular equivalents. It seems, moreover, that researchers who 'live' in the field (in whatever capacity and in whatever kind of society) are more likely to display a respect for their subjects and the lifestyles they embrace. Respect can include of course a critical perspective.

What next? Large numbers of researchers from many different disciplines are currently engaged in the study of religion – much of their work is innovative and insightful. In itself, however, this success suggests a further step: the need to

---

[15] On this point, Hans Joas is sharply critical of Jürgen Habermas (see in particular Joas 2002).

penetrate the philosophical *core* of the associated disciplines and to enquire what difference the serious study of religion might make to their ways of working. The size of the task should not be underestimated. Most of the disciplines in question have emerged more or less directly from the European Enlightenment, implying that they are underpinned by a markedly secular philosophy of social science. Interestingly it is precisely this point that Jürgen Habermas appreciates so clearly and addresses in his recent writing (for example Habermas 2006). He insists, moreover, that others have a similar responsibility: that is to rethink the foundations of their respective fields of study in order to accommodate fully the implications of religion and religious issues in their analyses of modern societies. This, moreover, means accepting religion as it is, not as we would like it to be. Above all, it must be driven by the data, not by the assumptions of overly secular social science.

References

Almond, G., Appleby, R.S. and Sivan, E. (2003). *Strong Religion: The Rise of Fundamentalisms around the World.* Chicago: University of Chicago Press.

Bäckström, A., Davie, G., Edgardh, N. and Pettersson, P. (eds) (2010). *Welfare and Religion in 21st century Europe: Volume 1. Configuring the Connections.* Farnham: Ashgate.

Bäckström, A., Davie, G., Edgardh, N. and Pettersson, P. (eds) (2011). *Welfare and Religion in 21st century Europe: Volume 2. Gendered, Religious and Social Change.* Farnham: Ashgate.

Baker, C. and Beaumont, J. (eds) (2011). *Postsecular Cities: Religious Space, Theory and Practice.* London: Continuum.

Berger, P. (ed.) (1999). *The Desecularization of the World: Resurgent Religion and World Politics.* Grand Rapids: Eerdmans Publishing Co.

Cox, J., Campbell, A. and Fulford, B. (eds) (2006). *Medicine of the Person: Faith, Science and Values in Health Care Provision.* London: Jessica Kingsley.

Davie, G. (1998). The Sociology of Religion, in *Encyclopedia of Religion and Society*, ed. W. Swatos. New York City: Alta Mira Press, pp. 483–9.

Davie, G. (2002). *Europe: The Exceptional Case. Parameters of Faith in the Modern World.* London: Darton, Longman and Todd.

Davie, G. (2007). *The Sociology of Religion.* London: Sage. A revised edition appeared in 2013.

Ferrari, S. and Cristofori, R. (eds) (2010). *Law and Religion in the 21st Century Relations Between States and Religious Communities.* Farnham: Ashgate.

Habermas, J. (2006). Religion in the Public Sphere. *European Journal of Philosophy*, 14(1), 1–25.

Joas, H. (2002). *Do We Need Religion? On the Experience of Self-Transcendance*. Boulder: Paradigm Publishers.

Joas, H. and Wiegandt, K. (eds) (2009). *Secularization and the World Religions*. Liverpool: Liverpool University Press.

Kepel, G. (1994). *The Revenge of God: The Resurgence of Islam, Christianity and Judaism in the Modern World*. London: Polity Press.

Martin, D. (1978). *A General Theory of Secularization*. Oxford: Blackwell.

Martin, D. (2011). *The Future of Christianity: Violence and Democracy, Secularization and Religion*. Farnham: Ashgate.

Marty, M. and Appleby, R.S. (eds) (1991). *Fundamentalisms Observed*. Chicago: University of Chicago Press.

Micklethwait, J. and Wooldridge, A. (2009). *God is Back: How the Global Rise of Faith is Changing the World*. London: Allen Lane.

Molendijk, A., Beaumont, J. and Jedan, C. (eds) (2010). *Exploring the Postsecular: The Religion, the Political and the Urban*. Leiden: Brill.

Rozenberg, J. (2013). Balancing Christian and Gay Rights isn't Easy – Give Strasbourg Some Credit. *Guardian*, 15 January [Online]. Available at www.guardian.co.uk/law/2013/jan/15/christian-gay-rights-strasbourg [accessed: 7 March 2013].

Chapter 2
What Sort of Social Theory Would Benefit the Sociology of Religion?

Steve Bruce

Introduction

This chapter considers the nature of social theory and its use in British studies of religion. It also offers what I hope are some improving suggestions. The British focus is deliberate. In part it arises from a desire to concentrate on material with which the reader may be familiar. In part it stems from a suspicion that the sociology of religion in Britain is somewhat unusual. Karl Marx, Max Weber and Emile Durkheim all studied religion and that heritage ensures the sociology of religion an honourable position in the British sociology canon but there is currently little British sociological interest in religion.[1] From its inception the British Sociological Association's Religion Study Group has always attracted a large number of non-sociologists to its annual conferences and a very large proportion of the empirical studies of contemporary religion in Britain are the work of people who are not social scientists. This impression can be quantified quite accurately. Linda Woodhead and Rebecca Catto's edited volume *Religion and Change in Modern Britain* (2012) includes the work of 36 researchers, many of them reporting on projects conducted under the AHRC/ESRC Religion and Society programme. Most of the contributors are familiar names from the *Journal of Contemporary Religion* and BSA Sociology of Religion conferences. Of the 36, 16 are theologians by current profession or by training, only six are unambiguously social scientists, and only three of them are sociologists.[2] Of

---

[1] I apologise to any colleagues I have forgotten but, as of 2013, I can think of only one professor in a British sociology department whose primary field is the sociology of religion.

[2] The breakdown is as follows: Theology/Divinity/Arts-based Religious Studies 16; Education 4; Sociology 3; History 2; and Law 2. Two contributors are church officials. Demography, Geography, Journalism, Architecture, Politics and Philosophy have 1 representative. The Civil Service and Anthropology have a half each. Two of the contributors now hold posts with sociology in the title but are theologians by training.

itself there is nothing wrong with this but it does have consequences for the theme of this collection and for my comments on the use of social theory. As will become clear, I find it difficult to separate the narrow question of how we use social theory from the wider issue of how we improve research which uses social scientific concepts and methods but is produced by scholars whose interest in social science is secondary.

Inter-disciplinary research is often excellent and I am not particularly precious about the discipline of sociology. However, academic disciplines are not merely flags of convenience. They have discrete bodies of knowledge, repertoires of questions and specialist skills, and the three are necessarily linked. In order to know certain things one has to ask certain things and be able to do certain things. For example, people who have not been trained to design and manage attitude surveys are more likely inadvertently to produce unrepresentative results than people who have taken quantitative social research methods courses. To give a recent example: a major project to assess the religious beliefs of English university students found over half describing themselves as religious or spiritual and just over a quarter describing themselves as Christian. Of those, almost three-quarters had attended church regularly. That is, some 18 per cent of students were regular churchgoers. This was presented as evidence of the growing popularity of religion among young people. And it would indeed be a remarkable finding were it not for the fact that it was based on a response rate of only 9.4 per cent to an email questionnaire sent to a sample of universities which included a disproportionate number of former Church of England training colleges. The students who were invited to complete the questionnaires were randomly selected but the colleges were not representative. It is almost certain that students who are religious or spiritual were more likely to respond than students who were indifferent or hostile to religion. Even worse, there was nothing to prevent early adopters (such as members of religious student societies) encouraging their friends to complete the form. The results still have considerable value for understanding those who completed the forms but they can tell us nothing about English university students in general.[3]

Of course the sorts of questions best answered by social science research do not exhaust what is interesting about religion. However, as this is an extension of a lecture given to a conference organized by the British Sociological Association,

---

[3] The project in question is Christianity and the University Experience in Contemporary England. Results are from the project website: cueproject.org.uk [accessed: 10 January 2011]. Of the four researchers two are theologians and two were trained in an inter-disciplinary religious studies department. None has any formal training in social science.

I will assume that, whatever their disciplinary background, its readers share a common interest in those aspects of religion that are best addressed through social science research. That is, our common subject matter is found in such topics as the social causes of church growth and decline, the social transmission of religious beliefs and practices, the social correlates and processes of religious conversion, patterned social differences in religious activity, and features and consequences of religious organizations. Although they require some knowledge of the content of religious traditions in order to identify salient differences in what is being explained, their currency is not the legal tender of religious exegesis or apologetics. So I can summarize my concern in this question: how can social theory best be used to advance the social scientific study of contemporary religious phenomenon?

The Nature of Social Theory

I will start by defining social theory in an entirely conventional manner as the stuff we find in social theory books and teach on social theory courses. Although much of the work I have in mind is broad enough to exhibit more than one of them, for heuristic purposes I want to identify four tendencies in social theory: normative theory, zeitgeist metaphors, agenda-setters, and social scientific explanation.

Normative theory tells us what the world should be like. It is not just description and explanation; it is also a blueprint for a better future. Overtly normative work is more common in political theory than in sociology but critical sociology and feminist sociology, for example, are generally normative: that is, they take sides.

Zeitgeist metaphors are works which try to capture the essence of the modern age in a single jaunty image. It is no accident that 'zeit' and 'cite' sound similar. The key to citation heaven is to coin a snappy new metaphor for the contemporary condition: disciplinary society; risk society; McDonaldization; network society; tribal society; the rhizome; bowling alone; liquid modernity; there is a lot of it about.

Then we have the agenda-setters. Feminist theory, queer theory and post-colonial theory are not primarily logically-connected explanations of related social phenomena, though they can be that. They are ways of looking. They alert us to topics which have not been given due attention and to questions about those topics which have not previously been asked.

I might add here that a lot of the social theory that is heavy on these three tendencies is not the work of sociologists but of philosophers, psychoanalysts and literary critics.[4] I don't want to get bogged down in boundary demarcation. Like W.G. Runciman I tend to the view that 'a distinction between sociology, anthropology and history will have meaning only in terms of incidental differences of technique' (1970: 12) but there is a clear difference between those subjects and, for example, philosophy. Philosophy and literary criticism could be conducted entirely in a sealed room; they do not require sustained observation. I would argue that much of the weakness of the three tendencies in theory I have thus far discussed is related to the fact that they are closer to philosophy than sociology.[5]

My fourth tendency in social theory might be thought of as social scientific explanation. Examples would include Emile Durkheim on suicide, John Goldthorpe on social mobility, Howard Becker on deviance or professional socialization, Harry Collins on science. Here theory is an attempt to explain research findings in general terms that allows further refinement, extrapolation and testing.

Theory in the Study of Religion

Before considering the merits (or otherwise) of each of these four tendencies for the social scientific study of religion, I would like to report a brief exercise in witless empiricism. I thought it would be useful to see just which social theorists figure most prominently in British sociology of religion. There are more rigorous ways of doing this but to get some idea of current usage I went through the bibliography of each article published in the *Journal of Contemporary Religion* (*JCR*) over the 15 years of volumes 11 to 25 and noted how often social theorists – defined in a cavalier fashion as those people who get anthologized and discussed in social theory books – were cited. The results were as follows.

---

[4] For example, Edward Said, whose claims about the nature of orientalism have been extremely popular, was a student of English literature and art. Judith Butler (1997), whose notions of performativity have been similarly popular, is a philosopher and literary critic.

[5] As an illustration of how remote from the matter-in-hand social theory can become, I offer Bryan Turner's brief judgement of the influence of religion in the United States (2011: 105) where an important argument about fact is dealt with by summarizing a debate between Jurgen Habermas and Pope Benedict XVI, neither of whom are known for their detailed empirical research.

In the last 14 years, the top 10 theorists in the *JCR* were, in reverse order: Theodor Adorno (with five mentions) and Clifford Geertz (with six). Roland Robertson shares the seventh equal spot with Michael Foucault. Zygmunt Baumann takes sixth place and just ahead of him is Anthony Giddens. Placed fourth is Emile Durkheim. And now we reach the top three. And they are, in third place, Pierre Bourdieu; in second place, Max Weber; and, at number one, the most popular sociologist of religion with contributors to the *Journal of Contemporary Religion* is Peter Berger.

In keeping with the principle that good research produces findings one did not expect, the most significant observation from my trawl is not the popularity contest result, though the presence of Weber and Durkheim and the absence of Marx are surprises. It is the relative absence of social theory. Almost half the 267 articles surveyed (48 per cent to be precise) cite no social theorists. In total, 38 theorists are cited but 17 of them (again almost half) are cited only once. Furthermore, at least half the citations are ritualistic. For example, almost all of Robertson's seven citations accompany a passing mention of globalization and what puts Berger in the top spot is not anything from his extensive work on religion: it is his popularizing of the phrase 'the social construction of reality'. Usually nothing in particular is said about how this or that bit of reality is socially constructed; the point being bolstered is almost always the very general one that culture matters.

Of course it does not follow that, because an article does not cite any social theory, it has not been informed by any. The work of Bryan Wilson and David Martin, for example, is thoroughly pervaded by sociological theory, though direct references to theory are rare. But actually many of the *Contemporary Religion* articles are primarily historical, descriptive or exegetical. There is nothing wrong with that except perhaps lost opportunity. It is routine that articles in more narrowly disciplinary journals such as the *Journal for the Scientific Study of Religion* (*JSSR*) or *Sociology of Religion* justify their publication both by the novelty of the substantive research reported and by their contribution to current theoretical debates. The high theory of social science supposes that empirical research should advance development by testing some general (that is, theoretical) ideas. We know that in practice the theory–substance link often works the other way round. We research some religious movement or activity because it intrigues us and then we search for some theoretical argument to which our material can be turned. Even this adventitious link between substance and theory is often missing. A long career of reviewing journal submissions leads me to conclude that one of their most common weaknesses is theoretical justification that is so obviously spurious that it borders on the cynical: for example, if nothing more germane occurs, almost any description of religious (or even 'implicitly religious' activity) can be justified by claiming that it refutes the secularization thesis. But nonetheless very many articles in such journals as the *JSSR* do manage a fruitful interaction of theory and substance. The absence of that interaction does not necessarily render a research publication pointless but it is reasonable to describe it as missed opportunity. Readers can, of course, make their own connections but as the researcher knows the material better than anyone, he or she is best placed to at least begin the work of trying to explore the research's wider implications.

As I am about to criticize much contemporary social theory, one might think the above regret at the absence of social theory is self-contradictory, like the judgement of the diner who complains: 'The food was disgusting. And such small portions.' There is something in that but rationality can be restored by noting in advance a point I will elaborate later: there is also a dearth of sociology in much superficially social scientific writing about religion in Britain.

What Sort of Theory Should We Use?

If we accept in principle that more social theory would be a good thing, we can go back to my four tendencies in theory and consider what might be gained from each of them.

There are two obvious difficulties with normative social theory. The first problem is that, while taken in isolation any one such theorist may be inspirational, it is hard to construct rational grounds for choosing between competing visions of the good life when there is more than one of them. For social scientists working within a generally positivist epistemology, the value of any theory is determined by how well it is supported by the available evidence and how well it survives repeated attempts to refute it. Some normative social scientists are pro-cake and pro-the-eating-of-cake. Classically Marxists claimed that their work was both thoroughly scientific and better than bourgeois science because it augmented description and explanation with radical praxis. But the cavalier treatment of evidence in much normative work generally shows disdain for the scientific method and makes it clear that understanding some past or present reality takes second place to promoting extra-social scientific goals or values.

Once one rejects conventional notions of evidence, it is not clear how one chooses between competing normative theories, unless one accepts the theorist's norms, which means one has already chosen. I would like to say that I am withholding his identity to spare his blushes. Actually the author in question had so little impact on the field that I have forgotten his name but I very clearly recall one 'critical criminologist' (critical in both the Marxist and the complaining sense) dismissing the work of the great American criminologist Edwin Sutherland with the rhetorical flourish of asking 'what has Sutherland ever done to promote popular struggles?'. Like Marx he clearly believed that the purpose of theory was to change the world rather than just explain it. But as any number of us are unlikely to agree on what would count as positive change, political rectitude is no help here.

Rather flippantly, I sometimes think we should judge models of the good life by how well their promoters exemplify the virtues of the good society in their personal lives. The record is not impressive. Karl Marx was clearly a sponger and arguably a hypocrite. Walter Benjamin and Nicos Poulantzas committed suicide. Felix Guattari was a philanderer who bullied his wife into having affairs so that he didn't have to feel guilty about his own infidelities. Louis Althusser did more than bully his wife: he murdered her. These are not people you'd invite round to your house so why look to them for instruction on the nature of the good life? To be more serious: the problem with normative or critical social theory is that it offers no principles that are agreed outside that theory's magic circle for distinguishing between alternatives. Old-fashioned social science as science has agreed rules for choosing between alternatives. Critical theorists reject those rules but cannot agree amongst themselves about alternatives.

My second difficulty is that I cannot see how the majority of the research that is done by sociologists of religion would be much improved by normative social theory. It often seems that normative theory is used more in order to establish one's loyalties, to show affiliation, than to cast new light on empirical material. Even if one thinks there are good political or ethical reasons to take sides, it is hard to see how being on the side of the poor, or of women, or of the subjects of one's fieldwork, helps develop accurate description and plausible explanation.[6] A case could be made for saying that some degree of sympathy or rapport is required for understanding one's subject or subjects but beyond establishing that research may be hindered by certain attitudes or relationships, it does not offer any guide to the conduct of the descriptive and analytical parts of the research process.

It is even more difficult to see the value of normative social theory for partisan or apologetic studies of religion. If the purpose of one's academic work is to

---

[6] For the debate in the sociology of deviance, see Howard Becker (1967) and the debate it occasioned. Hammersley (2000) offers sensible reflections on the debate.

promote a particular religion, there seems little point in wasting time citing some non-religious thinker whose vision of the good life is coincidentally compatible with the value position one is promoting. One adds some apparent authority but the bottom line remains what is always was. In any partisan borrowing from social science, the secular works of people are so obviously trivial compared to the Word of God that there seems little point in mentioning them beyond a little dishonest impression management.

I have as much difficulty seeing the point of zeitgeist metaphors. It is somewhat ironic, given that the theorist who is in the business of coining some telling new metaphor clearly thinks that he or she is uniquely capturing the essence of modern times, that such metaphors often seem interchangeable. Any reader of academic journals will be familiar with the sort of article I have in mind. The zeitgeist metaphor gets a big puff in the introduction. There then follows detailed analysis of some small slice of human life which makes no reference to the metaphor. In the conclusion the metaphor re-appears briefly to add some theoretical weight to the substance of the study. In some cases I am not sure whether the novel research supports or refutes the zeitgeist metaphor: that may be a fault of drafting but more often the ambiguity is inherent in the fact that the phenomenon being studied is too small to offer any kind of critical test of a depiction of society as a whole. The lack of close fit between the zeitgeist metaphor theory and what is being studied also runs in the other direction. Just as the original research cannot test the theory, the theory can have so little particular address to the research that one suspects any zeitgeist could be replaced by any other without loss. So the study of the Snibbo sect that is presented as an illustration of liquid modernity could equally well be framed as an example of the network society or the deleterious effects of bowling alone or McDonaldization.

If that conclusion seems jaundiced, consider the short career enjoyed by such metaphors. Were it the case that flashly-attractive depictions of the modern condition were of lasting benefit to empirical research, they should surely endure. But they do not. Twenty years ago Roy Wallis and I wrote a general review of the British contribution to the sociology of religion. In it we took issue with two esteemed colleagues, both of whom I am very pleased to say are still with us, literally as well as metaphorically. Bryan Turner's *Religion and Social Theory* (which can still be read with great profit) criticized the sociology of religion for not being involved in 'any major theoretical debate in modern sociology'. In particular we had failed to engage 'in neo-Marxist debates about modes of production and ideology, French structuralist discussions of subjectivity and power, and critical theory's discussion of knowledge, the state and legitimacy'

(1983: 3). James Beckford made the same point in his *Religion and Advanced Industrial Society* when he said that 'the sociology of religion has been intellectually isolated against, and socially isolated from, many of the theoretical debates which have invigorated other fields of modern sociology' (1989: 13). The important theorists we should have been attending to were, according to Turner, Louis Althusser, Nicos Poulantzas, Jurgen Habermas, Barry Hindess and Paul Hirst. Althusser and Habermas also appears on Beckford's list, which also contains Michel Foucault, Antonio Gramsci, Alberto Melucci, Claus Offe and Alain Touraine. Twenty years later, probably only Habermas and Foucault are still read and then not often.

If we could be confident that the decline in popularity of theorists was a consequence of refutation, it could be claimed as a mark of the health of a discipline. However, I suspect that zeitgeist metaphors are, like butterflies, doomed to a short life irrespective of their intrinsic merits because their success depends precisely on their novelty. Like every other sort of fashion, changes in this realm of social theory seems driven not by testing through some Popperian process of conjecture and refutation but by cohort replacement. Each generation of students is unduly attracted to something hip and novel and each generation thus dooms their heroes and heroines to be disdained by the next generation.

As with the value of normative social theory, we can add a secondary observation about the use of zeitgeist metaphors by partisan apologists for religion. As it seems likely that the writer's religious faith comes first and determines the selection of, and attitude to, social theorists, claiming that some secular image of the age confirms (or at least does not clash with) the faith that one is punting is simply a rhetorical device; little different to Billy Graham's fondness for decorating his sermons with references to this or that bit of recent scientific research which apparently showed that southern Baptist evangelical Protestantism was superior to all other religions.

The value of agenda-setting theory is clearer. Even if we do not believe that scholars are unable to transcend either the ideological limits of their upbringing or the current interests of their class, gender, national, ethnic or professional identity, we can accept that we can become blinkered. And here the outsider has an advantage. There is always value in asking new questions and a new set of interests will often cast new light on old problems. However, I would caution against two common dangers of agenda-setting theory: exaggerating novelty and exaggerating the defects of what is old.

As an example of exaggerating distinctiveness, I offer ethnomethodology, especially in its sub-field of conversation analysis or 'CA'. Harold Garfinkel and his students (particularly Harvey Sachs) made a great fuss of criticizing all previous sociology for relying on unproven assumptions about motives (Garfinkel 1967; Sacks 1963). Ethnomethodology was superior because it did not make contentious guesses about motives and intentions. And yet it seems clear to those who are interested in the social organization of talk, but are not CA partisans, that the most basic tools of conversation analysis do rely on guesses about actor motives and intentions. For example, a question and a request are distinguished not by their grammatical form but by the assumed intention of the first speaker in the adjacency pair. So the person who replies to 'Do you know the time?' with 'Yes' will almost certainly have either made a mistake or be teasing, as will become clear when one or other repairs the fracture. Either the first speaker adds 'No, I mean "what time is it?"' or the second speaker adds 'Ha. Only kidding. It's 3.30'. One could argue that the sorts of motives and intentions assumed in ethnomethodology are considerably narrower and more mundane than the causal connections assumed in conventional sociology (where, for example, we might interpret an interest in esoteric magic as evidence of status anxiety) and are thus less likely to be mistaken. But it remains the case that the research done within the ethnomethodology canon now seems far less novel than the paradigm shift advertised in the original programmatic statements.

The second danger of agenda-setting theory is the wrong solution to the baby-and-bathwater problem. Feminist social scientists are quite right to point out that until the 1970s much social science paid little overt attention to gender. That tells us what new work needs to be done but it does not tell us what to do about the old stuff. Mary Jo Neitz is clear that work done within the secularization paradigm is of little value: 'in telling the story of secularization in terms of decline, we tell a partial story of elite white men' (2008: 222). To the extent that we are influenced by any agenda-setting theory we can dismiss everything that has gone before or we can treat the effects of omission as a research problem in its own right and ask to what extent would a different set of questions have changed the research and its conclusions. I would argue that much of the explanatory part of the secularization paradigm stands up pretty well to a gender-minded re-examination. For example, the social-psychological claim that being exposed to a range of different religious perspectives creates problems of certainty and conviction for the believer is a properly universal claim. It rests on universal assumptions about the difficulty of believing one's own views to be uniquely correct when one enjoys pleasant and rewarding interaction with people who hold very different views. It may be wrong but, unless we are to suppose that women are naturally more (or less) anti-social, obstinate or dogmatic than men, it is not wrong because it fails to distinguish between the sexes. The same can be said for the proposition that effective technologies displace occasions for resort to religious solutions and thus reduce the presence of religious ideas. The illustrations that we could draw from the life experiences of women and men are different (as are the examples we would draw from different social classes) but the key principle – that religion loses authority as the range of events for which it appears to offers the best solution decreases – seems genuinely universal. Furthermore, gender differences in outcomes may be perfectly well explained by universal propositions. The universal proposition that rewarding social interaction with people of different faiths weakens dogmatism fits well with the observation that generally male church adherence declines before that of women: in many settings gender differences in domestic roles and in employment patterns meant that men were more likely than women to interact with strangers and to perform jobs that required the sublimation of private preferences to religiously-neutral public roles.

To summarize, there is obvious value in agenda-setting theory which alerts us to omissions and identifies new research problems but we should beware of exaggerating both the virtues of the new and the vices of the old.

Finally I come to sociological explanation. Not surprisingly, as a sociologist who just happens to study religion, it is in general sociological explanation that I find a body of knowledge from which students of religious phenomena can borrow with advantage. Before introducing an example, I will introduce a caution which takes us back to my introductory point about the downside of inter-disciplinary bricolage.

Within any discipline, concepts and observations generally have a history of elaboration and testing that means that, in borrowing some notion from an unfamiliar field, one may impute to an authority which it does not have within its home discipline and hence which arguably it does not deserve. Theologians will doubtless be horrified by the mess I have frequently made of using theological concepts. But my concern here is with arts and humanities scholars borrowing from the social sciences. The point is best made with a detailed illustration. In their deservedly well-known study of alternative spirituality and conventional religion in the small English town of Kendal, Paul Heelas and Linda Woodhead (2005) explain the appeal of New Age spirituality as a reaction to the frustrations caused by what Max Weber called 'the iron cage of rationality': a popular headline idea. That explanation suffers the flaw of there being a major discrepancy of scale between those of us whom Weber thinks are trapped in the iron cage of rationality (which is pretty well everyone) and those of us interested in alternative spirituality (which, by their own data, is less than 1 per cent of the population). But arguably it also suffers from giving too much weight to an idea that sociologists have long since questioned. Garfinkel

(1967) on good reasons for bad organizational records, Donald Roy (1959) on time and task management on a production line, Melville Dalton (1959) on personal relationships within complex organizations, and Jason Ditton (1977) on workplace fiddling; these and many others have raised important questions about the nature of bureaucratic rationality. We now know that even in the most straitened and bureaucratized circumstances, even relatively powerless people find creative ways of manipulating rules and procedures to serve their own local and immediate interests. And one of those interests is the re-gaining of the autonomy supposed lost to the iron cage. One may be sceptical of the possibility of social science research emulating the natural sciences in the gradual improvement of knowledge through theory-testing research but this example is offered as an illustration of the general observation that inter-disciplinary borrowing will be most beneficial when an idea is followed through its natural history rather than simply lifted out of a disciplinary context.

Now let me come to the positive. There is a great deal of sociological theory that can greatly improve our studies of religious phenomena but it is mostly to be found, not in the sweeping generalizations that appear in the social theory textbooks, but in next layer down: in the work of empirical sociologists who present their research findings in general and comparative terms that invite extension to other fields. What used to be called 'theories of the middle range' and is now called 'analytical sociology' (Demeulenaere 2011) or 'social mechanisms theory' (Hedström and Swedborg 1998) encompasses a very large body of pertinent sociological theorizing. To illustrate the claim I will describe one body of social scientific work which, I would argue, has been neglected by students of religion. To be more precise, there is no doubt about its neglect; what needs to be argued is its value for students of religion.

In stark contrast to those social theorists who are frequently cited but who have actually made little difference, Robert K. Merton is little known outside the profession but he was responsible for coining a surprisingly large number of terms and phrases that we now take for granted because they proved useful in research: the self-fulfilling prophecy, the reference group, and role strain are just three reminders of a long and influential career. Merton was introduced to communication research in the 1940s by Paul Lazarsfeld and colleagues, who were working on voter selection in a presidential election (Lazarsfeld et al. 1944). Merton researched a US war bonds radio sales campaign and the results were published as *Mass Persuasion* (1946). That slim volume included a thought-provoking section on the creation of 'pseudo-gemeinschaft' that was later much anthologized. In association with Elihu Katz, Lazarsfeld went on to develop the 'two-step flow of communication' thesis (Katz 1957; Katz and

Lazersfeld 1955), which argued for the importance of personal relationships in the mediation of effects of the mass media. The rural sociologist Everett M. Rogers studied the spread of new seed varieties and developed that work into *The Diffusion of Innovations* (1962), which remains one of the most cited works of social science. What Merton, Katz, Lazarsfeld and Rogers had in common was an interest in how people are persuaded to change their ideas and practices and what is particularly valuable about their work is that it does not radically separate the social structural elements of persuasion from attitudes to the ideas themselves. A persistent problem of much sociological treatment of religious change is that it tends to present causal explanations of conversion in a way that implies either that people are dopes (they convert because some social force makes them) or that they are cynics (they convert because they wish to achieve latent or secondary functions such as finding a new 'family' or achieving social advance). The great advantage of the two-step flow of communication and the diffusion of innovation work was that it treated the 'plausibility' of new ideas and practices as complex function of the interaction of social forces, individual preferences, interests, and the use value of innovations. The implications for the study of religion conversion and, in the wider sense, the growth and spread of new religions would seem obvious but I am hard pushed to recall any student of religion using it. The same could be said for the sociology of science: a body of research in which British academics have achieved international prominence and which is concerned with many of the questions which feature in accounts of contemporary religious change, but which is so rarely cited I cannot think of an example.

To summarize my main point, we can simplify my opening four types of social theory to one axis: at the high end we have abstract theorizing about the nature of society that is so removed from empirical support that it comes close to sealed room speculation; at the low end we have detailed sociological explanations of areas of human life. While the former can offer some inspiration and even orientation, it is the latter which offers the greatest benefits to the empirical study of religion. The best sources of explanations of the social structural elements of religious change are not texts which aim to characterize the nature of modernity in a few phrases; they are detailed studies of putatively similar secular behaviour.

Conclusion

I would now like to return briefly to two loose distinctions made at the start. The first is between those aspects of religious belief and behaviour that are best studied by social science techniques and those that are best served by the perspectives and assumptions of the humanities. There does not have to be an abrupt divide for us to appreciate that, for example, such questions as 'Is the charismatic movement growing?', 'How significant is the charismatic movement' and 'What sorts of people are attracted to the charismatic movement?' require a different set of skills to the questions 'Is the charismatic movement the work of God?' or 'How does the charismatic movement use scripture to justify itself?'. The second distinction is between scholars trained in the social sciences and scholars trained in the arts and humanities. I am concerned here only with the first sort of subject matter. In a long career of reading empirical studies of religious belief and behaviour, produced by both sorts of scholar, I have rarely thought 'This would be improved by some high theory', though I have sometimes regretted missed opportunities for generalization. Of work produced by social scientists, and I include myself in this criticism, I have more often thought that it would be improved by a better understanding of theological concepts and of religious ideas. Of work produced by arts scholars, I have more often thought that it would be improved by greater familiarity with social research: not so much in the narrow sense of mastering techniques (though that would be welcome); more in the sense of grasping principles of observation and inference. Arranging systematic comparison, attending to the boundaries of implied units, thinking about causal direction and the difficulties of inferring causation from correlation, considering representativeness and the limits of plausible generalization, being able to see what would count as refutation of some claimed causal connection; these are the sorts of intellectual activities least well managed issues in much cross-over research. And there is a particular blind-spot with measurement. Timothy Jenkins argues that because the ways in which people can be directly and indirectly involved with churches are complex 'it is possible to hold a reasoned distrust both of statistics and of attitude surveys' (2004: 120). True, but the same scepticism applied evenly would make us even more distrustful of the impressions of one person which are supported by at best a few selected illustrations: which is exactly what most ethnographies offer. And we should remember that good reason to be doubtful about one descriptive measurement is not itself a warrant for asserting any alternative. I add this because in presenting evidence of secularization to seminars in Religious Studies departments I have all too often been met with a sceptical response to one piece of evidence being followed with an assertion for which there is no evidence at all.

In brief, given that there is an interest among arts-trained scholars in studying the social causes, correlates and consequences of religious beliefs and behaviour,

I would rather more people became familiar with social research than with social theory. Which brings me back to my earlier line of argument.

It is entirely understandable that the most popular social theory is generally also the most philosophical and least well-grounded. The grander the assertion, the greater its possible application and hence the wider the range of scholars who can find some value in citing it. The drawback is that there is a corresponding lack of specific value in improving our understanding of the social phenomena we research. For all that we can find inspiration in all sorts of social theory, the sort of theorizing likely to be of the greatest value to the sorts of scholars who attend this conference and who read journals such as the *JCR* is that which Merton calls theory of the middle-range and which I call simply sociological explanation.

References

Becker, H. (1967). Whose Side Are We On? *Social Problems*, 4, 234–47.
Beckford, J. (1989). *Religion and Advanced Industrial Society*. London: Unwin Hyman.
Butler, Judith (1997). *Excitable Speech: A Politics of the Performative*. London and New York: Routledge.
Dalton, M. (1959). *Men Who Manage*. New York: John Wiley.
Demeulenaere, P. (ed.) (2011). *Analytical Sociology and Social Mechanism*. Cambridge: Cambridge University Press.
Ditton, J. (1977). *Part-Time Crime: An Ethnography Of Fiddling And Pilferage*. London: Macmillan.
Garfinkel, H. (1967). *Studies in Ethnomethodology*. Englewood Cliffs: Prentice-Hall.
Hammersley, M. (2000). *Taking Sides in Social Research: Essays on Partisanship and Bias*. London: Routledge.
Hedström, P. and Swedborg, R. (eds). (1998). *Social Mechanisms: An Analytical Approach to Social Theory*. Cambridge: Cambridge University Press.
Heelas, P. and Woodhead, L. (2005). *The Spiritual Revolution: Why Religion is Giving Way to Spirituality*. Oxford: Blackwell.
Jenkins, T. (2004). *Religion in English Everyday Life: An Ethnographic Approach*. Oxford: Berghahn.
Katz, E. (1957). The Two-Step Flow of Communication: An Up-To-Date Report on a Hypothesis. *Public Opinion Quarterly*, 21, 61–78.

Katz, E. and Lazarsfeld, Paul Felix (1955). *Personal Influence: The Part Played by People in the Flow of Mass Communications*. Glencoe: Free Press.

Lazarsfeld, P.L., Berelson, Bernard and Gaudet, Hazel (1944). *The People's Choice: How The Voter Makes Up His Mind In A Presidential Campaign*. New York: Columbia University Press.

Merton, R.K. (1946). *Mass Persuasion: The Social Psychology of a War Bond Drive*. New York: Harper and Brothers.

Neitz, M.J. (2008). Afterword, in *Women and Religion in the West: Challenging Secularization*, ed. K. Aune, S. Sharma and G. Vincent. Aldershot: Ashgate, pp. 221–4.

Rogers, E.M. (1962). *Diffusion of Innovations*. Glencoe: Free Press.

Roy, D.F. (1959). Banana Time: Job Satisfaction and Informal Interaction. *Human Organization*, 18, 158–68.

Runciman, W.G. (1970). *Sociology in its Place*. Cambridge: Cambridge University Press.

Sacks, H. (1963). Sociological Description. *Berkeley Journal of Sociology*, 8, 1–16.

Turner, B.S. (1983). *Religion and Social Theory*. London: Heinemann.

Turner, B.S. (2011). *Religion and Modern Society: Citizenship, Secularisation and the State*. Cambridge: Cambridge University Press.

Woodhead, L. and Catto, R. (eds) (2012). *Religion and Change in Modern Britain*. Aldershot: Ashgate.

PART II
History and Religion

Chapter 3
The Axial Age Religions: The Debate and its Legacy for Contemporary Sociology

Bryan S. Turner

Introduction: Classical Sociology of Religion

In his 'Nine Theses on the Future of Sociology', Giddens' first thesis was that 'sociology will increasingly shed the residue of nineteenth and early twentieth-century social thought' (Giddens 1987: 26). Whatever the relevance of that prediction to general sociology, in the sociology of religion the field continues to be influenced by two contrasted traditions that have their origins in Emile Durkheim's *The Elementary Forms of Religious Life* (1961 [1912]) and Max Weber's *The Protestant Ethic and the Spirit of Capitalism* (2002 [1905–6]) and *The Sociology of Religion* (1966 [1922]). Despite significant developments in the study of religion, Weber and Durkheim continue to define the basic parameters of the sociology of religion. They remain important because they recognized the centrality of religion to social life, they understood how secularization posed critical problems for the continuity of social forms, and in order to understand the problem of religion in relation to modernity both sociologists looked beyond Europe to obtain a comparative, if not universal, perspective on religious institutions. Durkheim was influenced by William Robertson Smith's reflections on the functions of ritual in Semitic cultures in his *Lectures on the Religion of the Semites* (Smith 1997 [1889]). More importantly, he provided a brilliant analysis of the religious rituals and totemic beliefs of aboriginal communities from Central Australia (Spencer and Gillen 1997 [1904]). Weber, as we will see, undertook an ambitious study of religions in India and China as part of his broad project into the economic consequences of the world religions. Perhaps the only competition in this arena of classical sociology comes from Georg Simmel's *Essays on Religion* (1997) and *The View of Life* (2010), but this revival of interest is relatively recent.

On the basis of their studies, they provided a vocabulary and research agenda that, however much disputed, continues to influence contemporary research. However in modern sociology, large-scale comparative research has been largely abandoned, because contemporary epistemological debate has undermined confidence in claims about generic definitions of 'religion' across cultures and through history. The critique of universalism has also thrown doubt on such large-scale historical and comparative claims, and the legacy of the secular Enlightenment, specifically Immanuel Kant's philosophy of religion, is seen to be problematic. Against the background of the modern critique of evolutionary and universalistic approaches, the work of the late Robert Bellah stands out as exceptional and in this chapter I explore his contribution to the sociology of religion through a commentary on his relationship to the legacy of Max Weber and Karl Jaspers. My purpose is to defend comparative and historical research against epistemological scepticism. However, before launching into that defence, some preliminary observations about the legacy of Durkheim and Weber are in order.

To start with Weber, his work has been narrowly and conventionally conceived as the comparative study of the social and cultural conditions that gave rise to rational capitalism in the west and more generally to secular modernity. In this respect, *The Religion of China* (1951 [1916]), *The Religion of India* (1958 [1916]) and *The Sociology of Religion* (1966 [1922]) represent major contributions towards what Friedrich Tenbruck (1980) has identified as the 'thematic unity of Weber's work', namely the study of the economic ethics of the world religions. I propose that, while Weber clearly had in mind the study of the origins of rational capitalism, these interpretations (rationalization, routinization of charisma, origins of capitalism, economic ethics and so forth) are, while accurate, perhaps the least interesting or important aspect of the Weber legacy. In this discussion, I am more concerned with the underlying moral vision of Weber's work in the context of understanding other cultures (Peel 1969) or, in modern parlance, of understanding religious traditions from a cosmopolitan perspective and outside so-called 'methodological nationalism' (Delanty 2012).

We can more broadly interpret Weber's project in terms of the analysis of the religio-cultural complexes shaping human choices in relationship to empirical reality. In this more expansive interpretation, Weber's sociology of religion was a contribution to the comparative study of 'personality and life orders' (Hennis 1988; Schluchter 1988). In this respect the distinction between mystical and ascetic orientations becomes the central issue, and therefore the *Zwischenbetrachtung* or 'The Religious Rejections of the World and their Directions' (Weber 2009 [1915]) is the decisive text. Within this framework we can study religions, specifically modern religious movements in their urban settings, as systems of rules of personal piety, especially in terms of the disciplining of the human body (Turner 2011). The emphasis here is on practices and rituals in the everyday world or habitus that are designed to produce virtue or religious excellence.

There is however another way in which we might think about Weber's comparative and historical sociology of religion which is brought to light by considering his legacy within the debate about the religions of 'the Axial Age' that has revolved around the work of Robert Bellah on religion and human evolution and the work of the late Shmuel N. Eisenstadt (2000) on 'multiple modernities' and his reflections on the Axial-Age thesis (Eisenstadt 1992). As we will see shortly, Bellah brought our attention to the importance of Weber's idea of 'acosmistic love' or 'life-denying love' and following Bellah's lead we can approach Weber's sociology as the study of the inevitably tragic relationship between politics, which requires violence as a means, and religious traditions that attempt to institutionalize an ethic of brotherly love. In this struggle between politics and religion, the demand for peaceful co-existence (in the ethic of absolute commitment) is sacrificed to the mundane requirements of politics and reasons of state (in the ethic of responsibility). In his late work, Bellah proposed that this debate culminated towards the end of Weber's life around the figure of Leo Tolstoy. In the relationship between 'the religious and the political' (Turner 2013), religious values are, in the last analysis, typically compromised in favour of political necessity. Hence life is tragic from a religious perspective.

In Karl Jaspers' *The Origin and Goal of History* (1953 [1949]) these religions or ethical systems failed ultimately to control violence in human societies, and hence there is a tragic element to these diverse movements. Jaspers (1953: 20) specifically recognized that the Axial Age had 'ended in failure'. How does this relate to Weber's own implicit ethical position vis-à-vis violence? One answer is to be found in *The Religion of China*, namely that 'China in particular has become a crucial case to test the empirical soundness of the Axial Age theory' (Roetz 2012: 255). For Weber, Chinese civilization never experienced the tension between 'the world' and the religious imagination, mainly because Confucian values were always absorbed into the state without any tension or ambiguity. Most of the 'revisions' of Weber's account of the Orient have sought to challenge not only his interpretation of Confucianism, but more generally his approach to Asian cultures (Busse 1985).

These developments open up at least two interesting lines of inquiry. The first is simply to ask whether Weber's description of Chinese religions is empirically valid. In general, modern scholars have argued that his interpretation of religious life in China cannot be easily supported. A second question strikes me as obviously more interesting, namely whether it is possible to see Weber's sociology – despite all the debate about his philosophy of the social sciences in terms of its objectivity and value neutrality – as an ethical inquiry that was conducted on the stage of world history into the tragic and fateful relationships between the means of violence in politics and the quest for brotherly love in the legacy of the Axial Age religions? And as an additional line of thought, what is the relationship between Durkheim and Weber in terms of this larger ethical question about the conditions that make social life satisfactory, or at least possible as a consequence of the regulation of violence? I conclude that much contemporary sociology of religion has become trivial and local by comparison with the classical legacy of Weber and Durkheim. The exceptions to this harsh judgment would include the authors who conributed to *The Axial Age and its Consequences* (Bellah and Joas 2012). Two other noteworthy exceptions in historical sociology are Peter Stamatov's *The Origins of Global Humanitarianism* (2013), which examines religious responses to slavery and the genocide of Native Americans, and David G. Hackett's *That Religions in which all Men Agree* (2014), an historical sociology of Freemasonry in the formation of civil society in the United States. Having noted these contributions, one can only agree with Ates Altinordu (2013: 67) that, given Weber as the starting point, 'It is surprising that a vast majority of recent work in the American sociology of religion is characterized by a presentist and non-comparative outlook, with most studies focusing on contemporary American congregations'.

Generally speaking, large-scale comparative and historical sociology did not flourish in the post-war period, especially in American sociology. In retrospect, one can always think of exceptions – Guy E. Swanson's *Religion and Regime* (1967), Talcott Parsons' *The System of Modern Societies* (1971) and Benjamin Nelson's *On the Roads to Modernity* (1981) – but the generalization will hold. Today in British sociology, David Martin (2011), working on Pentecostalism and the future of Christianity, continues the tradition of large-scale sociological analysis. Another recent example in the United States would be Philip S. Gorski's *The Disciplinary Revolution* (2003). However, other major figures in historical and comparative sociology often ignored religion. For example Norbert Elias (2000 [1939]) in his study of European manners was more or less silent about the impact of Christianity on 'the civilizing process'. While focusing on the emergence of the state in relation to different patterns of self-regulation, he did not attach any significance to the role of the Church. The contrast with Weber, who in many ways was the inspiration behind Elias' magnum opus, is striking. The exceptions to this observation that sociology abandoned large-scale comparative studies of religion, include, as I have already observed, Eisenstadt and Bellah. While Eisenstadt did not write extensively on China, he disputed Weber's interpretation of the religions of Asia in *Japanese Civilization* (1996) by claiming that Weber had not fully appreciated the theme of transcendence in Confucianism. Bellah, in contrast to scholars of his generation, has done much to revive the Weber tradition in his monumental *Religion in Human Evolution* (2011).

Bellah plays an important part in my exposition, not simply because he was inspired by both Durkheim and Weber, but because he is one of the few major figures in mainstream American sociology to have taken Asian cultures seriously. One can simply refer here to his *Tokugawa Religion* (1957) and *Imagining Japan* (2003). From his study of Jaspers and early Chinese society, he departed from Weber's interpretation in arguing that there was a sense of transcendence in Confucianism and therefore Confucian ideas cannot be interpreted as merely a secular ideology of the state and a system of ethics for the literati. His use of the Axial Age framework to analyse the transcendental character of Confucianism is perhaps the most important work to be published within the Weber legacy for many decades. Bellah (1999) approached Weber's sociology of religion from the perspective of 'an object-less life-denying love' (*ein object-lösen Liebesakosmismus*) better to understand the nature of Confucianism not as a state ideology but as a genuine world religion that is a religious tradition with a strong sense of transcendence.

In this introductory comparison of Weber and Durkheim, one might start simply by noting that, whereas Durkheim was interested in the generic notion of *religion* (specifically the classification of the sacred and profane), Weber was concerned with the historical and comparative importance of *religions*. Durkheim famously observed it to consist of 'a unified system of beliefs and practices relative to sacred things' (Durkheim 1961: 62). Weber (1966: 1), by contrast, declared in *The Sociology of Religion* that defining '"religion", to say what it *is*, is not possible at the start of a presentation such as this. Definition can be attempted, if at all, only at the conclusion of the study'. While Weber examined for the consequences of the 'economic ethics' of the world religions, Durkheim examined the 'elementary forms' of religious classification, the impact of their emotional framing, how these classificatory systems were embedded in ritual practices, and finally how the 'collective conscience' was an essential foundation of the social. If there is a point of convergence between Weber and Durkheim, it is that authentic religion is characterized by its seriousness either because it involves for Weber an overriding vocation or because for Durkheim human contact with the sacred is dangerous and sacred spaces and practices are not to be approached frivolously or carelessly. This idea of taking religion seriously from a scientific perspective was probably influenced by William James (1929 [1902]) in *Varieties of Religious Experience* from the Gifford Lectures in 1901–2. It may be a sweeping exaggeration but one could plausibly argue that Durkheim was not interested in religion as such. His focus was on the collective experiences of the sacred, which we can argue is the real foundation of everything that gets defined as religion.

With respect to specific religious traditions, Durkheim did not undertake any extensive study of Chinese religion. However *Primitive Classification* (Durkheim and Mauss 1963 [1903]) offered a characteristic investigation of Chinese religion in terms of its classificatory significance. More precisely, he argued that the underlying principle of Asian religions (at least in China, Cambodia, Thailand, Tibet and Mongolia) was 'Tao', which he translated as 'nature'. Durkheim and Mauss noticed that the underlying logic of Chinese classification was complex – often involving multiples of eight. They also observed that the classificatory system facilitated the 'reduction of multiplicity of gods to one, and consequently they have prepared the way for monotheism' (Durkheim and Mauss 1963 [1903]: 78). Did the classificatory principle anticipate the universal monotheism of the Axial Age?

While Durkheim was not especially interested in Asian religions, we can treat Marcel Granet (1884–1940) as a substitute, so to speak, for Durkheim. We can compare Weber's treatment of China with the legacy of Marcel Granet whose *The Religion of the Chinese People* (1951 [1922]) and *Chinese Civilization* (1930 [1929]) were influential in French historiography in the 1930s. Granet was a member of the Durkheim circle, and was influenced by Edouard Chavannes, Marcel Mauss and Henri Hubert. Granet's oeuvre illustrates his interest in rituals and customs within a framework derived from Durkheim and Mauss. The study of religious festivals was dedicated to Durkheim and Chavannes. As a professional Sinologist, Granet was in fact interested in more general social phenomena. His work was a major contribution to the sociology of knowledge but *Chinese Civilization* had relatively little to say about the sacred, concentrating instead on power structures in the feudal system and their eventual evolution towards an imperial political and urban culture. If Durkheim's sociology was a study of morality or mores – for example in *Professional Ethics and Civic Morals* (1992) – we may not be surprised to find Granet placing considerable emphasis on Chinese moral codes such as filial piety. He (1930 [1929]: 310) declared filial piety to be 'The foundation of domestic and even of civic morality'. Weber went in a similar direction, observing that 'piety, the mother of discipline, was the only true absolute duty and a literary education was the only true means of perfection' (Weber 1951 [1916]: 163).

As we know, Weber was reluctant to describe Confucianism as a religion and in *The Religion of China* described piety (especially filial piety) as the basis of moral conduct. An important aspect of Christianity, in contrast to other world religions, was its decisive break with kinship ties and familial relationships. The charismatic authority of Jesus, and the promise of a coming world, overturned any mundane loyalty to parents or the wider kinship group. As a development within Judaic millenarianism, Jesus and his disciplines did not anticipate the continuity of this world and therefore the family as a reproductive unit was irrelevant to early Christian eschatology. In Pauline Christianity, the faithful are commanded to abandon their duty to family in order to respond to the pure charismatic demands of the gospel of Jesus – Follow me! In his account of the city and citizenship in *The City*, Weber also noted that the Christian congregations were not familial or kinship organizations, because the Christian community was based, to quote St Paul, on the 'circumcision of the heart'.

Weber's notion of 'religion' is that it exists in perpetual tension with 'the world' made up of the various value spheres. For Weber, insofar as we are in the garden of 'disenchantment', what remains of the moral or serious life can only be conducted as a vocation in either science or politics. In what we might call the charismatic challenge to established routines, Weber followed Adolf von Harnack (1912 [1908]) who had elaborated a notion of the conflict between inspiration and tradition in his *The Mission and Expansion of Christianity in the First Three Centuries*. This theme has been taken up by Gerd Theissen in his controversial *The First Followers of Jesus* (1978) in which he described different types of 'wandering charismatics'. However Weber extended Harnack's ecclesiology of western Christendom into comparative religion by looking at religious tensions with the world and their eventual rationalization and standardization. Thus Confucianism had no such tension with the world, the emperor and the family. Hence 'in sharp contrast to Buddhism, Confucianism meant adjustment to the world, to its orders and conventions. Ultimately it represented just a tremendous code of political maxims and rules of social propriety for cultured men of the world' (Weber 1951 [1916]: 152). Given this pragmatic orientation to the secular world, he concluded that Confucianism had no notion of individual salvation from sin and redemption through grace. In the Confucian ethic, the literati 'had no desire to be "saved" either from the migration of the souls or from punishment in the beyond' (Weber 1951 [1916]: 156). If this tension with the world provided the underlying dynamism of the Puritan world, it was also the source of its tragic vision.

If this comparison with Durkheim is worth making, one needs to ask whether there was any parallel moral argument or sentiment in Durkheim's work equivalent to Weber's lecture on 'politics as a vocation'? Perhaps the underlying moral theme in Durkheim's sociology was that a meaningful life (or the serious life as he once defined 'religion') is only possible in a society that is normatively coherent. For Durkheim, the social and moral coherence of traditional European societies had been shattered by the First World War as a consequence of which he came to develop a notion of cosmopolitanism (or 'world patriotism') in response to nationalism and international conflicts. Perhaps we have here a possible point of convergence between Durkheim and Weber insofar as both men turned to the problem of violence with the industrialization of warfare. Durkheim died in 1917 and Weber in 1920. The classical sociology of religion was a product of urbanization and secularization after the French Revolution but perhaps it was terminated as a consequence of the social and moral problems thrown up by the mechanized violence in modern warfare. Joachim Radkau (2009: 540) suggests that Weber's sociology in general was haunted by the problem of death, namely that death no longer has any meaning in modern society. The mass slaughter of men in the trenches raised issues for which there was no convincing religious answer. The tragic dimension of Weber's sociology was perfectly captured by Jaspers in his 'commemorative address' in 1920 when he noted that Weber 'was also no Christian. For him, to be a Christian was to accept the commandment of the Sermon on the Mount: do not succumb to evil. He did not want to fulfil this commandment, because it was incompatible with operating in the world' (Dreijmanis 1989: 22).

Karl Jaspers, Max Weber and the Axial Age

Jaspers' *The Origin and Goal of History* was published in 1949; to Hannah Arendt, he had described his ideas on the Axial Age as 'a presumptuous project' (Arendt and Jaspers 1992: 109). In the English-speaking world, the debate was launched by a publication in *Commentary* (Jaspers 1948). Of less importance were the essays on great philosophers that included works on Socrates, the Buddha and Confucius (Jaspers 1962 [1957]). The subtitle of the *Commentary* article – 'A Base for the Unity of Mankind' – adequately captures the moral purpose of his 'presumptuous project'. In many respects Jaspers was writing against the legacy of Hegel arguing that the notions of history, criticism, transcendence and humanity were already highly developed well in the Axial Age before the rise of the modern world. While Jaspers is obviously the author of the concept of an Axial Age, Hans Joas (2012: 17) proposed that Weber has to 'figure prominently' in any debate about the Axial Age, noting in passing that in *Economy and Society* Weber (1978 [1928]) made various comparative references to Greek and Indian parallels to the prophets of early Judaism. Indeed for Weber the age of prophets constitutes '*the* crucial event in the history of religions'.

Jaspers is important for my interpretation of the history of the sociology of religion, because his work is directly influential in Bellah's approach to the evolution of religion and specifically to the religions of China. Bellah's *Religion in Human Evolution* falls into two sections. In the first section, his interests and approach are distinctively Durkheimian. Following the work of Merlin Donald (1991) in his *Origins of the Modern Mind*, Bellah developed the idea of religion passing through three stages or themes: the mimetic, the mythic and the theoretic. This scheme owes something to Durkheim's focus on early rituals as elementary forms. The idea that as modern religions evolve they shed their mythological forms probably grew out of Jaspers' encounter with Rudolf Bultmann who was at the time working towards his idea of the de-mythologization of Christianity (Jaspers and Bultmann 2005 [1953–4]). According to Bellah in the mimetic stage, it was through play and associated rituals that early humans began to develop religion, but it was only in the Axial Age that these warm-blooded mammalian creatures became recognizably human (through their religious and critical collective conscience). The second half of the study is indebted to Weber, being concerned primarily with religious responses to violence (in the shape of war and politics). It is in this second section that the theme of acosmistic love comes into its own as basic to the Axial Age. It is in Bellah's analysis of Confucianism that Durkheim and Weber were finally reconciled in a macro-comparative history of religion in the course of human history.

For Jaspers the Axial Age was the transformative period of the prophets and religious leaders such as Confucius and Lao-Tse in China, the Buddha in India, Zoroaster in Iran, the prophets of ancient Israel, and finally the poets and philosophers of ancient Greece. Through the idea of revelation, the prophets offered humanity a notion of a different superior world beyond or one distinctively contrasted with the mundane world of the here and now. Through reason and revelation, these leaders developed ethical codes of conduct that established norms of virtuous behaviour and that constituted a breakthrough in human history. These early religio-ethical movements therefore established a division between a spiritual sphere and the everyday world of violence, need and interest. These prophets and philosophers established 'the age of criticism' (Momigliano 1975: 9). For example, Plato looked towards Socrates the philosopher as the kingly personality and not to military heroes such as Achilles.

In China it was Mencius who championed the legacy of Confucius as the wise official whose political vision promised peace and stability. In South Asia, it was the Buddha who challenged the legacy of caste and preached the supreme doctrine of non-involvement through a spiritual path. Finally the prophets of ancient Israel condemned the corruption of the monarchy and the temple priests in the name of a single transcendent God. In summary these religious leaders separated the spiritual world of self-development from the mundane callings of kings and warriors through critical worldviews that were revolutionary. In so doing, they set up a lasting tension between the political and the religious.

These religious movements emerged on the basis of important social and economic changes. Axial Age worldviews came into existence against a background of growing literacy, complex political organizations, early urbanization and advances in metal technology. There was a transition from bronze to iron, and importantly the emergence of coinage. The Axial Age was characterized by both rising prosperity and constant warfare between small states and occasionally by the rise of powerful empires. While these factors in the rise of the Axial Age have been challenged by historians, the work of Jaspers has been important in shaping modern historical sociology. As Bellah (2011: 271) has pointed out, although it is difficult to discover overt references in Weber's sociology to an Axial Age, there is a reference to the 'prophetic age' (Weber 1978: 441–2). For Weber, religious or charismatic movements for social change depend on a conflict between secular and religious values or between this-worldly and other-worldly orientations. The idea of 'religious orientations' to the world, conflicting with dominant economic and political realms, was pivotal to his analysis of the significance of 'world religions'. In both Judaism and Christianity, Weber found the roots of an ethic of brotherly love in opposition to this-worldly greed, selfishness and violence. Generally speaking, Weber did not see Islam in the same light despite the theme of suffering in both Sunni and Shi'ite traditions (Turner 1974). This sociological vision of an ethical realm standing over and against politics was tragic in the sense that love (*agape* not *eros*) is always compromised in this world. In a secular age, the best that ethically-driven people can achieve is a calling in science or politics wherein they might exercise some vestige of virtue.

Bellah's sociology of religion is exceptional in terms of its evolutionary framework and its large-scale perspective. Eisenstadt was perhaps the only other figure in modern sociology to have worked on such a wide ranging comparative scale. Eisenstadt (2000, 2002) has played an important critical role in the Axial-Age debate by exploring an alternative notion of 'multiple modernities' or what we might call 'second wave Axial Ages'. Heiner Roetz (2012: 253) observes that modern social science has abandoned the normative features of Jaspers' thesis in favour of a descriptive account of religious change, and he went on to claim that 'what Weber offers is a sociologically enriched reformulation of the same Hegelian view of non-Occidental cultures that Jaspers attacks'.

The idea of historical breakthroughs driven by religious ideas was at the heart of Weber's comparative sociology and hence he thought that the 'Asian religions', especially Hinduism and Confucianism, lacked both universalism and a sense of transcendence. As we have already observed, he regarded Confucianism as a moral code rather than a religion. In this respect Bellah, building his argument on Herbert Fingarette's *Confucius: The Secular as Sacred* (1972), rejected Weber in arguing that there was an important sense of transcendence in Confucianism and therefore Confucian ideas cannot be interpreted as merely a secular ideology. While Weber regarded this worldly asceticism as the driving force behind religious universalism, Bellah adopted an alternative approach to Weber's sociology of religion, namely from the perspective of 'an object-less life-denying love' (*ein object-lösen Liebesakosmismus*) to recognize Confucianism as a genuine world religion, that is a religious tradition with a strong sense of transcendence.

The Axial Age was defined by a growing appreciation of the unsatisfactory nature of the empirical world and in response the prophets and philosophers conceived of a transcendental and universal realm as an alternative to the grim humdrum routine reality of human existence. They conceptualized a world in which humans could flourish if they were once freed from the shackles of profane reality. More importantly, this world-to-come was in principle available to all human beings. The goal of history was to convert this moral vision into a social reality. However in *The Axial Age and its Consequences*, there is scepticism about the value of the general architecture of the theory. This sceptical reservation is summarized by Jan Assman (2012: 398): 'I cannot bring myself to believe in the "Axial Age" as a global turn in universal history occurring *grosso mondo* in the middle of the first millennium BCE. These "breakthroughs" occurred in different civilizations at different times and to different degrees under different conditions and with different consequences.'

The Axial-Age thesis has been much criticized in contemporary research (Boy and Torpey 2013). There are three basic objections to the Axial Age thesis. The first problem is the matter of chronology. It is striking that Jaspers and Momigliano identified the end of the Axial Age as occurring before both Christianity and Islam emerged. Was the Sermon on the Mount, to take one example from the New Testament, fully anticipated by the prophetic message of the Israelite prophets, or was the vision of justice in the Qur'an fully worked out in the original Axial-Age principles? It is not entirely convincing to suggest that the prophetic message of Jesus and Muhammad contributed nothing to the stock of ideas that had appeared between 800 and 200 BCE.

The second issue, which is important in the work of Weber, concerns the 'religion of China' and especially Confucianism, and the status of the 'religion of India', namely the Vedic and Brahminical movements of spirituality. The tendency of modern scholarship is to question the whole notion of 'the world religions' and scholars argue that what we now know as 'the religions of Asia' arose out the encounter between the west and Asia in the age of imperial expansion. Thus what we now know as 'Hinduism' was created in British India by the administrative difficulties of creating a census. It has been argued that there was no notion of 'religion' in Japanese culture until the fateful collision between Japan and the west when American warships appeared off the Japanese coast on 8 July 1853. As Americans began to demand the right to practice religion freely in their trade agreements with the Japanese courts, Japanese intellectuals had to develop a notion of religion (Josephson 2012). By contrast, neither Weber nor Durkheim confronted this epistemological criticism of 'essentialism'. The constitutive principle of Weber's comparative sociology of religion is that 'religion' implies some systematic tension with empirical reality of 'the world'. Religions that compromise their values and practices under pressure from economic and political institutions begin to lose their status as religions, becoming instead useful ideologies that legitimize hegemonic systems of power (from kings to modern presidents). As we have seen, Durkheim's generic definition of religion was aimed to overcome narrow understanding of religion in terms of supernatural beings that would have ruled out early Buddhism. Durkheim ends up treating the social and the religious as co-terminus; therefore religion is universal. I shall return to this problem in my conclusion.

Despite criticisms, the Axial-Age thesis remains important for us today. Firstly Jaspers' work and its legacy sought to avoid any notion of western supremacy and therefore the selection of religious leaders (the Buddha, Confucius, Socrates and Jesus) was overtly eclectic and global. This selection and Jaspers' general approach indicates the fact that the tradition of humanities in Germany was not invariably Orientalist in denying the value of the religions and philosophical systems of Asia. On the contrary, Jaspers put Confucianism and Buddhism on the same moral and civilizational plain as Israelite prophecy and the philosophy of Plato and Socrates. Jaspers (1962 [1957]) described Socrates, Buddha, Confucius and Jesus as 'paradigmatic individuals'. However, in making this point, we have to keep in mind the problem in his version of world history that it did not engage with either the Americas or Africa. Jaspers' legacy – the quest for the bases of the unity of mankind – was an antidote to the idea of a deep and inevitable clash of civilizations. The Axial Age points to a common origin to religions in human evolution and therefore this debate has an important moral dimension. Despite their global significance, for Jaspers and subsequently for Bellah, the religions and philosophies of the Axial Age with their theme of acosmistic love were failures in the sense that they ultimately offered no satisfactory answer or practical solution to the institutionalized presence of violence in human societies. What connects Weber, Jaspers and Bellah then is a moral vision of the evolutionary dilemma of humankind faced with the failure of the Axial Age religions to resolve the deep fissure between the ethic of brotherly love and the political necessity of violence. This dilemma was presented in Bellah's study of evolution through the story in the *Mahabharata* of the encounter between Krishna and Arjuna before the battle of Kauravas, when Arjuna recognized that to fulfil his obligations in the warrior caste he would be forced to kill members of his own kith and kin. There was therefore an inevitable conflict between the *dharma*, the way of the religious ascetics of Hinduism and Buddhism, and the political power of the princes (Bellah 2011: 561).

Weber, Universalism and China

Despite criticisms of western notions of world religions (Masuzawa 2005), did Weber engage in a similar universalizing account of religion? Weber's study of Chinese civilization was his first large-scale study of religion outside the west, and was designed as a volume within his larger project on the economic teachings of the world religions. His analysis of China concentrated on the powerful role of the traditional literati and their control over the centralized state bureaucracy, the traditionalism of Confucian teaching, and the conservative effects of family and kinship. Although the book is overtly about the contrast between Confucian orthodoxy and Taoist traditionalism, over half of the volume is devoted to an analysis of the social structure of traditional China. There is also the substantial chapter on the literati, which Weber's biographer Joachim Radkau (2009: 474) claimed was uppermost in Weber's mind, because at the time he was engaged with a bitter political fight with the German bureaucrats or literati.

Following the way in which Weber's argument unfolds, he began with the analysis of money, claiming that China failed to develop an integrated and effective monetary system, and this failure produced a significant brake on the development of rationalism in monetary exchange. Secondly, and following his thesis in *The City*, Weber (1958) noted that autonomous and vibrant cities were absent, and hence there was no space in the social structure for a genuine bourgeois culture to emerge and survive. He recognized that guilds were widespread in Chinese society, but they did not enjoy adequate legal protection. Instead China was characterized by a top-heavy centralized bureaucracy, which was run by a traditional Confucian literati. In short, China represented a clear example of what Weber described as a 'patrimonial bureaucracy', the centralization of which meant that state officials had little connection with local culture at the village level. He was also interested in the geography of China and its system of landownership. He believed that Chinese history had been characterized by recurrent attempts at land and taxation reform, but these official policies had been forcefully resisted by the peasantry which had a deep suspicion of state interference. Weber blamed much of the ineffective approach to land reform and the 'largely irrational conditions of landownership' on 'fiscal policies which alternated between arbitrary interventions and complete laissez-faire' (Weber 1951 [1916]: 80). In the absence of primogeniture and with a growing population, there was a tendency for the land to be continuously divided up into holdings of ever decreasing size, and as a result large-scale capitalist agriculture failed to develop. Finally he noted that the local organization of kin groups meant that the villages were highly traditional and resistant to change. Having discussed the social structure, Weber concluded the study of China with the famous analysis of Confucianism as an ethical system and Taoism as a magical heterodoxy within which he argued that the notion of *tao* in emphasizing stability and tranquillity never offered a radical challenge to the secular world. In short the 'Chinese "soul" has never been revolutionized by a prophet' (Weber 1951 [1916]: 142).

Much of the critical literature on Weber's thesis regarding Asia has been edited by Wolfgang Schluchter (1983). This literature is unsurprisingly focused on the causes of the failure of capitalism in China. However *The Religion of China* should not be seen simply or narrowly as an addendum to the famous 'Protestant Ethic Thesis' about the religious inspiration of rational capitalism (Love 2000). The grand theme of the final stages of Weber's sociology was the rationalization of culture in the west and its consequences. We might further specify the emerging theme as involving a deeper analysis of the nature of religion as such around the contrast between inner-worldly asceticism and mysticism, between religion as a 'cultural instrument' to re-shape the world or as an experience in which the human subject becomes a 'vessel' of grace. One of the central issues in Weber's work on China is the simple but profound underlying question: is Confucianism a religion? Much contemporary research continues to debate the religious character or otherwise of Confucianism (Sun 2013).

Weber's answer was quite emphatic and explicit. Firstly the Chinese language, he asserted, has no distinctive term for 'religion', but 'there was first: "doctrine" – of a school of literati; second – "rites" – without distinguishing whether they were religious or conventional in nature. The official Chinese name for Confucianism was "doctrine of the Literati" (*ju chiao*)' (Weber 1951 [1916]: 144). He concluded that 'Confucianism, like Buddhism, consisted only of ethics and in this *Tao* corresponds to the Indian *Dharma*' (Weber 1951 [1916]: 152). The point of this argument becomes more obvious if we turn to chapter six on the sociology of religion in volume one of *Economy and Society* where Weber gave a more explicit account of the differences between Oriental and Occidental religions. Recognizing that the distinction between asceticism and mysticism is fluid, he proposed that the Occident, or at least the Protestant version of Occidental culture, was dominated by an ascetic drive to confront and struggle with the world. In the Orient there was by contrast a greater emphasis on contemplative mysticism. There were in addition important organizational differences around law, congregations and priesthood. It was significant that in the Orient the 'Asiatic salvation religions' were produced and promoted 'as pure religions of intellectuals who never abandoned the "meaningfulness" of the empirical world' (Weber 1978 1:553). In the Occident, asceticism took the discipline of the monastery out into the everyday world of the laity and this creation of inner-worldly ascetic discipline led to rational control over sexuality, family life and economic activity. The outcome was the man of vocation and 'its unique result was the rational organization of social relationships' (Weber 1978 1:556). Thus Weber's sociology involved, not so much the narrow study of capitalism, but rather the life disciplines or 'life orders' that produced particular personality forms, especially the historical eruption of the men of vocation (Stauth and Turner 1986).

Conclusion: A Future for the Sociology of Religion?

Weber's comparative sociology of religions has remained controversial because of the influence of the quest to establish an agenda for world history or indeed universal history (Buck-Morss 2009). Weber has been accused often enough of 'Orientalism' (Turner 1978) or at least of approaching world religions from the perspective of the Calvinistic sects and within the framework of Kant's *Religion within the Boundaries of Mere Reason* (1998 [1763]). His theory of modernization rejected cultic or magical practices in favour of religions of personal discipline and piety (Turner 2009). Indeed religion starts where magic ends. The defining characteristic of Axial Age world religions for Weber was focused on prophecy. Bellah's work has the consequence of putting Weber's moral or tragic vision back into perspective thereby overriding or diluting some of the Orientalist critique. Here we can also see the difference between Durkheim and Weber. Durkheim (1961: 15) argued that no religions are false; all are true in the sense that they play a crucial role in sustaining social life. In this sense he cannot be accused of Orientalism and indeed Durkheim was not interested in universal religious history but rather sought out the generic features (or 'elementary forms') of religion. Granet's vision was by contrast not inclusive and in *The Religion of the Chinese People* (1975 [1922]: 103) he made the following judgement, in referring to the legacy of the disciples of Confucius and the institutions they created:

> It is doubtless thanks to them that Chinese civilization and the Chinese empire were not ruined by Buddhism, while Christianity was ruining the Graeco-Roman world. The Chinese literati were able to save the State, because, at their Master's invitation, they had penetrated the nature of the links which in their country tied men together in society and had become aware of the interdependence of human society and natural conditions.

We might say that while Granet did not follow Durkheim's dictum (all religions are true) he did recognize the necessary tie between the social and the religious.

Are Durkheim (and Granet) and Weber (and Jaspers) pointing in the same direction, and how do they stand in relation each other? Durkheim was interested in securing a generic definition of the sacred rather than studying religious institutions from a comparative and historical perspective. Weber and Jaspers were both interested in the long-term contribution of religions to modern civilizations. While both men had a moral vision of history, Weber was not offering a universal history; he believed that the direction of the civilizations of Asia was very different from the trajectory of the Protestant Reformation, and he never offered a systematic definition of religion. Nevertheless Durkheim and Weber were deeply troubled by the violence unleashed during the First World War, and retained an understanding of how deeply religion had shaped human cultures.

Classical sociology remains important because it raises problems, not just about the empirical characteristics of modernity, but also because it poses ethical (indeed theological) questions about the meaning of modernity and about how we might, in human terms, survive the process of modernization. Modern thought increasingly sees the modern world as catastrophic. Given the catastrophic events around the First World War, the prominence of the sociology of religion in classical sociology – Marx, Durkheim, Weber, Simmel and Parsons – perhaps comes as no surprise. There is a tragic element to both Durkheim and Weber's sociology, because both men had to rethink their early sociology in the light of the mechanization of mass warfare. Could Christianity or religion or indeed society in general survive the onslaught of modern warfare? Their ambiguous answer was 'probably not'. Perhaps we can see Weber's study of China (and India) in the context of this broader question about war, the ethics of warfare, the religions of brotherly love, and the complex relationships between the religious and the political.

This interpretation is based in part on the idea in Jaspers that the religions of the Axial Age (therefore including Confucianism) were failures in the sense that they were unable to come to terms with the role of violence in human societies. In this context, China was important in western thought because it was (however falsely) interpreted as a stationary (albeit violent) society and therefore set against the crisis-ridden and catastrophic nature of western capitalism, it was blessed with continuity. The paradox is that the twentieth-century history of China has been one of endless crisis. Now that all modern societies are in some sense capitalist, all are crisis prone and hence there is in the twenty-first century the widespread presence of what I will call 'the catastrophic imagination'.

In conclusion, as we have seen, Heiner Roetz (2012: 253) observed that modern social science has abandoned the normative features of Jaspers' thesis in favour of a descriptive account of religious change, and he went on to claim that 'what Weber offers is a sociologically enriched reformulation of the same Hegelian view of non-Occidental cultures that Jaspers attacks'. Weber, Jaspers and Bellah shared this moral vision of the dilemma of humankind faced with the contradictions between the ethic of brotherly love and the inescapable connection between politics and violence. By contrast to the expansive vision of classical sociology of religion, modern scholars work increasingly within a professional framework that is more inclined to reward descriptive accounts of religiosity such as private, subjective, post-institutional 'spirituality'. Contemporary sociologists of religion look for religion in everyday life where religious beliefs and practices are typically post-institutional and post-orthodox (Ammerman 2014). Two important exceptions are Jason Ananda Josephson's *The Invention of Religion in Japan* (2012) and David Martin's *The Future of Christianity* (2011).

However, if Protestant discipline was one factor in the rise of rational capitalism, was it also, through its individualism and emphasis on the emotional dimension of personal conversion, the midwife of contemporary post-orthodox and post-institutional religiosity? Weber was struck by the emotional appeal of Wesley's preaching style and Methodist hymns were characteristically emotionally charged. An emotional and expressive religion of sexual satisfaction rather than love probably had its origins in the United States in the 1960s in such movements as Esalen which combined massage, yogic meditation, sexual freedom and eastern spirituality (Goldman 2012). This therapeutic hybrid religiosity of the erotic self has continued to flourish among youthful seekers (Wuthnow 1976). Of course, we have to thank Bellah for also recognizing this evolution of religion towards emotive individualism in his famous essay on 'Religious Evolution' (1964) where, influenced by both twentieth-century sociology and theology, he argued that religion had come to flourish outside the limitations of the mainstream denominations. Youth, in the search for a meaningful interpretation of the modern world, no longer had any need for institutional religion.

However, anticipating the retrospective analysis of our epoch in another age, I doubt that modern-day spirituality can qualify either as the serious life in Durkheim's sociology or as Weber's notion of a religion of self-denying acosmistic love. The challenge facing modern sociology of religion is to decide whether spirituality in the west has any significant implications, especially for the long-term shaping of modern secular culture, precisely because it is a product of the secular world rather than an agent to change it. These developments are not confined to the west. These forms of youthful religiosity are erupting in a global world and therefore small-scale studies of the local manifestations of spirituality will not provide satisfactory insights or answers to important sociological questions. At present the modern world is being shaped by major conflicts between Shia and Sunni Muslims, between Buddhists and Muslims, and between Copts and Muslims. The global Shia–Sunni conflict not only threatens to destabilize societies in the Middle East and Asia, it is also re-shaping the borders between societies (Nasr 2006). Consequently we need large-scale, comparative and historical studies in the tradition of Weber, Jaspers and Bellah if sociology is to remain a significant discipline not only within religious studies broadly conceived, but in the social sciences generally.

References

Altinordu, Ates (2013). Toward a Comparative-historical Sociology of Religious Politics: The Case for Cross-religious and Cross-regional Comparisons, in *Religion on the Edge: De-Centering and Re-centering the Sociology of Religion*,

ed. Courtney Bender, Wendy Cage, Peggy Levitt and David Smilde. New York: Oxford Unversity Press, pp. 67–91.
Ammerman, Nancy Tatom (2014). *Sacred Stories, Spiritual Tribes: Finding Religion in Everyday Life*. Oxford: Oxford University Press.
Arendt, Hannah and Jaspers, Karl (1992). *Correspondence 1926–1969*. San Diego: Harcourt Brace.
Assman, Jan (2012). The Cultural Myth of the Axial Age, in *The Axial Age and its Consequences*, ed. Robert N. Bellah and Hans Joas, Cambridge, MA and London: The Belknap Press of Harvard University Press, pp. 366–410.
Bellah, Robert N. (1957). *Tokugawa Religion*. Glencoe: Free Press.
Bellah, Robert N. (1964). Religious Evolution. *American Sociological Review*, 29, 358–74.
Bellah, Robert N. (1999). Max Weber and World-Denying Love: A Look at the Historical Sociology of Religion. *Journal of the American Academy of Religion*, 67(2), 277–304.
Bellah, Robert N. (2003). *Imagining Japan: The Japanese Tradition and its Modern Interpretation*. California: University of California Press.
Bellah, Robert N. (2011). *Religion in Human Evolution: From the Paleolithic to the Axial Age*. Cambridge, MA: The Belknap Press of Harvard University Press.
Boy, John D. and Torpey, John (2013). Inventing the Axial Age: The Origins and Uses of a Historical Concept. *Theory and Society*, 42(3), 241–59.
Bellah, Robert N. and Joas, Hans (eds) (2012). *The Axial Age and its Consequences*. Cambridge, MA and London: The Belknap Press of Harvard University Press.
Buck-Morss, Susan (2009). *Hegel, Haiti and Universal History*. Pittsburgh: University of Pittsburgh Press.
Busse, Andreas E. (ed.) (1985). *Max Weber in Asian Studies*. Leiden: E.J.Brill.
Delanty, Gerard (ed.) (2012). *The Routledge Handbook of Cosmopolitan Studies*. New York; Routledge.
Donald, Merlin (1991). *Origins of the Modern Mind, Three Stages in the Evolution of Culture and Cognition*. Cambridge, MA: Harvard University Press.
Dreijmanis, John (ed.) (1989). *Karl Jaspers on Max Weber*. New York: Paragon House.
Durkheim, Emile (1961) [1912]. *The Elementary Forms of Religious Life*. Oxford: Oxford University Press.
Durkheim, Emile (1992). *Professional Ethics and Civic Morals*. London: Routledge.

Durkheim, Emile and Mauss, Marcel (1963) [1903]. *Primitive Classification*. London: Cohen and West.
Eisenstadt, Shmuel (1985) [1983]. This Wordly Transcendentalism and the Structuring of the World: Weber's 'Religion of China' and the Format of Chinese History and Civilization. *Journal of Developing Societies*, 1, 168–86.
Eisenstadt, Shmuel N. (ed.) (1992). *Kulturen der Achsenzeit. Ihre institutionelle und kluturelle Dynamik*. Frankfurt am Main: Suhrkamp.
Eisenstadt, Shmuel (1996). *Japanese Civilization: A Comparative View*. Chicago: University of Chicago Press.
Eisenstadt, Shmuel N. (2000). Multiple Modernities. *Daedalus*, 129(1), 1–29.
Eisenstadt, Shmuel N. (ed.) (2002). *Multiple Modernities*. New Brunswick: Transaction Books.
Elias, Norbert (2000) [1939]. *The Civilizing Process*. Oxford: Blackwell.
Fingarette, Herbert (1972). *Confucius: The Secular as Sacred*. Prospect Heights: Waveland Press.
Giddens, Anthony (1987). *Social Theory and Modern Sociology*. Stanford: Stanford University Press.
Goldman, Marion (2012). *The American Soul Rush, Esalen and the Rise of Spiritual Privilege*. New York and London: New York University Press.
Gorski, Philip S. (2003). *The Disciplinary Revolution: Calvinism and the Rise of the State in Early Modern Europe*. Chicago and London: University of Chicago Press.
Granet, Marcel (1930) [1929]. *Chinese Civilization*. London: Routledge & Kegan Paul Ltd.
Granet, Marcel (1951) [1922]. *The Religion of the Chinese People*. Paris: Press Universitaires de France.
Granet, Marcel (1975) [1922]. *The Religion of the Chinese People*. New York: Harper & Row.
Hackett, David G. (2014). *That Religion in which all Men Agree: Freemasonry in American Culture*. Berkeley: University of California Press.
Hennis, Wilhelm (1988). *Max Weber: Essays in Reconstruction*. London: Allen & Unwin.
James, W. (1929) [1902]. *Varieties of Religious Experience: A Study in Human Nature*. New York: Modern Library.
Jaspers, Karl (1948). The Axial Age of Human History. *Commentary*, 6, 430–435.
Jaspers, Karl (1953) [1949]. *The Origin and Goal of History*. London: Routledge and Kegan Paul.

Jaspers, Karl (1962) [1957]. *Socrates, Buddha, Confucius, Jesus*. San Diego: Harcourt Brace Co.

Jaspers, Karl and Bultmann, Rudolf (2005) [1953–4]. *Myth and Christianity: An Inquiry into the Possibility of Religion without Myth*. New York: Prometheus Books.

Joas, Hans (2012). The Axial Age Debate as Religious Discourse, in *The Axial Age and its Consequences*, ed. Robert N. Bellah and Hans Joas. Cambridge, MA and London: The Belknap Press of Harvard University Press, pp. 9–29.

Josephson, Jason Ananda (2012). *The Invention of Religion in Japan*. Chicago: University of Chicago Press.

Kant, Immanuel (1998) [1763]. *Religion within the Boundaries of Mere Reason*. Cambridge: Cambridge University Press.

Love, John (2000). Max Weber's Orient, in *The Cambridge Companion to Max Weber*, ed. Stephen Turner. Cambridge: Cambridge University Press, pp. 172–99.

Martin, David (2011). *The Future of Christianity: Reflections on Violence and Democracy, Religion and Secularisation*. Farnham: Ashgate.

Masuzawa, Tomoko (2005). *The Inention of Word Religions, or, How European Universalism Was Preserved in the Language of Pluralism*. Chicago: University of Chicago Press.

Nasr, Vali (2006). *The Shia Revival: How Conflicts within Islam will Shape the Future*. New York and London: W.W. Norton and Company.

Momigliano, Arnaldo (1975). *Alien Wisdom: The Limits of Helenization*. Cambridge: Cambridge University Press.

Nelson, Benjamin (1981). *On the Roads to Modernity: Conscience, Science and Civilization*. Totowa: Rowman & Littlefield.

Parsons, Talcott (1971). *The System of Modern Societies*. Englewood Cliffs: Prentice Hall.

Peel, J.D.Y. (1969). Understanding Alien Belief Systems. *British Journal of Sociology*, 20, 69–84.

Radkau, Joachim (2009). *Max Weber: A Biography*. Cambridge: Polity Press.

Roetz, Heiner (2012). The Axial Age Theory: A Challenge to Historism or an Explanatory Device of Civilization Analysis? With a Look at the Normative Discourse in Axial Age China, in *The Axial Age and its Consequences*, ed. Robert N. Bellah and Hans Joas. Cambridge, MA and London: The Belknap Press of Harvard University Press, pp. 248–73.

Schluchter, Wolfgang (1983). *Max Webers Studie uber das Konfuzianismus und Taoismus*. Frankfurt: Suhrkamp.

Schluchter, Wolfgang (1988). *Religion und Lebensfuhrung. Vol.1. Max Webers Kultur – und Werttheorie*. Frankfurt am Main: Suhrkamp.

Simmel, Georg (1997). *Essays on Religion*. New Haven and London: Yale University Press.

Simmel, Georg (2010) [1918]. *The View of Life: Four Metaphysical Essays with Journal Aphorisms*. Chicago and London: University of Chicago Press.

Smith, William Robertson (1997) [1889]. *Lectures on the Religion of the Semites*. London: Routledge/Thoemmes.

Spencer, Baldwin and Gillen, Francis James (1997) [1904]. *The Northern Tribes of Central Australia*. London: Routledge/Thoemmes Press.

Stamatov, P. (2013). *The Origins of Global Humanitarianism*. New York: Cambridge University Press.

Stauth, Georg and Turner, Bryan S. (1986). Nietzsche in Weber oder die Geburt des modernen Genius im professionellen Menschen. *Zietschrift fur Soziologie*, 15(2), 81–94.

Sun, Anna (2013). *Confucianism as a World Religion: Contested Histories and Contemporary Realities*. Princeton and Oxford: Princeton University Press.

Swanson, Guy E. (1967). *Religion and Regime: A Sociological Account of the Reformation*. Ann Arbor: University of Michigan Press.

Tenbruck, Friedrich (1980). The Thematic Unity in the Works of Max Weber. *British Journal of Sociology*, 31(3), 316–51.

Theissen, Gerd (1978). *The First Followers of Jesus: A Sociological Analysis of the Earliest Christianity*. London: SCM Press.

Turner, Bryan S. (1974). *Weber and Islam*. London: Routledge & Kegan Paul.

Turner, Bryan S. (1978). *Marx and the End of Orientalism*. London: Allen & Unwin.

Turner, Bryan S. (2009). Max Weber on Islam and Confucianism: The Kantian Theory of Secularization, in *The Oxford Handbook of the Sociology of Religion*, ed. Peter B. Clarke. Oxford: Oxford University Press, pp. 79–97.

Turner, Bryan S. (2011). *Religion and Modern Society: Citizenship, Secularisation and the State*. Cambridge: Cambridge University Press.

Turner, Bryan S. (2013). *The Religious and the Political*. Cambridge: Cambridge University Press.

von Harnack, A. (1912). *The Mission and Expansion of Christianity in the First Three Centuries*. London: Williams and Norgate.

Weber, Max (1951) [1916]. *The Religion of China: Confucianism and Taoism*. New York: Macmillan.

Weber, Max (1958). *The City*. Glencoe: Free Press.

Weber, Max (1958) [1916]. *The Religion of India: The Sociology of Hinduism and Buddhism*. New York: The Free Press.
Weber, Max (1966) [1922]. *The Sociology of Religion*. London: Methuen.
Weber, Max (1978) [1928]. *Economy and Society: An Outline of Interpretive Sociology*, 2 vols. Berkeley: University of California Press.
Weber, Max (2002) [1905–6]. *The Protestant Ethic and the 'Spirit' of Capitalism and Other Writings*. New York: Penguin.
Weber, Max (2009) [1915]. The Religious Rejections of the World and their Directions, in *From Max Weber: Essays in Sociology*, ed. Hans Gerth and C. Wright Mills. London: Routledge, pp. 323–59.
Wuthnow, Robert (1976). *The Consciousness Revolution*. Berkeley: University of California Press.

Chapter 4

Hope and Religion

David Lehmann*

Introduction

Hope, like its twin, despair, is obviously an enduring and pervasive human emotion, and one common feature of religion in its innumerable forms is that it is sought by people in search of hope and of relief from despair. But the management of the supernatural does not stand still, and I will argue in the following pages that by examining some of the ways in which religion responds to despair and provides hope we can learn about how religion is changing in quite fundamental ways.

The Abrahamic religions, it is argued, offer a solace which is intangible, unknowable and distant, and in that they stand in contrast to the thaumaturgic and the shamanistic which offer remedies that are uncertain, but knowable. Both display elaborate ritual procedures, but the Abrahamic religions clearly mark themselves out at least in their official versions: shamans do not have 'official versions'. But, as is well known, this contrast, based on the Abrahamic religions' theological or Rabbinic traditions,[1] sets aside the Abrahamic religions' rich and ancient undergrowth of popular religion. The thesis of the chapter is that popular religion exists in a dialectic relationship with institutionalized official religion, that it embodies a sense of tradition, but of a living tradition, and that like shamanic ritual it offers solace and occasionally healing. Examples drawn are mostly Catholic and Jewish. This dialectic relationship between the official and the unofficial, the erudite and the popular, is one of mutual interdependence. It is not destructive.

---

* A shorter and earlier version of this paper appeared in Portuguese in *Estudos Avançados* (University of São Paulo), 26, (75) 219-236, 2012.

[1] I do not regard Judaism as having a theology in the same sense as Christianity – that is an elaborate theodicy and philosophy of existence constructed in a manner aspiring to complete coherence and closure. Judaism, to summarize another massive issue, is rather a tradition revolving around a legal heritage in the Talmud.

Obviously this model is presented not as a summary of thousands of years of civilization, but as background to an interpretation of the ways in which contemporary charismatic movements are changing the location and the meaning of religion in Latin America in particular, but by extension throughout Western Christianity. The chapter tracks the transformation of the erudite–popular relationship as it is transformed and dissolved by contemporary charismatic movements, by Pentecostalism and especially neo-Pentecostalism, in an evolution which I describe as the secularization of religious reason – a tendency shared also by non-charismatic movements such as the Theology of Liberation, bearers of a project profoundly different from the charismatic. The interpretation relies on the idea of exchange with the supernatural, of institutionalization and of the trust which institutionalization is designed to instill and maintain – exchange, therefore, which is variously mediated by a lone shaman, by a hierarchical institution, directly as in popular religion, or with the institution itself as in Pentecostalism. When the exchange is with the institution itself religion has somehow been remade and relocated. Popular religion is discarded with the heritage or tradition which sustains it; erudite religion is discarded because doctrine and theology are despised; but the state is still expected to grant this sort of religion the same kind of exemptions and privileges which it grants to institutionalized religions.

The Supernatural, Ritual and Uncertainty

Despite the apparently enormous variation of what goes, somewhat intuitively, by the name of religion, and despite the statement by Maurice Bloch that anthropologists have found it impossible 'to ... isolate or define ... religion' (Bloch 2008), I think that cognitive anthropologists and psychologists have demonstrated that a common core does exist. The cognitivists are dealing not with institutionalized religion but rather with how we invoke and mobilize the supernatural or how the supernatural is built into our evolution. This is manifested in popular religion, not in institutionalized religion. Popular religion does have common features across cultures and through time, because of its deep involvement with curing or preventing illness, with warning of and warding off rumour and gossip, with divining and controlling the future and with life after death. Cognitive psychology, as applied to religion in the work of Boyer and Atran (Boyer 2004, 2001; Atran 2003; Lehmann 2005) tells us that these accounts rely on several evolved modes of operation of the mind: one is the inclination to search for agency in explaining obscure and disconcerting phenomena: this is essential to enable us to survive but it can also be excessive, as in paranoia. Alertness to danger/risk which leads us to associate strange or threatening noises and visions with agents like ghosts or with a warning from a supernatural godlike agent. The need to know what is going on in other people's minds – as in the 'theory of mind' which to varying degrees is recognized to be lacking in autistic individuals (Baron-Cohen 1995) – is also an essential feature of human interaction which leads us to look for all-knowing entities like an omniscient God or, in more everyday terms, to consult a shaman or witch or therapist who has privileged knowledge and offers to diagnose plots against us and to provide weapons to counter them. Risk plus uncertainty plus information combine with plausible advice in areas where certainty is not available. (The shaman is powerful because since everyone consults him he has privileged information and may provide the right advice. The trouble is that one cannot always trust the shaman to be impartial, and we shall see that this issue of trust is important to the demarcation of institutionalized religion in the Abrahamic traditions.)

The cognitivists do not claim that the bundle of ideas and behaviours we intuitively describe and package as 'religion' make a coherent or homogeneous whole; rather in Atran's words, religion as we know it encompasses 'a variety of cognitive and affective systems, some with separate evolutionary histories, and some with no evolutionary history to speak of. Of those with an evolutionary history, some parts plausibly have an adaptive story, while others are more likely by-products' (Atran 2003: 265). The line between features with an 'original' adaptive function and others which are 'exaptations', by-products, is somewhat notional, but for our purposes the point is that they have come to form common underlying features of the popular religion which is at the heart of all religion, despite the diversity of its institutional forms across time and space.

Dealing with the uncertainties of gossip, illness and death requires experts and specialists, and so individuals carve out or inherit expert roles with esoteric knowledge and access to the supernatural realm. But there has to be some sort of 'system' for building trust in individuals who help us to cope with uncertainty, who cure illness and who manage the transition from life to death and communication with the dead, even while also protecting us from confidence tricksters. And so we must add ritual and exchange to these psychological propensities to look for solutions. Ritual institutionalizes or essentializes a practice, marking it as standard procedure but also introducing extensive elements which are not present for any practical reason related to the context, but fix social roles in relation to the procedure: ritual should induce trust and it also should confer privileged knowledge on the part of the person performing it.

Exchange is deeply embedded in our evolved psychology from the exchange of glances in recognition, to sex, to economics and guilt – the guilt we experience when we do not fulfil the obligations of reciprocity. In our relationship with the supernatural the exchange is also ritualized so that the successes of the past can be repeated and the failures explained. In explaining how religion – which has ritual as an indispensable component – manages hope and hopelessness, ritual and exchange are intimately connected. Such ritual exchanges depend on the meticulous fulfilment of esoteric procedures, yet they remain bedevilled by uncertainty – and the word 'bedevilled' is probably appropriate in this context. In Dan Sperber's words: 'only misfortune always begs for an explanation': if things go fine then questions are not asked. But 'when failure to adhere to the practice is followed by misfortune, it may appear to have caused it' (Sperber 1996: 51–2). Sperber's formulation includes the words '*strict* adherence' (my emphasis), reflecting the ritual character of these procedures, and that is in turn related to the belief in their efficacy. They do not claim to be 100 per cent successful, but that is not the point: the point is that (1) if you haven't performed the ritual and the misfortune arises you could be held responsible; (2) that it ties people in to a social network of responsibility who might hold you responsible or, alternatively, forgive you – or indeed be grateful if the ritual is perceived to have had the desired effect, and (3) it allows for mistakes to explain failure. So long as you have performed the ritual, the system is set up so that even if it does not achieve the desired or anticipated outcome you will not be held to account.

The ritual distributes roles, thus evoking reciprocity in others, be they those who suffer the misfortune directly or those who are linked to the sufferers. It also creates a set of idealized, 'essentialized' figures (Bloch 2008) who act in the name of supernatural powers and incur costs on their own behalf (the accoutrements of ritual, renunciation of their daily needs) but attract donations, reciprocity, from those who stand to benefit from their renunciation. The stricter the requirements of the ritual the higher the cost, but as the ritual becomes more costly so more participants are required and more people can join in support. If the central figure is a celebrity, enjoys a cult of personality, then people may be prepared to pay a higher cost, even pay with their lives, but more usually the cost is low because of the uncertain outcome, balanced by the comfort of shared reciprocity.

In a ritual involving exchange with a supernatural agent there is always an intermediary: a medium, or an institution – the Church. These exchanges have to be public: just as a Pentecostal cannot claim to have received the Holy Spirit in private, a vision of the Virgin Mary is of no value if it is not recognized, and an exorcism, for example has to be witnessed.

In non-institutionalized religious cultures the intermediary wields real, sometimes frightening power. Geschiere (1995) describes the sorcerers and witch-hunters who are indispensable associates of Cameroonian politicians: the mystery surrounding them is whether they are themselves responsible for the possession which they diagnose. Likewise neo-Pentecostal churches (of which more later) practise exorcism to help their followers recapture a lover or expel drugs from their households: if it doesn't work then the sufferer is told that the procedure had a defect or the exorcist him/herself was possessed or was an agent of diabolical forces, or the sufferer has not tried hard enough. There is always an answer and reassessments go round and round in a never-ending circle. So paranoia is fed, but so also social actors in the long run have an incentive to try to create trust and institutions.

It is precisely the uncertain efficacy of these procedures that cultivates their ritual character – the 'strict adherence' in Sperber's formulation. The managers of the supernatural in non-institutionalized religious possession cults manage a relationship of exchange between their devotees and the supernatural and between themselves and their adepts, keeping initiation for themselves, thanks again to elaborate esoteric rituals. And so this sort of religion handles, manipulates and perpetuates the hope and hopelessness of individuals. It was classically described by Evans-Pritchard for the Zande, though he studiously avoids mentioning emotions such as hopelessness at all: for the Zande, in his account, witchcraft is an everyday matter of social and physical explanation. But the ambiguity is patently present, as when he describes how oracles may lie – and how everyone knows that they are lying – in circumstances when to do otherwise would create social tension (Evans-Pritchard 1965: 77). A similar pattern appears in Joel Robbins' account of the conversion and subsequent religious life of a tiny community in Papua New Guinea – the Urapmin – who had converted en masse to evangelical Christianity. The Urapmin confessed innumerable sins in extended and very frequent public meetings in their church building, but these were mostly trivialities. When a transgression was serious and affected the stability of their own social relationships, for example an extra-marital affair, then they waited for it to pass or the personal conflict to be resolved before confessing it (Robbins 2004: 276).

The Hereafter and its Rewards

In contrast to 'non-institutionalized' religions, Abrahamic religious traditions, Judaism, Christianity and Islam provide a soteriology, an eschatology, a narrative about life and death, a set of abstract principles for living one's life, and an ethos. These religions offer hope to the hopeless in different ways, and on a far, far grander scale than shamans and possession cults. Instead of a cure for your stomach pains or revenge on your enemies, they offer unlimited happiness and prosperity for generation after generation, and for eternity. And how does one earn this bounty? Not by making ever greater donations, nor by upping the stakes in reciprocity, but by obeying commandments, and following laws. Not only is none of this claimed to benefit the supernatural source of this authority, but even the benefits for the faithful and the followers are only for a distant future – for future generations in 'the land that I have given you' when the 'you' will long be dead (like Moses) or in the life hereafter when we will be saved.

And what of the punishments for the disobedience of a stiff-necked people?

In the Book of Deuteronomy Chapter 28 has 68 verses, of which 14 tell of the wonderful blessings which will come upon the people if they diligently observe all God's commandments. But the remaining 54 verses list curses and misfortunes so shocking and frightening that when they are reached in the annual cycle of Torah readings in the synagogue they are not chanted but hurriedly recited in a low voice.

In the works of the Old Testament Prophets, when the children of Israel suffer, it is *their* fault, *they* have brought it upon themselves by abandoning the laws, as in the Book of Lamentations, written after the Babylonians had laid waste to Jerusalem, in which the theme is the punishment by God of the people who disobeyed or forsook his laws, ending with the hope that the Lord will turn his people 'back to thyself', that they will return to him. The Babylonians are not mentioned: they are the mere instruments of God's wrath against his disobedient people.

Neither the Prophet Jeremiah, presumed author of Lamentations, nor the other Old Testament Prophets, needed a magician to convince themselves, or to convince their followers. When misfortune struck the explanation was not individual and the remedy did not lie in ritual or charms or esoteric remedies, or in casting of a curse on an enemy. The explanation was moral: the people had transgressed and God was punishing them. The remedy was in God's hands alone.

But this is not of course the whole story, for there can be no supernatural agency without supernatural intervention in human interaction – that is, without magic, and one should not forget that Israel's austere law-giving God was not above proving his superiority by performing very earthly miracles, especially in enabling his people to triumph over their enemies and discrediting the priests who served rival gods.[2] But the idea of a covenant, a contract, with a whole people, to ensure their future, rather than ongoing endless wheeling and dealing on an individual basis, does set the God of the Old Testament apart. And the curious thing is that, in exchange for these long-term unknowable benefits this tradition demands much more costly sacrifice – not donations, not trinkets or offerings, but moral sacrifices, obedience and ritual sacrifices of animals. The only immediate benefit was a negative one: to be spared the punishments.

Old Testament Judaism lays down a legal system for a people as a whole, underpinned by the contract/covenant. Christianity, in contrast, provides individual salvation in the next world, so that we can never know for sure if we will be rewarded for good behaviour. This, again, is not a God who can be appeased by offering sacrifices and exchanges, or at least not officially. It is a God who died so we might all be saved, whose grace is free and unconditional, yet whose followers established a vast apparatus which has lasted 2,000 years, which has regulated the lives of millions, which developed elaborate visions of hell and eternal damnation and role models of self-sacrifice in monks and martyrs, in people who abstain from sex, from normal social intercourse and so on. Far from exchanges with supernatural entities, certain strands of Christianity seem to be telling us 'the more you sacrifice the less you will be rewarded in this life' – sacrifices embodied in a hierarchy of abstinences from 'no sex before marriage' for lay people to total silence and withdrawal from the world for Trappist monks. But at the same time they create institutions which enable the rest of us to benefit from their sacrifice – a feature which, as Danièle Hervieu-Léger has explained, is central to the Catholic heritage and which stands in stark contrast to the evangelical churches which we shall discuss later (Hervieu-Léger 2001: 141).

The Dialectic of the Popular and the Erudite

That, however, is far from the whole story, for side by side with the ethos of abnegation and sacrifice Christianity exhibits an intricate dialectic of popular and official religious practices. If the exchanges managed in official rituals are extremely opaque for individuals, popular religion amply compensates. The promise of salvation is hard to sell to individuals, but the rites which are attached

---

[2] Cf. among innumerable examples 1 Kings 18. Not only did the Prophet Elijah demonstrate that his God could burn an offering without setting fire underneath it while Baal's priests could not: he also immediately slew all 450 of them at the brook Kishon.

to it (namely, Holy Communion, baptism, fiestas, saying the rosary, etc.) and communal activities like maintenance of church buildings and servicing its many activities and charitable works both create multiple mechanisms of common identity among the faithful and also reward contributions of time and energy with status, respect and the pleasure and pride of collaborating with a great institution.

Thanks to popular religion the Church has been able to go well beyond (or below) the austere mission of saving souls and focusing on the after-life. It sponsors, maybe oversees, but rarely directly manages pilgrimages and local fiestas, it welcomes prayer groups in its churches, celebrating and venerating local saints, Corpus Christi and the like, but with some notable exceptions (see below) leaves all these to be self-managed by the laity and sometimes the organizations in charge have large memberships and substantial resources – like the fraternities (*cofradias* in Spanish) which manage fiestas (Molinié 2004; Brandão 2007: 55).

Of particular interest to us are activities and rituals which are a response to hopelessness or which provide hope. In Catholicism these follow the pattern of exchange: *votos* and *ex-votos*, and pilgrimages. But there is sometimes complicated negotiation with the hierarchy, as at Lourdes where a young girl's story about 'that thing' (*acqueyro* in the local dialect) she had seen in a grotto in the Pyrenees developed into a worldwide cult (Harris 1999). On the one hand the French bishops and the opponents of anti-clericalism seized upon the incident to transform this obscure village into a world centre for divine healing. But on the other the hierarchy has gone to great lengths to maintain control during the 150 years since Bernadette's vision, establishing an office to certify miracles and setting such a high standard that in 2006 a bishop called for it to be relaxed in the light of competition from Pentecostals and their healing industry (*Le Monde*, 25 March 2006).[3]

A similar pattern developed around Padre Pio, a Franciscan friar in a tiny convent in the Southern Italian village of San Giovanni Rotondo (Puglia): after he received the stigmata in 1918 a cult grew up around him attracting pilgrims from all over Southern Italy who came to attend his celebrations of

---

[3] Sixty-eight miraculous cures have been recognized by the 'Bureau des Constatations Médicales' whose rulings must themselves be confirmed by the Comité Médical International de Lourdes. The last miraculous cure took place in 2002 but was only confirmed in 2011. In 2012, according to the website of the Comité, a miracle was confirmed which had taken place in 1964. See http://fr.lourdes-france.org/approfondir/guerisons-et-miracles/serge-francois-guerison-remarquable and http://fr.lourdes-france.org/approfondir/guerisons-et-miracles/68eme-miraculee.

Mass, which tended to last for many hours (Luzzatto 2007). But for decades the Vatican remained sceptical, sending inquisitorial missions to the monastery and subjecting the friar to periods of withdrawal when he could neither say Mass nor preach nor hear confession – the three activities for which he was most sought after. All sorts of political and even financial scandals arose in the little village, especially during and after the Second World War when it became the beneficiary of the combined support of the Christian Democratic Party and Marshall Plan assistance – both interested in countering the strong influence of the Communist Party in Southern Italy at that time (Tarrow 1967). This patronage led to the construction of a very large hospital which continues to function. The friar was meticulously obedient and orthodox: he never said anything controversial apart from the claim to have received the stigmata – whose lesions have indeed been documented, though of course their cause remains forever a matter of controversy. He simply 'stood there' and allowed the cult to develop. Eventually John Paul II, well known for having multiplied beatifications and canonizations on an unprecedented scale, and himself a devotee of Padre Pio, beatified him and then elevated him to sainthood in 2002.

The case of Padre Pio shows the hierarchy struggling to control a cult which might get out of hand: control over the shrine in San Giovanni Rotondo was first transferred from the Franciscans to the local bishop and later the renowned architect Renzo Piano was commissioned to design a vast sanctuary which, while perhaps better adapted to receive pilgrims in large numbers, is utterly out of keeping with the needs of visitors who continue to prefer the older church where the saint had been buried and which offers the niches and intimacy which they seek (Mesaritou 2009). In 2008 Padre Pio's body was exhumed for reburial in the sanctuary and his hands and chest were found to be intact.

Exchange with the supernatural involves a dose of ambiguity, manipulating the balance between hope and despair and insuring against failure. But with institutionalization the ambiguity becomes less threatening, more routinized, more consolation than cure, more discipline or doctrine than manipulation of an individual's state of mind. We see this in accounts of pilgrimage sites where a routine is established for visitors who are inclined, as if programmed, to believe that visiting is a matter of following a routine, of participating in notionally set rituals of touching certain objects or places, of doing what they assume has to be done. Stadler and Luz describe the careful control of pilgrims' movements through the tomb of Mary in Jerusalem (Stadler and Luz, 2014), while Bax's account of Medjugorje, for example (Bax 1995), describes pilgrims being taken off by a tour company on a preset route, making confession and attending Mass. Medjugorje, located in a particularly contested part of Croatia, is the site of several instances of visions of the Virgin Mary by seers in 1981 who have remained there and continue to receive messages from her which they convey to the public in daily sessions. The content of the messages, at least as filtered by the Franciscan friars who manage the site, is inoffensive and in conformity with Church doctrine. By touching objects in the vicinity of the site, by taking home stones, rosaries and other trinkets, and by physical contact with the seers, to whom they attribute quasi-medical powers (p. 39), pilgrims return home armed with the power of the site. Inevitably, visitors have introduced healing into their routine, while the persons responsible try to strike a balance between that pressure and the risks of sanctions by the authorities in old Yugoslavia, for illegal practice of medicine. Unlike Lourdes, the Medjugorje claims of visions, ongoing ever since 1981, have not been endorsed by the Vatican, so there is no certification procedure. On the other hand, the Franciscans (who have a long and combative history of involvement with Croatian nationalism) have not been punished for their involvement. In San Giovanni Rotondo, on the other hand, they have been marginalized by the bishop, to whom the Vatican has granted control of the Padre Pio sites. The visits to Medjugorke incorporate much standard Catholic ritual – Mass, confession – thus adding to the routinization effect and tempering hopes of instant solutions. To illustrate the flexibility of meaning beside the constancy of ritual, John Eade, author of numerous important contributions to the literature on pilgrimage, has provided an up-to-date account in an unpublished paper, of how the rituals of Lourdes now begin to transcend Catholic identities and acquire a dynamic all of their own for people of different obeisances (Eade 2013).

The difficulty represented for modernism by the exchanges which lie at the heart of popular religion is well illustrated by the late Olivia Harris's account of a young Spanish priest schooled in post-conciliar (i.e. post-Vatican II) modernism and social commitment trying to perform his duties properly in a highland Bolivian parish: he drives away in his jeep overloaded with corn and potatoes and much besides, after enduring an interminable Mass – interminable because of the votive offerings, promises and exchanges which had to be dealt with individually (Harris 2006: 56). He is embarrassed by what he sees as gifts – gifts pressed upon him despite his insistence that the Communion is offered freely, and that all that is required is for a person to be in a state of grace. But for the faithful these are precisely not gifts because they form part of the reciprocity which is essential to their relationship with the supernatural. They, after all, are heirs to 500 years of coexistence between Catholic divinity and their 'own' mountain spirits.

The substratum of popular religion is evident in Catholicism worldwide, but it is also present in Judaism and in Islam. In Judaism the most visible expression of Ashkenazi popular religion has been in the Chassidic sects which arose in Eastern Europe in the late eighteenth century and flourished thereafter until the Shoah – since when they have had a worldwide renewal. The Chassidim developed from a movement following a particular mystical figure (the Baal Shem-Tov, d. 1760) into a movement of millions of followers of pious or righteous men (*tzaddikim*) who had 'collapsed the distinction between normative and popular religion' (Sharot 2011: 77). The tzaddikim were not precisely intercessors, in the manner of Christian saints, but rather a channel to God. The usual term used in English is that they 'cleaved' to God, they were people possessed of a 'higher', more mystical religiosity which brought them close to the divine, and their followers cleaved to them in the same way. The tzaddik was 'able to capture divine power and channel that power down to his earthly dependents' (Sharot 2011). But they also looked to him for cures and blessings as well as advice: the tzaddik somehow managed to combine 'the high status of the mystic with engagement in popular religion', and he would receive a 'redemption fee' when followers came to ask for his intervention (Sharot 2011).

Yet this apparently uncontrollable effervescence, which encountered fierce internecine opposition from the learned centres of Vilna (today Vilnius) especially, eventually was institutionalized in dynasties in the nineteenth century, and this continues today.[4] The followers of the Talmudic scholars of Vilna came to be described as the opponents (*mitnagdim*), associated with an austere religiosity centred on study of Rabbinic texts and today known as Lithuanians. So one might suppose that the popular religion of the Chassidim, whose dynamic core was composed of business people rather than the unlettered masses (Dynner 2006), has been tamed or neutralized, but there is another interpretation which sees a continuation of popular religion in Torah study, for all its erudition.

Today the practice of Torah study, which has become a mass phenomenon (Friedman 1986; Soloveitchik 1994), is itself a type of popular religion, justified in terms of keeping a tradition alive, and even of saving the state of Israel. Torah study has many of the attributes of popular religion: it follows rhythms of the day, the month and the year; it rests on esoteric story-telling and the combination and recombination of elements from a vast corpus, it is oblivious

---

[4] The notion of dynasty though is relativized in the sense that since they usually have many children, and since both sons and sons-in-law compete for succession, much 'politics' accompanies the succession process.

to modern scientific scholarship, it relies heavily on oral communication, and its leading lights, who are honoured with rituals of deference and never retire, have an extraordinary array of esoteric and linguistic learning. Yeshiva students learn, typically, in pairs which stage ritualized disputes on abstruse points. This is not study in the secular sense of learning to master a body of knowledge, let alone of acquiring a certificate, not in the sense of training for the priesthood – which is secular learning: for yeshiva students, examinations are a formality and the resulting qualifications are more an entitlement than an achievement, counting for less than the recommendation of the yeshiva head and the opportunity to find a suitable wife (Lehmann and Siebzehner 2009).

So in Judaism the culture of learning, for all its esotericism and erudition, does not count as an official culture in the way that Catholic seminaries or Anglican theological colleges might: it is too much subject to unwritten and uncodified habits and customs which are variously certified and debated by rabbis who forever reach differing conclusions. Only in Israel is there something like a codification because of the official character of the Rabbinic Courts, but the scope of their rulings covers only the narrow issue of qualifying people for citizenship under the Law of Return, plus kosher certification and the yeshiva heads and dynastic leaders have little respect for the state's Chief Rabbis, even though they have a preponderant voice in their appointment. The puzzle for outsiders accustomed to a theologically driven notion of religious adherence arises from the embeddedness of Jewish strictness and Orthodoxy in daily life. Ultra-Orthodoxy is immersion in a life suffused with habits and rituals which consist of automatic, almost compulsive, practices. If you ask about their 'origins' or justification, you may be given an esoteric interpretation buried in the mists of time, but it will be vague and the interlocutor will regard it as a silly or irrelevant question: touching the scroll on a doorpost as you enter a room; washing left and right hands before a meal in a specified order, pouring water three times over each hand using a two-handled jug; keeping one's head covered at all times; maximizing the number of children ... the list is endless, and is constantly being augmented. In addition, it is by no means clear that the apparently unending tightening of stringency in contemporary ultra-Orthodoxy derives from pressure from the rabbis: it may well be that it comes from 'below', from anxiety among followers, especially those newly returned to strict observance (*t'shuva*, or 'repentance', 'return').

Aside from this merging of the popular and the erudite, Judaism also exhibits the classic exchange relationship with the supernatural mediated by tzaddikim of various kinds, especially in North African and Middle Eastern (Sephardi) traditions. These fit more with the model of exchange, and are very similar to that of the neighbouring Muslim populations, to the point that according to Issachar Ben-Ami out of '656 Jewish saints' in modern Morocco '126' were venerated by both Jews and Muslims (Ben-Ami 1998; Sharot 2011: 74), before the Jewish culture of the Maghreb was destroyed by mass emigration in the wake of Israel's creation and the subsequent wars. It survives in modern Israel, in the form of cultural celebrations and veneration of rabbis of distinguished lineage (Bilu and Ben-Ari 1992).

Many practices which are standard in the ultra-Orthodox world fit well with the model of relating to the supernatural or fending off misfortune described earlier. In case of illness, people may say 'check the mezuzah': this refers to small devices attached to doors in many Jewish houses, for these contain tiny scrolls on which a prayer is written: the sick person or their kin are advised to check that the prayer does not contain a mistake. If a child misbehaves parents or others concerned are advised to check into the background and see whether perhaps there is not a mixed marriage in the genealogy somewhere, or a liaison with a non-Jewish employee. Of course people consult their doctors, but not always and they also consult rabbis on these matters, or several rabbis if the opinion or ruling they hear is not to their liking. They owe less to expected rewards than to the pressure to keep on the right side of 'the law'. This law is inherently uncertain, subject to multiple interpretations, whose obedience is unforgivingly enforced by gossip. Indeed, most customs are derived from tradition and no 'system' or set of principles is invoked to encompass them. Not for nothing did Isaac Bashevis Singer once write: 'the first words I can remember hearing were "It is forbidden"' (Bashevis Singer 1979: 11).

The Abrahamic traditions have institutionalized religion and as a result they can create relationships of trust which underpin a postponement of salvation or redemption until an unknown and unknowable future. The devotion of their followers thus does not seem to have an immediate return. However, this official religion exists in a dialectic relationship with a popular religion which is concerned with this-worldly rewards, with the ties of community and with a built-in message that those ties are ancient, have 'roots'. The idea is very similar to Linda Woodhead's terms strategic and tactical religion and indeed she also uses the word 'dialectical':

> strategy and tactics form and shape one another dialectically. The strategist cannot merely impose, for the tactical will find ways over, under, through, and around strategic plans, targets, rewards and sanctions. But if the strategist plans for such things, his plans contain the impress of the tactical, and the tactical inheres in the strategic. Likewise, the tactical may anticipate and try to foil the

strategic, thereby internalising it and bowing to its logic. And the strategic, when it resorts to trickery and deception, dissolves into the tactical. Thus the tactical and strategic form the conditions of the other's possibility, the potential pathways of realisation, and the horizons of one another's dissolution – within an unequal exchange. (Woodhead 2012)

If my concept is different from hers, it is in its addition of the dimensions of time, or history, and of the ways in which popular religion creates ties of interdependence among people who live together in neighbourhoods, villages and so on. So to some extent it is a dated concept which may require recasting in contemporary conditions. But whereas Woodhead, in a lecture at the 'New Forms of Public Religion' conference in Cambridge later in 2012, focused on personal spiritualities which exhibit a highly fragmented and dispersed organization, characteristic of Western Europe and North America in particular, I will present a rather different, parallel, evolution dynamized by Pentecostalism in Latin America but which also is widely observed in Africa, and in Europe among immigrants from Africa, the Caribbean and Latin America.

Latin America: The Dialectic Transcended in a Time of Both Religious Revival and Secularization

Pope John Paul II undertook a campaign of beatifications and canonizations with the intention – presumably – of encouraging a revival of popular religion. But if we look more carefully at the sort of revivals which Catholicism is currently experiencing, can they be called 'popular religion'? They are led by a multiplicity of devotional movements such as the Neocatechumenals or Neocatechumenates, the *Sodalitium Christianae Vitae* (a Society for Apostolic Life), Communione e Liberazione, Opus Dei, the Legionaries of Christ and more besides. Each has distinctive features, so these few paragraphs cannot do justice to the variety. Among the most visible is the Charismatic Renewal and its multiple offshoots and loosely connected branches, in the massive Youth Festivals which Popes have attracted in Paris, in Sydney and Rio de Janeiro (2013) and in the mediatic success of celebrity priests like Brazil's Marcelo Rossi whose little book of moralisms entitled *Agape* ('Hope' or 'Love') (Rossi 2010) sold two million copies in its first six months in 2010–11. The revival is patchy but intensely expressed in local charismatic groups across the world whose practices are often largely indistinguishable from those of Pentecostal churches. Despite their advertised mysticism, their direct receipt of Gifts of the Spirit and their inclination towards corporeal expressiveness, the charismatic movement is developing a religious culture which is distinguished by its this-worldly orientation in contrast to the traditional themes of the eternal, the Kingdom, the transcendent, and does not share the dimensions of community and heritage associated with classic conceptions of popular religion, of which that of Carlos Brandão seems to me the one which best combines theoretical and practical dimensions (Lehmann 2002; Brandão 2007). Marcelo Rossi's book consists of a series of moralisms and exhortations to love and do good with little reference if any to salvation and few exhortations to sacrifice: the themes include 'love', 'light – which brings lies and vice out of the shadows' – and persistence, more even than faith. In a series of studies of new Catholic communities, Brenda Carranza and Cecilia Mariz describe ventures (not only charismatic in style) like the creation of abstemious alternative communities, charitable works, evangelizing activities, self-realization programmes, evangelizing radio stations – but the common factor is their vocation to change people and to make them live better lives in accordance with officially approved Catholic morality and also in accordance with their own inner selves (Carranza et al. 2009). Catholic popular religion in the classic image, whether veneration of world-famous patron saints or innumerable local saints and Virgins, or prayer groups led by lay women saying their rosary, is not particularly concerned with the policing or reform of morals, let alone with self-realization.

What Carranza calls 'a new religious genre oriented by emotion' (Carranza 2009: 50) has much in common with Woodhead's 'tactical religion', like a religious version of the vast culture of self-realization and self-exploration described by Eva Illouz and many others as a pervasive feature of modernity (Illouz 2008, 2012). It calls on adepts to abandon a world of superficiality and consumerism by, for example, embracing the opportunity to serve (looking after street children among many other possibilities), or to retreat from the world and take a vow of poverty or chastity: a 'utopia of a profane neo-Christendom' (Carranza et al. 2009: 143). Taken together the studies by Carranza and her colleagues reveal a space within Catholicism for choice and entrepreneurship: numerous alternative paths to the life of a good Catholic. Even the fasting and abstention is not for the sake of the rest of us, as it is in traditional Catholicism: as part of the therapy culture of self-exploration and self-improvement, such sacrifices and bodily afflictions are chosen by individuals as and when they see fit rather than as part of a ritual cycle as in heritage religion (Jews fast on Yom Kippur and certain other specified days; Catholics used to abstain from meat on Fridays, etc.). Woodhead in her Cambridge lecture specifically mentions this shift whereby devotions or supernatural communication cease to be dictated by official calendars and follow instead the needs or desires of the subject. But Véronique Altglas has cast some doubt on the spiritual explanation of these phenomena, bringing to light the ways in which their sponsors and entrepreneurs respond to the material and emotional needs of their adepts, as well as the sometimes quite ephemeral affiliations they involve. Altglas has brought a more down-to-earth interpretation which undermines much current interpretation in which spirituality is accorded an unjustified analytic status (Altglas, 2014).

So in delineating these new forms of non-official Catholicism from what I have called classic popular religion, three themes stand out: (1) 'tradition'; (2) therapy or healing; and (3) authority. The new forms detach themselves from tradition and heritage as expressed in public celebration at local, national and global levels; they distance themselves from the immediacy of healing but delve instead into therapy and self-exploration; but they share with classic popular religion a conformity with the hierarchy and erudite religion. To be sure, classic popular religion may engage in unorthodox practices (animal sacrifices in the highland Andes for example), but these are not of the kind to undermine priestly or episcopal authority. The Lourdes and Padre Pio examples show that the hierarchy can regain control when, so to speak, 'things get out of hand'. The difference, in the relationship with authority, is that the devotional movements place much more emphasis on morals and doctrine than these saintly cults, not departing one iota from the Papal message.

This can be interpreted as a modern, secular ethos which propagates hope as the building of a new world on earth and in this life: the element of exchange with the supernatural, in the way of *votos* and *ex-votos*, of pilgrimages and sacrifices, is out of the picture. Charismatics invoke gifts of the spirit which are bestowed upon them for the sake of achievements in this world – for example that they can preach, that they can heal or be healed. They need priests and bishops as safeguards or guarantors of the acceptability of their practices, but they tend to invent ritual 'on the hop'. Even the most deeply traditionalist of devotional movements, Opus Dei, has also engaged, so we understand, in liturgical and ritual innovation forms – the classic modernist device of reinventing tradition and, in this case, making it more rigid than ever, like the Jewish ultra-Orthodox.

The Secularization of Religious Reason in Liberation Theology

This-worldly concerns are by no means confined to conservatively inclined movements, as the history of Latin American Catholic *basismo*, inspired by the Theology of Liberation, amply testifies. Priests and male and female religious put their lives in danger and some were killed in fighting for social justice, standing in the way of land grabs in Amazonia, and in the civil wars in Salvador and Guatemala. None, such as the martyred Archbishop Oscar Romero,[5] have ever been beatified. These people certainly sacrificed themselves for the rest of humanity, but for humanity to be protected in this world.

Liberation Theology orientates Christians towards a Kingdom of social justice in this world, in a vision inspired by a concept of 'structural sin' affixed to social structures, not to individuals. Salvation, in Gutierrez's classic work (Gutierrez 1973), is an intra-historic matter; it transforms history in this world. In this theology care of one's neighbour is something other than a good deed to achieve eternal salvation – the 'neighbour' stands for society as a whole, and to work for social change is to do the work of God; eschatology is not an escape from history but involvement in the political field and in social praxis. Charity is not about pity but about the pursuit of social justice (1973: 278). The argument is not pamphleteering: it is developed in conjunction with close readings of biblical and theological texts. The word salvation is gradually, though not fully, replaced by the word liberation; the Kingdom is not brought down to earth, but the announcement of the Kingdom is one of brotherhood of men as a part of the pursuit of the full communion of all people with God (1973: 309). Liberation Theology sees Christianity as so non-sectarian as to be uninterested in converting those it seeks to save: they would be saved by living in a more just world.

It is often said that Liberation Theology (*Teología de la Liberación* – TL) is a Marxist politicization of religion and that it took the religious life out of Catholicism. This is unfair and partial, as I explained many years ago (Lehmann 1990, 1996): Gutierrez used a Marxist method in his 1967 book and thereafter studiously avoided it. The word was used to denigrate their ideas by tarring them with the brush of materialism, as well as by accusing the priests and religious among them of disregard for authority. But in many ways TL was a branch of the modernist trend in Christian theology, focusing on the living Jesus and an activist Church, but retaining the idea of doctrine and theology, retaining the separateness of clergy and laity, and retaining the idea of a Church sacrificing itself for the good of others – of society. TL does not focus on the personalized religion which some devotional movements promote, nor on the ritualization of daily life which Opus Dei and the Legionaries seem to promote. For TL popular religion has not always served the interests of the people and its heritage and community dimensions should be made more relevant to their sufferings

---

[5] Assassinated while saying Mass on 24 March 1980 in San Salvador.

and their daily lives: thus in the 1990s in Brazil a group of religious in Rio de Janeiro developed a 'Missa Afro' (a liturgy for the Mass in African style) which incorporated elements aiming to show a recognition of the African heritage of Brazil's black population. So this is a secularization of religious reason, but along quite different lines from the devotional movements which to some extent were encouraged to counter the influence of TL.

The heyday of Liberation Theology coincided with a spurt in the growth, or at least the visibility, of Pentecostalism in Latin America. When that Pentecostalism started out in the early twentieth century, embedded in rural areas and the poorest urban strata, it emphasized self-discipline and respectability, as well as healing and the struggle against the forces of evil. But with the rise of neo-Pentecostalism at the turn of the century, a strong element of self-realization and the therapeutic moves centre stage. The most extreme expression of the self-realization strand, which does stretch most common-sense notions of what can count as religious, is described in a US context by Tania Luhrmann (Luhrmann 2012): this is a religious subculture with barely any institutionalization or any limitations on what can be done in the name of religion, less breathlessly analysed by Altglas than by Luhrmann (Altglas, 2014).

The Dialectic Transcended: Beyond Popular Religion

Popular Catholicism revolves around rituals which take place at particular times, in accordance with long-established formulae, and in particular places, conducted by designated persons (not always priests, but always with priestly approval) in fixed roles. Although these practices change over time, they do so incrementally and imperceptibly and they carry an aura of faithfulness to deep tradition, with a strong sense of origins and authenticity. Official ritual shares these characteristics but, in addition, carries the imprint of faithfulness to ancient texts and recorded commandments, in addition to institutionalization, traditions of music and bodily expression, liturgy carried out by personnel invested with charisma and versed in esoteric procedures whose meaning is enshrined in age-old interpretations. The official rarely suppresses the popular even if the latter strays from strict orthodoxy: indeed very often it is encouraged, as we saw earlier on, and the popular is usually respectful of official orthodoxy. But the popular does respond to the demand for immediate this-worldly solutions to life's problems in a way that the official does not.

Pentecostal churches, in contrast, cannot be said either to have stable sets of rituals or to have a codified, written liturgy in the Catholic, Anglican or Jewish sense. However, they certainly have recourse to an identifiable repertoire of calls on supernatural forces, but these are short invocations rather than ritual procedures, and their services do not follow a fixed set of written invariant prayers. Many invocations are in the form of exchanges between preachers and their listeners, when the preacher calls for a response and the congregation cry 'Amen!' or 'Hallelujah!'. They can be thought of as cues: during services preachers at several points make apparently improvised perorations often backed up with sound effects designed to manage emotion. This absence of elaborate ritual procedures is related to the core Pentecostal doctrine that gifts of the spirit are precisely that – gifts – not learnt in prolonged training – and to the concomitant idea of the potential for priesthood on the part of all believers, and is incompatible with the notion that a particular status conferred by the hierarchy or organization (comparable to that of a priest in the Catholic or Anglican churches) would bring with it charismatic gifts or a privileged role of intermediary with the supernatural. If Pentecostal services nevertheless exhibit a remarkably uniform set of speaking styles, iterated across the globe, this is not because they are subordinated to any sort of common authority.

Despite this democracy of the spiritual, decision-making authority in most evangelical churches in Latin America and Africa is usually heavily concentrated and exercised in impenetrable ways. To be sure there is enormous variation, but accounts of pastors who involve their congregants in decision-making are unusual (Garma Navarro 2004; Englund 2007), and unheard of in large-scale neo-Pentecostal organizations.[6]

Among Pentecostals there is not a set of procedures to be executed at fixed times of a life cycle, an annual cycle, or a seasonal cycle. When an *obreiro* or *obrero* (Portuguese/Spanish for church workers, usually volunteers) approaches you, places three fingers of one hand on your forehead and yells 'Out, out, out', that is hardly an esoteric procedure. Pastors, preachers, *obreiros* are authorized or empowered to bless congregants, to invoke the supernatural power of Jesus to heal physical and psychological ailments, and to exorcise the forces of evil from their lives, their families, their homes.

Neo-Pentecostalism is in many ways an even more radical break than its predecessor Pentecostalism. At its core is a model of a highly centralized and global Church organization in which the themes of donation, diabolic possession and exorcism take pride of place. Pentecostalism, in contrast, is

---

[6] Garma does describe a pastor opening up decision-making in a medium-sized church in Mexico City. Englund describes an attempt by a pastor to hold elections in his church in an impoverished township in Malawi, which failed because members were afraid that the process would become enmeshed in witchcraft and did not credit the secrecy of the vote.

more discrete on these subjects and is highly decentralized, so that pastors have to manage their own churches and if they want to be professionals it is their business to achieve a corresponding growth in their churches. The earliest model of neo-Pentecostalism is probably the Brazil-based Universal Church of the Kingdom of God, which has millions of followers in Brazil and millions more across the world, especially in other Latin American countries, in Portugal and in Africa. The Universal Church has also been strongly influenced by the prosperity Gospel, but that is only one, and perhaps not the principal, feature distinguishing it and others like it from classic Pentecostalism (Lehmann 2011a, 2011b).

Roles in Pentecostal churches – which still have many more adherents – and neo-Pentecostal churches relate more to organizational than to ritual responsibilities: *obreiros* undertake practical tasks, patrol the aisles in the larger churches, and ensure everything is in order. In the Universal Church I have encountered pastors responsible for tasks like education, public relations or security, as well as preaching or managing a church, and, at the upper end, there is something like a senior management whose members are known as bishops. When I sought to interview their leading architect, responsible for the massive 'Temple of Solomon' which the Church opened in São Paulo in 2014,[7] for example, I was told that this required the 'permission of the top management' – which was eventually obtained. In the classic model of small churches and chapels the dynamic is quite different: one individual controls all aspects of the church, material and spiritual, and if someone in the congregation has leadership ambitions he will set up a separate church or chapel. The context is however a dynamic one, and the Pentecostal field is changing, so that we observe a trend towards the neo-Pentecostal model even among the pastors of the Assemblies of God, a loose worldwide confederation which is the umbrella group for the classic model.

Little is known about training in neo-Pentecostal churches, and they are certainly not keen to open it up to researchers: to judge by their conduct of

---

[7] Costing a reputed $300 million, this monumental construction measures 55 metres in height and 75 metres along its frontage, covers an entire street block and in addition to a hall to accommodate 10,000 people, with replicas of the two pillars at the entrance to the original temple (Boaz and Jachin) and, in its precincts, of the tent which housed the Ark of the Covenant as it was carried across the desert. The building contains broadcasting studios, classrooms, a large baptismal pool, and the future burial place of the Church's leader and his family. The design is inspired by the Roman concept of Herod's Temple and can be appreciated on the Church's many websites worldwide including www.templodesalomao.com. The inauguration was a rolling event over a month in July-August 2014.

services, they may learn techniques of effective preaching and management of the emotional state of a congregation. The widespread distrust in Pentecostal culture of erudite knowledge and of the sort of theological training which is required of Catholic and mainstream Protestant clergy, is well documented (Anderson 2004): such learning is regarded as detracting from the spiritual and inspirational, though there are variations and exceptions. Nonetheless, as evidence of the constantly changing landscape of evangelical Christianity, the leaders of the Igreja Apostolica Unidade em Deus in the Ilha do Governador in Rio de Janeiro who have developed programmes and initiatives in religious tourism, social work in local communities, and hospital visiting and hope to establish a recognized university level course in Ministry, precisely because they see a need for a more intellectual sort of training for evangelical pastors.

Exchange in a Secularized Religious Setting

The exchange in Pentecostalism is with the Church, which expects members to contribute tithes amounting to 10 per cent of their income (before tax). In small chapels where congregants are part of a network of known individuals, contributions can be thought of as a way of affirming membership in an identifiable group and church, and of funding a pastor with whom the members are all familiar. According to observation in the early 1990s, in the large-scale also Brazil-based Deus é Amor church, people who are not up-to-date with their tithe (*dízimo* – recorded in a little notebook called the *Caderneta da prosperidade* – 'Prosperity Notebook') are not allowed to take part in the monthly ritual of the 'Holy Supper' (Santa Ceia) – a ritual common among Pentecostals which mimics the Catholic Holy Communion, distributing grape juice and a wafer. In the Universal Church there is no such concrete exchange, nor can congregants be said to form a community: they are too numerous to know one another, the churches are located increasingly in non-residential areas which can accommodate their imposing size, and the organization itself discourages communal interaction for example by constantly rotating its pastors and preachers – a 'Church of Strangers' as in the title of a remarkable book on its expansion into South Africa (van Wyk 2014).

But how then can such churches persuade people to become regular attenders and workers? They do not want them to drop in for a 'fix' and never reappear, thus circumventing the commitment to make contributions or pay their tithes. As an illustration, in September 2011 in a large temple of the Universal Church in the Boa Vista neighbourhood of Recife (capacity c.

3,000 plus offices and underground car park) I asked an attendant whether they still distributed plastic bags with water from the River Jordan to be used in purifying a dwelling: the reply was that they had been instructed to stop this practice because people would just come in to pick up the miraculous water but would then not return. It may sound like a detail, but the underlying structure is important: these churches may seem to offer well-being and God's blessings for free but attracting and retaining converts is their raison d'être. They have to persuade their followers that adherence and contribution are part of the effort at 'helping themselves'. The exchange is not with the supernatural, but with the organization itself, whose agents are the volunteers, the preachers and the pastors. It is not easy to interpret what congregants think they are getting out of the Church: in interviews the standard narrative is about the renunciation of vice-ridden ways, about a life which changed in a fundamental way, about the healing of physical and mental illnesses but it sounds too much like a ready-made formula to be entirely convincing, as do the life stories told by followers on their TV programmes which all seem to follow a standardized format culminating in eventual rescue and financial success notably in small businesses like hairdressing and skincare. Maybe what people really mean when reciting the narrative is that they found someone to listen to them – and pastors and preachers sometimes say they offer counselling as if they were doing so in a quasi-professional way. It is not uncommon to observe these consultations, which are not very prolonged and tend to conclude with a brief invocation or a cry of 'Out!' to free the individual of demonic possession. They may even offer a house visit by a team to remove evil spirits.[8] The leadership no doubt hopes that its services – personal and collective – will encourage people to become regular members and regular contributors.[9] A recent newcomer to the Brazilian Pentecostal field, the Igreja

---

[8] I watched as a preacher arranged this with a family of women who came to the Universal Church in Boa Vista, Recife, in September 2011. The mother described how her son had killed their dog and their cat and drank the animals' blood. The pastor concluded the house was under the power of the devil and promised to send a team along to exorcise it. He spoke to me in quite a matter-of-fact way about this exchange immediately afterwards.

[9] Ronaldo de Almeida has conducted some analyses of a 1998 Ministry of Health survey on the sexual behaviour of the Brazilian population and of his own 2003 survey in the São Paulo Metropolitan Region and these showed that respondents had changed their religious affiliation during their lives – indeed the São Paulo survey showed that one third had done so. It also showed that Pentecostal churches were the primary gainers from these shifts, but neither survey distinguished between Pentecostal and neo-Pentecostal adherents and retention rates cannot be deduced from the analysis. It should be said that in a fast-moving and crowded environment it would be very difficult to capture retention. Putnam and Campbell did chart changes of affiliation in their US survey but they did not attempt

Mundial do Poder de Deus (World Church of God's Power) led by Valdemiro Santiago, a breakaway from the Universal Church, has had a meteoric success offering a reduced diet of little but healing: people are exhibited in outdoor events as having recovered from all sorts of ailments and these are broadcast on the Church's own cable television channel. Since 2013, however, this venture seems to have fallen back, apparently ceding physical and especially mediatic space to the Universal Church.

In her remarkable account of the Universal Church in South Africa, Ilana van Wyck devotes a lengthy section to explaining the rationale for giving large sums, often sums which the giver cannot afford, to the church. She begins by quoting the church's leader, Edir Macedo who defines sacrifice both as 'the shortest distance between a wish and its materialization' and as 'the act of voluntarily giving something up in exchange for something else of much greater value'. Macedo also reminded his followers that 'giving and receiving has always been present in the relationship between man and God' and the greater the benefit one wants to receive the greater the sacrifice. This last of course is quite out of keeping with liturgical practices where the sacrifice is a matter of symbolism and ritual not of quantity (viz. the red bull of the Temple or the goat sacrificed at Yom Kippur – the 'scapegoat') (Macedo 2003: 70–71, van Wyck 2008: 185). The element of gambling is also there in the immediacy of the (desired) return and in the disproportion between the value of the sacrifice and that of the desired return. The church displays its psychological insight by separating the moment of promising from the moment of giving: followers, or for that matter incidental visitors, are invited to make an extravagant promise of donation and to bring the donation at a later date. This plays on a sense of guilt which in some cases will haunt them if they do not make the donation. Thus van Wyck quotes the case of a desperately poor follower who promised far more than she could afford: her friends were divided as to the 'efficacy or wisdom' of her sacrifice, but all agreed that 'you had to fill your campaign jar with the amount you promised because it was God's money'. In addition, the churchgoers whom she frequented lived in constant fear that forces of evil would be transmitted by objects and money which they received, whatever the good intentions of those transmitting them. This extended to bank loans, and so they chose to take a wager by making a donation to the church in the hope of receiving a boon from God (van Wyck, 2014: 192).

---

to describe the retention rates for different types of churches (Almeida and Monteiro 2001; Almeida 2004; Putnam and Campbell 2010).

If a person publicly contributes money, responding at the extreme by giving more than he or she can afford, for all that it is part of an exchange, the experience of failure will also be an experience of shame or guilt, and so the incentive to overcome his or her misfortune is increased, an incentive accentuated by the churches' own message that each person must give yet each person is responsible. To say, in the wake of disappointment, that it is all the fault of the Church is to expose oneself to the accusation of gullibility, to feel a fool, something most people would prefer to avoid. This is unlikely to be the rationale consciously followed by all adepts of the neo-Pentecostal churches, who may donate for all sorts of reasons, but it does offer a coherent structure to explain what many observers believe to be incomprehensible behaviour or else simply the actions of suckers. To dismiss the actions of millions of people in this way is to abandon the task of explanation.

In constructing a model of an adept's motivation, we must recall the extreme diversity of evangelical and Pentecostal churches, and remember that we are referring principally to Latin American and Africa. Innumerable small Pentecostal churches still account for the vast majority of Pentecostal faithful in Brazil (Almeida 2004) and probably everywhere, and in these the motivation to make donations is probably simply to enable the chapels to exist and to fund a pastor. There are no doubt other motivations as well, but that one is the simplest. Neo-Pentecostal churches are quite different: they are almost business ventures. The explanation offered here in terms of exchange and self-respect as well as fear of the powers of darkness, is not intended to be more than partial: motivations are many and varied, but the pattern is by now so standardized across geographical and cultural boundaries, that a model is nevertheless called for.

Ritual Promiscuity

The Catholic Church is not a closed institution which keeps a list of members: one may have to fulfil some minimum conditions to take communion, but services and the churches are open. For centuries Catholic bishops took a prominent role in events of national importance in countries where the state recognized the Church. Likewise, Catholic popular religion belongs to a community, not just to the members of a Church or organization. The spirit of inclusiveness goes even further with the incorporation or co-optation of indigenous practices and ideas into popular Catholicism as we saw in Olivia Harris' description of the Andean village, and as Antoinette Molinié describes for a Castilian village (Molinié 2004). Pentecostalism and neo-Pentecostalism emphasize joining, membership and tithing, and whereas a Catholic or Anglican, once baptized, remains a Catholic or Anglican, membership in Pentecostal churches has to be constantly renewed through tithing and attendance. Pentecostal pastors do not attach much importance to their role in celebrating marriages and Pentecostal churches do not own cemeteries: for that one goes to the mainstream religious institutions.

The larger-scale, more centralized neo-Pentecostal churches are more open and less interested in creating a tightly-knit community linked to a church. Rather they throw open their doors, keep them open all day long every day, and provide a service: the Universal Church calls itself a 'spiritual emergency service'.[10] It aims to rival the Catholic Church for hegemony in the religious field by building imposing pastiche neo-classical façades in prominent locations and establishing a prominent media presence. The instability of its ritual and symbolic formulae indicates that the leaders are still experimenting. The example of the water from the River Jordan was one instance: another is the oscillating relationship with the Afro-Brazilian – or African – imaginary: its preachers and workers oscillate between mocking the paraphernalia of possession cults and encouraging followers' fear of the devils which lie within them.[11] The IURD collects prayer notes ('pedidos de promessa') like Catholic *votos* which are collected and deposited in a simulacrum of the Ark of the Covenant for transport to Israel and offering as a kind of burnt sacrifice on Mount Sinai.[12] It also forefronts Jewish themes by displaying seven-branch candelabras on the podiums of its meeting halls, and its infatuation with Judaism reaches a new height with the 'Temple of Solomon'. So while rejecting the nearby heritage of Catholicism, they reach out to a distant one in Judaism, and one which is not connected to the lives of their followers.

Whether the churches indulge the spirits from the cults or try to stamp on them, they are adopting an approach which demystifies them, and they are not engaging in elaborate esoteric procedures to fight them off. There is a matter-of-factness to their response which is disconcerting for someone who seeks an

---

[10] 'Um pronto-socorro espiritual' in Portuguese.

[11] In a paper delivered in Cambridge in May 2011, Linda van de Kamp described how in Mozambique pastors sent by the Universal Church sometimes make fun of images and devices from the country's indigenous cults, yet at other times advise followers to avoid confrontation and indeed to engage and tame the devils which might be attacking women through their husbands' misbehaviour (van de Kamp 2013).

[12] Israeli tour guides confirm that Universal Church pastors do arrive with suitcases full of these notes, though there is some doubt if the ceremony, which is filmed, always takes place on Mount Sinai.

interpretation in terms of ritual and symbolism. A distant example, from New Guinea again, illustrates this rather well: Robbins recounts that the Urapmin, having renounced the cult of their ancestors, took their bones away, holding them at the end of long poles, and burnt them; nonetheless, in the case of particularly important ancestors they did not burn them but placed them in a safe hiding place. Later they started hunting in a taboo area, previously reserved for the ancestors, but when some people fell ill after eating the meat from the animals they had been hunting, the big men quickly declared the ground taboo again. Nevertheless, in a delightful phrase the Urapmin said they saw no return: 'after how we treated those ancestors, there is no way they would have us back' (Robbins 2004: 146–50).

Saying the Unsaid

And yet, and yet ... remember how the Urapmin in their prolonged truth-speaking sessions, were frank to one another about trivialities, but held back what really mattered – their squabbles and disputes – until they had been resolved. Similarly the neo-Pentecostal churches are physically open all day seven days a week, always providing an *obreiro* or pastor to listen to someone's troubles. But the structures which underpin the listening pastor are hermetic: they reveal nothing about their finances, save to the tax authorities, nor about their training methods, nor about their management methods, nor about how their bishops and pastors are paid. They have extensive interests in the media and have accumulated untold riches: according to *Forbes Brasil*, the head of the Universal Church, Edir Macedo, is worth US$950m, and two of the next four richest are former associates of his: the leader of the very recently founded Igreja Mundial do Poder de Deus (World Church of God's Power), Valdemiro Santiago, is worth $220m, and the leader of the Igreja Internacional da Graça de Deus (Internal Church of the Grace of God), R.R. Soares, a brother-in-law of Macedo, $125m. Two others are worth respectively $150m and $65m. A similar pattern is observed in Nigeria (Marshall 2010). While millions of Brazilians follow these men and not infrequently attribute their happiness or success to their attendance at their churches and even to their contributions to them, millions of others regard them as cynical opportunists profiting from the naïveté of the poor. The TV Record network is owned, as far as is known, by Macedo himself but its relationship with the Universal Church and with the money donated to the church is unknown. Officers of the Church can be met at the TV Record offices and TV Record has recording studios at its Rio de

Janeiro 'Cathedral of Faith'. No wonder some Brazilian commentators have asked whether the Constitutional separation of religion and the state, which allows churches and other religious institutions exemption from tax on the basis that religion is not a business, has not been overtaken by events.

So the church doors are wide open, but behind the podium there is mystery, and apart from their perfunctory encounters in the church hall, the pastors and preachers are kept isolated from the followers. The parking lots at Universal Church meeting places seem to be venues for *obreiros* and pastors gossip away from the limelight. The esoteric, the mysterious is there, but it is not in the ritual, which as we have explained has none of the impenetrable symbolism which characterizes shamanic ritual or the mystery of transubstantiation in Catholicism. The mystery is in the organization.

So where have we arrived? The most dynamic form of Christianity, or at least of organized faith in Jesus Christ, in the world today, professes no theology, speaks little if at all about the life hereafter, demands that its followers make sacrifices for the sake of their Church not for the sake of their salvation, demands no sacrifice of its personnel save full-time dedication to the Church and its management, and offers followers an exchange not with the supernatural, but with the organization itself. The reward promised to its followers, *if they too make the effort*, is success in this life – a happy family, a secure marriage, a comfortable lifestyle. It would seem that the old certainties may have to be discarded, even categories like popular religion – for in neo-Pentecostalism there is no heritage and no community and the ritual is denuded of mystery or of its binding quality, leaving a repertoire of gestures and imprecations whose meaning has no mystery at all.

References

Almeida, R.D. (2004). Religião na metrópole paulista. *Revista Brasileira de Ciencias Sociais*, 19(56), 15–27.

Almeida, R.D. and Monteiro, P. (2001). Trânsito religioso no Brasil. *São Paulo em Perspectiva*, 15(3), 92–100.

Altglas, V. (2014). *Religious Exoticism: the Logics of Bricolage in Contemporary Societies*. New York, Oxford University Press.

Anderson, A. (2004). Pentecostal-Charismatic Spirituality and Theological Education. *PentecoStudies*, 3(1).

Atran, S. (2003). *In Gods We Trust: The Evolutionary Landscape of Religion*. New York: Oxford University Press.

Baron-Cohen, S. (1995). *Mindblindness: An Essay on Autism and Theory of Mind*. Cambridge, MA: MIT Press.

Bashevis Singer, I. (1979). *Shosha*. Harmondsworth: Penguin.

Bax, M. (1995). *Medjugorje: Religion, Politics and Violence in Rural Bosnia*. Amsterdam: VU.

Ben-Ami, I. (1998). *Saint Veneration among the Jews in Morocco*. Detroit: Wayne Sate University Press.

Bilu, Y. and Ben-Ari, E. (1992). The Making of Modern Saints: Manufactured Charisma and the Abu-Hatseiras of Israel. *American Ethnologist*, 19(4), 672–87.

Bloch, M. (2008). Why Religion is Nothing Special but is Central. *Philosophical Transactions of the Royal Society*, 363, 2055–61.

Boyer, P. (2001). *Religion Explained: The Human Instincts that Fashion Gods, Spirits and Ancestors*. London: Heinemann.

Boyer, P. (2004). Religion, Evolution and Cognition. *Current Anthropology*, 45(3), 430–3.

Brandão, C.R. (2007). *Os Deuses do Povo: um estudo sobre a religião popular*, new and unabridged edn. Uberlândia: Editora da Universidade Federal de Uberlândia.

Carranza, B. (2009). Perspectivas da neopentecostalização católica, in *Novas comunidades católicas: em busca de um espaço pós-moderno*, ed. B. Carranza, C. Mariz and M. Camurça. Aparecida: Ideias e Letras.

Carranza, B., Mariz, C. and Camurça, M. (eds) (2009). *Novas comunidades católicas: em busca de um espaço pós-moderno*. Aparecida: Ideias e Letras.

Dynner, G. (2006). *Men of Silk: The Hasidic Conquest of Polish Jewish Society*. Oxford and New York: Oxford University Press.

Eade, J. (2012). "Pilgrimage, the Assumptionists and Catholic Evangelisation in a Changing Europe: Lourdes and Plovdiv." *Cargo. Journal for Social/Cultural Anthropology* 10(1-2): 29-46.

Englund, H. (2007). Pentecostalism Beyond Belief: Trust and Democracy in a Malawian Township. *Africa: Journal of the International African Institute*, 77(4), 477–99.

Evans-Pritchard, E.E. (1965). *Witchcraft, Oracles and Magic among the Azande*. Oxford: Clarendon Press.

Friedman, M. (1986). Life Tradition and Book Tradition in the Development of Ultra-Orthodox Judaism, in *Judaism Viewed From Within and From Without: Anthropological Studies*, ed. H. Goldberg. Atlantic City: SUNY Press, pp. 235–55.

Garma Navarro, C. (2004). *Buscando el espíritu: Pentecostalismo en Iztapalapa y la Ciudad de México*. Mexico City and Barcelona: Plaza y Valdés.

Geschiere, P. (1995). *Sorcellerie et Politique en Afrique: la viande des autres*. Paris: Karthala.

Gutierrez, G. (1973). *Theology of Liberation*. New York: Orbis Books.

Harris, O. (2006). The Eternal Return of Conversion: Christianity as Contested Domain in Highland Bolivia, in *The Anthropology of Christianity*, ed. F. Cannell. Durham, NC: Duke University Press, pp. 51–76.

Harris, R. (1999). *Lourdes: Body and Spirit in the Secular Age*. London: Penguin.

Hervieu-Léger, D. (2001). *La Religion en Miettes ou: la Question des Sectes*. Paris: Calmann-Lévy.

Illouz, E. (2008). *Saving the Modern Soul: Therapy, Emotions, and the Culture of Self-help*. Berkeley: University of California Press.

Illouz, E. (2012). *Why Love Hurts: A Sociological Explanation*. Cambridge: Polity Press.

Lehmann, D. (1990). *Democracy and Development in Latin America: Economics, Politics and Religion in the Post-war Period*. Cambridge: Polity Press.

Lehmann, D. (1996). *Struggle for the Spirit: Religious Transformation and Popular Culture in Brazil and Latin America*. Oxford: Polity Press.

Lehmann, D. (2002). Religion in Contemporary Latin American Social Science. *Bulletin of Latin American Research*, 21(2), 290–307.

Lehmann, D. (2005). The Cognitive Approach to Understanding Religion. *Archives des Sciences Sociales des Religions*, 131–2, 199–213.

Lehmann, D. (2011a). Introduction to Volume 3, in *Fundamentalism and Charismatic Movements*, ed. D. Lehmann and H. Iqtidar. London: Routledge, pp. 1–9.

Lehmann, D. (2011b). The Latin American Religious Field, in *Latin America, 1810–2010: Dreams and Legacies*, ed. C. Auroi and A. Helg. London: Imperial College Press, pp. 419–58.

Lehmann, D. and Siebzehner, B. (2009). Power, Boundaries and Institutions: Marriage in Ultra-Orthodox Judaism. *European Journal of Sociology*, 50(2), 273–308.

Luhrmann, T.M. (2012). *When God Talks Back: Understanding the American Evangelical Relationship with God*. New York: Knopf.

Luzzatto, S. (2007). *Padre Pio. Miracoli e politica nell'Italia del Novecento*. Turin: Einaudi (English translation: *Padre Pio: Miracles and Politics in a Secular Age*. New York: Metropolitan Books, 2010).

Macedo, E. (2003). *Change your Life through Sacrifice*. Johannesburg, UCKG Publications.

Marshall, R. (2010). The Sovereignty of Miracles: Pentecostal Political Theology in Nigeria. *Constellations*, 17(2), 197–223.

Mesaritou, E. (2009). The Dialectics of the Sacred: Institutionalization, Power and Transformation of Padre Pio's Charisma at the Shrine of Santa Maria delle Grazie. PhD thesis, Social and Political Sciences, Cambridge, University of Cambridge.

Molinié, A. (2004). The Revealing Muteness of Rituals: A Psychoanalytical Approach to a Spanish Ceremony. *Journal of the Royal Anthropological Institute*, 10(1), 41–61.

Putnam, R. and Campbell, D. (2010). *American Grace: How Religion Divides and Unites Us*. New York: Simon & Schuster.

Robbins, J. (2004). *Becoming Sinners: Christianity and Moral Torment in a Papua New Guinea Society*. Berkeley, CA and London: University of California Press.

Rossi, M. (2010). *Agape*. São Paulo: Globo.

Sharot, S. (2011). *Comparative Perspectives on Judaisms and Jewish Identities*. Detroit: Wayne State University Press.

Soloveitchik, H. (1994). Rupture and Reconstruction: The Transformation of Contemporary Orthodoxy. *Tradition*, 28(4), 64–130.

Sperber, D. (1996). *Explaining Culture: A Naturalistic Approach*. Oxford: Blackwell.

Stadler, N. and N. Luz (2014). "The Veneration of Womb Tombs: Body-Based Rituals and Politics at the Tomb of Mary and Maqam Abu al-Hijja." *Journal of Anthropological Research* 70(2): 183–205.

Tarrow, S.G. (1967). *Peasant Communism in Southern Italy*. New Haven: Yale University Press.

van de Kamp, Linda (2013). South-South Transnational Spaces of Conquest: Afro-Brazilian Pentecostalism, *Feitiçaria* and the Reproductive Domain in Urban Mozambique. *Exchange*, 42, 343–65.

van Wyck, I. (2014). *The Universal Church of the Kingdom of God in South Africa: a Church of Strangers*. New York, Cambridge University Press.

Woodhead, L. (2012). Strategic and Tactical Religion. Sacred Practices of Everyday Life, Edinburgh, 9–11 May 2012. Available at www.religionandsociety.org.uk/attachments/files/1337692875_Woodhead-Tactical%20Religion-Edinburgh%20May%202012.pdf [accessed: 23 June 2014].

Chapter 5

The Sacramental Mechanism: Religion and the Civilizing Process in Christian Western Europe with Particular Reference to the Peace of God Movement and its Aftermath

Andrew McKinnon

In the modern world, religion sometimes fosters, channels and perpetuates violence (cf. Juergensmeyer 2003), a fact that has been difficult to ignore after 11 September 2001 (Lincoln 2006). At the same time, contemporary research has also shown that religion is far from an insignificant force in the processes of peace-building and post-conflict resolution (Brewer 2010). In his important survey of social scientific attention on the topic, Scott Appleby sensibly suggests that the role of religion in the violent conflicts of the modern world is profoundly ambivalent (2000).

Much of the attempt to understand the relationships between religion, violence and peace-building is marked by a decided concern with contemporary religion. While this is of undoubted value, and reflects well-intentioned concern over contemporaries suffering from religiously inspired violence, and the potential contributions of religion towards peace, the discussion can sometimes seem characterized by the 'retreat of sociologists into the present' (Elias 1987). It would seem important to try to situate the relationship between religion and violence in the context of long-term changes in dispositions towards violent acts that Norbert Elias referred to as *The Civilizing Process* in his masterwork of that same title (2004).

Religion and the Civilizing Process

That the relationship between religion and violence has not been previously considered from the perspective of *The Civilizing Process* (2004) is not particularly surprising, since Elias himself sidelines the role of religious belief, practices and institutions (Bax 1987; Van Krieken 1989; Mennell 1992; Goudsblom 2004; Turner 2004), seeing it as largely irrelevant to the fostering of either violence or peaceableness, or shaping the course of historical change. Indeed, Elias is explicit that he sees

> religion, the belief in the punishing or rewarding of an omnipotence of God, never has in itself a 'civilizing' or affect-subduing effect. On the contrary, religion is always exactly as 'civilized' as the society or class which upholds it. (2000: 169)

While the direct consequences of such beliefs may well be limited, religion entails far more than this narrow (and somewhat ironically, markedly Protestant) conception of individual actors whose conduct is guided by their convictions. The dismissal of religion as inconsequential is difficult to reconcile with the history of Western Europe, and its exclusion seems incongruent with Elias' own theoretical inclinations towards sociology as a relational science (Bax 1987; van Krieken 1989). If we pause to consider the power and wealth of the medieval religious elite (Wood 2006), its role in legitimating and coordinating relations among the three orders of medieval society (Duby 1980), and its role as the primary carrier of trans-continental communication and interchange (Mann 1986; Le Goff 2005) it is difficult to see how it can be treated entirely as a 'dependent variable', as 'epiphenomenal', or as institutions with even 'relative autonomy' (Bax 1987). None of these are terms Elias would endorse, but it is difficult to see how he treats religious belief and practice as anything other in the context of the *Civilizing Process* (2000).

For the most part, scholars working in the school of Elias have followed his lead in this respect, though the work of Mart Bax (1987) and Robert van Krieken (1989, 1998, 2011) stand out as partial exceptions. Bax (1987) shows how Elias' analysis of the civilizing process can be used to great profit for understanding the trajectory of religious evolution in the west, without neglecting its relative autonomy from the emerging state. Unfortunately, Bax contributes little to understanding the role of religious institutions in the major civilizing processes of western European history. Van Krieken (2011) has recently argued that in Ireland at least, the Church played an important role in re-organizing the practices and institutions of marriage and family, with long-term, independent consequences for the civilizing process.

A fall-back position in the face of criticisms that Elias' sins of omission are potentially mortal for a historical social psychology of Western Europe, would be to recall that Elias' self-defined limits to his project are that his stated interest is in the 'secular elite' (Goudsblom 2004). Given Elias' own insistence on the importance of interdependencies (Mennell 1992), however, we can hardly treat the secular elite as entirely independent of the religious elite. Rather, the lives of religious and secular elites in medieval Europe are intertwined in any number of significant ways. The religious elite has long played a central role in educating the children of the secular elite, ever since the development of the cathedral schools (Jaeger 1985), and exemplified by the priest and humanist Desiderius Erasmus, whose *De Civilitate Morum Puerilium Libellus* plays such an important role in volume one of the *Civilizing Process* (Knox 1995; Bast 1995). The religious elite were, furthermore, typically kin relations of the secular elite. Finally, and in this context perhaps most importantly, the religious elite had considerable powers of consecration *and* de-consecration. These powers could, and sometimes did, change the this-worldly fortunes of the secular elite. Bishops had the power to declare someone a sinner or an excommunicate (and with some more effort as a heretic). This may have been perceived to have other-worldly consequences for the fortune of the excommunicate's soul, but it could also have very real, concrete and this-worldly consequences, as I will discuss in what follows.

If medievalists have taken issue with the omission of religion in Elias' account of the civilizing process, they have also found it difficult to recognize the face in his portrait of the medieval *habitus* (Rosenwein 1998; Meyerson et al. 2004, Thiery 2009; see also van Krieken 1989). While Elias is always careful to argue that the civilizing process has no historical degree zero, and that the difference between the dispositions that developed during the Renaissance and those of our medieval forebears is one of degree. In practice, however, he often treats the medieval *habitus* as qualitatively distinct, and he often allows a caricature to make his case (Borkenau 1938, 1939; Arnason 1989; van Krieken 1989).

Assessing a range of critical appraisals of *The Civilizing Process*, Barbara Rosenwein writes that although Medievalists have generally been unwilling to accept Elias' view of emotionally unrestrained medievals, his implicitly Freudian conceptions of human personality, or his exclusive emphasis on secular courts, and, although they have tended to push the civilizing process several centuries further back in European history, Elias nonetheless remains an important touchstone. Despite the many reservations Medieval historians have of the *Civilizing Process* as it pertains to their period, she writes, '[i]n general, then, historians of the West have accepted the thrust of Elias's model' (1998: 240). Given how much of Elias' 'model' she has summarily sent to the scrap heap, I am not sure that it is his 'model' that has been generally accepted, even as it is equally true that his 'general thrust' has.

In their introduction to *A Great Effusion of Blood* (2004) Meyerson et al. concur with Rosenwein's assessment:

> Few scholars today would subscribe to Elias's notion that the development of a court society and the taming of the European nobility, especially from the end of the Middle Ages, effected a change in norms and a reduction of violence throughout society. Medievalists in particular have criticized his characterization of medieval people as irrational, given to extreme emotions, and uncontrollably violent. They have also questioned his almost exclusive emphasis on the lay aristocracy, his assumption that new aristocratic mores necessarily percolated down to or were aped by the lower classes, and his relative neglect of the latter and the church in his treatment of the ideological and social changes essential to the civilizing process. (2004: 5)

If this seems like a damning indictment from specialists in the period, they do offer a reason why Elias' account of the civilizing process is sent to be redeemed in purgatory, rather than consigned to the burning lake of fire. Their provisional verdict is that:

> however medievalists and others have criticized and qualified the work of Elias, it is difficult to avoid concluding that medieval people used and understood violence differently, and that what separates us from our medieval forebears is not just the greater efficacy of modern states in controlling and suppressing violence but, more importantly, fundamental modifications in mentality and behaviour. (Meyerson et al. 2004: 5)

In this chapter, I want to contribute to paying down the debt of indulgences owed for the *Civilizing Process*, proposing a way to include religion and the religious elite in the model, whilst avoiding any suggestion that medievals were enslaved to their passions but recognizing that there is a difference between their *habitus* and ours. In this chapter I argue that what I will term the *sacramental mechanism* is vital for understanding the civilizing process in western European history, suggesting that it may be of importance on a par with the *monopoly mechanism* and the *royal mechanism*, two of the primary levers of the civilizing process. My concern in this chapter is with the sacramental mechanism itself, largely leaving aside the relation between the different mechanisms, a full conception of which would ultimately be necessary for understanding the complex web of relations that drive the civilizing process as a whole. To analyse these interconnected forces would require far more than I will be able to accomplish within the limits of this chapter; my ambition here is simply to provide this first and, in my view, necessary, step.

There are a number of historical cases that could be used to show the importance of religious forces and institutions for diminishing the proclivity towards violent means, for fostering self-restraint and taming passions. For example, Daniel Thiery (2009) has written a compelling book on the role of the late-medieval English parish in the civilizing process, and there are encouraging beginnings of the consideration of Protestant institutions in the promotion of self and social control (Bast 1995; Knox 1995). Likewise, although not framed in terms of the civilizing process, both Philip Gorski's *The Disciplinary Revolution* (2003) and Michael Graham's study of the discipline in Scottish Kirk Sessions (1996) are both important studies that have much bearing on the questions raised here.

I will address the question of religion and the civilizing process by inspecting a rather different case: the *pax Dei* movement (from the late tenth century) and its after-effects through the eleventh century (including the canons of *treuga Dei* and the preaching of the First Crusade) proves instructive for the consideration of Elias' account of the civilizing process for several reasons. First, in the Peace Councils, we find the violent, unruly warrior class of castellans (the very group that will develop into Elias' court nobility) being shaped and constrained by ecclesiastical elites and by the peasants, in response to the acts of violence and exploitation perpetuated against them. While these castellans certainly do not become the purveyors of courtly manners at this point, here we find a fundamental step along that path. Second, following from this, an examination of this case shows that, at the very beginning of the process of feudalization, Christian ideals and institutions played a formative role that is decisive for the course of both the monopoly mechanism and the royal mechanism. Third, the church acted to constrain the violence of the castellans by Christianizing it. Although such sacralization of violence was by no means ineffective in constraining the warrior nobles, the church was unable to control their violent impulses completely, at least in part due to the relative religious independence of the knights (Kaeuper 2009); the church also played no inconsiderable role in the formation of the First Crusade. This last point is important, especially given Elias's insistence that the crusades were primarily driven by economic pressures, particularly the finite amount of land and the primogeniture of the French landowning classes. More recent research on the Crusades casts that empirical claim into very serious doubt, but there is an important theoretical point that this example forces us to confront directly in the theory of the civilizing process. This means that the same means of restraining violence and the passions 'at home', may at the same time foster them at a distance; it also shows the importance of religion in fostering both peace and directing violent impulses.

The Civilizing Process

Elias's masterpiece is a book that defies simple summary without gross distortion: it is a brilliant, nuanced and detailed work of historical sociological analysis, 500 pages in length and covering 1,000 years of history, even if it is primarily focused on about three or four centuries, and primarily concerned with French history. Nonetheless, it is an argument that may be sketched out in the broadest brushstrokes, indeed, it must be so delineated so that the reader may see my addition of the sacramental mechanism to the conception of the civilizing process and its relation to the whole.

Volume One of the *Civilizing Process* charts the development of courtly manners in the Renaissance. Elias largely follows Johan Huizinga's (1924) portrayal of the medieval *habitus*, judging it as characterized by what

> in comparison to later times might be called its simplicity, its naïveté. There are, in all societies where the emotions are expressed more violently and directly, fewer psychological nuances and complexities in the general stock of ideas. There are friend and foe, desire and aversion, good and bad people. (2004: 55)

Table manners, the exercise of bodily functions, sexual restraint and the exercise of violent passions are not isolated aspects, but form a 'definite social structure' that is 'a total way of life' (59) that is quite radically different from our own more civilized dispositions. The pictures of these dispositions, largely painted by clerics, and for that reason

> the value judgements they contain are therefore often those of the weaker group threatened by the warrior class. Nevertheless the picture they transmit is quite genuine. 'He spends his life', we read of a knight, 'in plundering, destroying churches, falling upon pilgrims, oppressing widows and orphans. He takes particular pleasure in mutilating the innocent. In a single monastery, that of the black monks of Sarlat, there are 150 men and women whose hands he has cut off

or whose eyes he has put out. And his wife is just as cruel. She helps him with his executions. It even gives her pleasure to torture the poor women. She had their breasts hacked off or their nails torn off so that they were incapable of work'. (2004: 163)

This story of medieval violence, often quoted because it sums up Elias' picture of medieval violence, is, as Elias notes, contained in a work of propaganda, though it is not the account shaped by Nietzschean ressentiment. Rather, it tells of the evils of an opponent of the good Catholic Lord Simon de Montfort. It appears in Pierre des Vaux-de-Cerny's *History of the Albigensian Crusade* where, even in a catalogue of horrors of those opposed to the Lord's Peace, it stands out as an example of truly exceptional pagan wickedness (see van Krieken 1989).

Elias' account of the civilization of manners takes off with his consideration of Erasmus' *De civilitate morum puerilium* (1530) the first, and, in terms of literary merit, undoubtedly the greatest, of humanist manners books. In Volume One, Elias charts the trajectory of increasingly civilized dispositions through what is advised, and how it is advised, in these manners books of the succeeding several centuries. Elias uses these manners books to great effect, showing the increasingly sensitive dispositions of the European (mostly French) elite, their inclination to hide bodily functions, to restrain the emotions, to maintain distance from the bodies of others, and to show superiority by avoiding causing offence to others rather than by a show of force.

In Volume Two, Elias begins to explain the trajectory he charts so effectively in the first volume. The explanation for the course of civilization is not derived from a single cause, but rather it involves the relationship among elements in a web of social relationships (prefiguring his later concept of 'figurations'). Two of the most important elements in the narrative, however, are the process of state formation, and social differentiation and their relation to what he identifies as the 'monopoly mechanism' and the 'royal mechanism'.

The process of state formation leads to an increasing monopoly of force, such that nobles have ever greater reason to train and keep a reign on their passions, and to express their superiority over others by means acceptable at court: the ethos and aesthetics of courtesy, which becomes a 'second nature'. Equally important in this story, and bound up with the courtization of the nobility, is the increasing differentiation of society: an increasingly complex and specialized division of labour and function results in long chains of interdependency and mutual dependence which encourage and facilitate the restraint of the passions. This latter factor was facilitated by the growth of (urban) trading networks and the money economy. The civilizing process implies a particular trajectory towards ever greater constraint, but it is by no means linear, and it can entail multiple contradictions and cross-currents.

If the courts are important in Elias' account, it is not because what happens at court 'causes' the civilization of the rest of society. Rather, he argues, that court society is the place where the civilizing process crystallizes (2004: 99). Nonetheless, the courts are the place where we first find what Elias refers to as the psychologization of experience, where people learn to observe and make sense of their own behaviour and that of others, watching for clues to its hidden meaning. The jockeying for position becomes subtle and strategic, rather than simply a test of strength, and it does so first of all at court.

Elias identifies two mechanisms that are particularly important contributions to state formation and that combine with increasing economic and social differentiation to drive the civilizing process: the monopoly mechanism and the royal mechanism. His conception of the monopoly mechanism seems to draw on observations about competition between modern capitalist firms: each unit finds itself in a competitive situation with other units, and will either get bigger, or else risks getting swallowed up by others that have gotten bigger, to the theoretical end-point of a monopoly. From early Capetian France (late tenth century), the warrior elites and their retinues are engaged with one another in the absence of a strong central power; indeed, the Dukes of l'Île de France, who became the Capetian dynasty, were at this point, less powerful than many of their competitors. They were, in fact, chosen from the nobility of Western Francia to replace the Carolingian dynasty precisely because, in their private capacity, they did not have the wealth and power to threaten a monopoly on the other noble families.

Given the increasing differentiation of society and the mutual interdependence mediated by an increasingly monetized economy, we find an increasing ambivalence of interests among competing warrior elites. A situation where power is distributed relatively evenly among powerful actors tends to privilege the central power. This is what Elias referred to as the royal mechanism: although the medieval nobles were collectively far more powerful than the king, their power relative to each other tended to encourage them to tie each others' hands, a kind of Hobbesian compromise to prevent a war of all nobles against all nobles. The authority of the central power is advantaged, but it is in large measure derived power, rather than being the outcome of monopoly competition.

Where Elias discusses the role of the church in the early Capetian period (2000: 328–9), he treats the church elites simply as contributors to the royal mechanism, aiding the centralizing power of the king in order to prevent the violence and exploitation of other (secular) elites against them. While the church did indeed show considerable nostalgia for the Holy Roman Empire of Charlemagne, where churches and monasteries were less vulnerable to predators (and the castellans did not yet exist as a class), this is far too simple. Church elites were not just another segment of the secular elite inclined to support the prerogative of royal power because it was consonant with their interests. Even if their innovations were later clearly appropriated for the centralization of power, they ought not be reduced to a contribution to the royal mechanism from the start. A closer examination of the *pax Dei* movement suggests the need to consider the power of the church as a relatively autonomous institution (Bax 1987), and to conceptualize its distinctive form of power as *sacramental power*.

Pax Dei and its Reverberations

Norbert Elias' description of the tenth century in western Europe as 'anarchic' was certainly in keeping with the adjectives used by many historians from the late nineteenth century to the middle of the twentieth (Huizinga 1924). The aftermath of the collapse of the Carolingian Empire, the slower dissolution of the dynasty's power in Western Francia, and the rise of the castellans certainly meant for a chaotic and violent time. Following Georges Duby (1953), the consensus is now to see this as a period of transition, where power arrangements were being contested and rearranged: violent and unstable, but by no means anarchic. The courts of Carolingian counts were losing authority over their territory (*pagus*), and power was being devolved to the castellans' *districtio*. Often the castellans were little more than local warrior lords who were able to set up a 'castle', often without the authority of the higher authorities (dukes, counts and certainly not the king). The castellans' 'castles' were initially heaped earth with a drawbridge and a wooden palisade; these were warriors' forts, not nobles' courts. The local lords were increasingly surrounded by bands of warriors, the most important of which were armoured and on horseback (*chevalier*), the higher status of which were armed and supported by their own wealth, the lesser were retained by their lord. In the last third of the tenth century, the king's presence (spread over two dynasties) was entirely absent from all of Aquitaine, and much of the rest of southern France (Debord 1992: 156).

If the Holy Roman Emperor had been anointed to maintain the peace and defend the church, responsibilities delegated to his counts, the upstart warriors in their castles did not have this same sense of *noblesse oblige*. This was the primary reason for clerical nostalgia for the power of the Carolingian Empire. Local rustics, including the free peasantry, fared even worse than the church in this emergent set of relations and became, in many instances, exploited to the brink of starvation, given the vastly superior force of the local lords and their mounted warriors.

As H.E.J. Cowdrey observes, the period around the turn of the millennium was marked by numerous significant famines and outbreaks of disease, including ergotism, widely thought to be God's punishment on a sinful society (1970). The Peace Councils sought the intervention of the God through the saints, present in the holy relics, and demanded that the sinners turn from their sinful ways in the hope that God would spare the people from plagues both 'natural' and 'social' (to use an anachronistic distinction).

In the Peace of God movement, church leaders did not, as Elias implies, demand a restoration of monarchical power, but they asserted the rights and responsibility of the episcopate to assert and to maintain God's peace. The Peace Councils begin in southern France (Aquitaine, Auvergne and Vellay), in the areas furthest from the reach of the last of the Carolingian kings or the early Capetian kings, and in response to the rapid growth of lesser lords taking control of, though not responsibility for, much of the region. The dramatic rise in the number of warlords' 'private' castles (those not authorized by the rightful authority) marks shifting power relations in the region (Debord 1992).

The first Peace Council took place at Le Puy (Auvergne) in 975 CE. Bishop Guy convened a meeting of the faithful in his diocese, held in an open field to accommodate a far larger crowd than could be accommodated in the cathedral. To create a sacred space, many relics were brought from the cathedral, as well as from surrounding monasteries. There Guy made peasants and knights alike swear to keep God's peace, with the explicit threat of excommunication for those who broke the oath, and the only slightly more implicit threat from his nephews, the counts of Gévaudan and Brioude who were present with their assembled troops (Lauranson-Rosaz 1992).

As the Peace Councils took hold, they tended to use the broad template developed by Guy, first in surrounding dioceses, spreading further afield and peaking sometime in the late 1020s or 1030s. An account of an early Peace Council, probably written in the 990s, by Letaldus of Micy, has left us with a vivid description:

> At that time sinners were rising up like stalks of wheat. Evil people wasted the vineyard of the Lords just as briars and thorns choke the harvest of the land. Therefore it pleased bishops, abbots, and other religious men that a council be held at which the taking of booty [*praeda*] would be prohibited and the property of the saints, which had unjustly been stolen, would be restored. Other evils that

fouled the fair countenance of the holy church of God were also struck down by the sharp points of anathemas. I think that this council was held at the monastery of Charroux and that a great crowd of many people [*populus*] gathered there from the Poitou, the Limousin and neighbouring regions. Many bodies of saints were also brought there. The cause of religion was strengthened by their presence, and the impudence of evil people was beaten back. That council – convoked, as it was thought, by divine will – was adorned by frequent miracles through the presence of the saints. Along with these various relics of the saints honoured by God, the remains of the glorious father Junianus were brought with proper honour. (Head and Landes 1992: 328–9)

The crimes upon which anathemas are placed are first and foremost offences against the church, secondarily the peasantry, and thirdly against merchants: both theft, and the use of violence (often, no doubt, committed in the act of theft). Often the prohibitions are rationalized in terms of a prohibition against the use of violence towards the unarmed. Special protection is conferred upon churches and abbeys, guarded by the threat of special anathemas.

Peasants, while not primary actors in the dramas (at least as they are recounted by the literati), they are nonetheless notable participants, even if they may have been drawn as much by the presence of so many holy relics in one place as by the promise of peace. This, in all likelihood, is what drew the warriors, as well, even if the general thrust of the Peace Councils was a finger pointed in their direction. The peasantry, while not orchestrators of the Peace, were not simply passive victims to be protected by the bishop; their enthusiastic, and potentially unruly, presence at the councils acted to pressure the warrior nobility into compliance (Duby 1953; Lauranson-Rosaz 1992). Later, when several bishops organized 'Peace Armies' to avenge the breakers of the Peace, the peasantry formed one of the army's most feared 'columns'.

The role of the holy relics was not only to draw a crowd, but also to guarantee that oaths would be kept. This is not to say that concrete measures were not also taken, including threat of military reprisal for those who broke their oaths, and the exchange of hostages to reinforce them (Lauranson-Rosaz 1992).

Later Peace Councils (from the 1030s) spread geographically through the whole the kingdom of France, but they also expand the scope of the earlier Peace Councils in a number of ways, first expanding the prohibition to include not only the unarmed, but all Christians. As we find in a canon from the council at Narbonne from 1054: 'No Christian should kill another Christian, since whoever kills a Christian doubtless sheds the blood of Christ' (Head and Landes 1992: 8). These later councils are often referred to as the Truce of God (*treuga*

Dei) because they increasingly defined not only whose blood could not be shed, but when warfare could be conducted at all. Specifically, warfare was prohibited not only on the Sabbath, but to make sure that it did not overflow, the Truce of God included a day or two on either side, as well as the holy days of the Church Calendar, particularly the Lenten season.

The prohibitions of the Truce of God (which include and build on those of the earlier Peace) are increasingly appropriated by the secular elite, particularly in the Ducal and Royal courts, who find that they can use them to their advantage, as well as by those who preached, encouraged and engaged in the First Crusade. Thomas Bisson has divided the movement into two phases: the first phase, the Bishop's Peace, he referred to as 'sanctified peace', the second, the Duke's Peace, he referred to as the 'organised' or 'instituted' peace (1977). The former was more popular in character, consisting of councils gathered in fields surrounded by holy relics; the instituted peace had less need of the mass gatherings, and becomes increasingly typical in the second half of the eleventh century.

Elias' account of the Crusades simply allows no room for the religious constraint or encouragement of violence, and gives the church only a very limited means of channelling it. For Elias the basic issue is 'the desire for land and bread', and the church simply 'steered this pre-existing force' (2000: 216). His contention about the Crusades is a basically neo-Malthusian argument – the growing population was less unchecked at the higher eschelons of society creating a '"reserve army" of the *upper class*, of knights without property' (217). These were predominantly younger sons who, because of local laws of primogeniture, faced landlessness. This argument received some measure of support from Georges Duby (1953), although more recently it has been observed that Duby's tentative analysis was based on an examination of one family in one corner of Burgundy (Riley-Smith 2009). Jonathan Riley-Smith has shown that the costs of taking the cross, particularly in the First Crusade, before effective mechanisms of finance and operational infrastructure would have been an exorbitant burden to bear. If the cost of a campaign, for a fully equipped knight, to nearby Hungary would cost something like twice a year's income for a minor noble, taking up the cross to Jerusalem likely cost four to five times as much. The undoubted need for land could certainly be met much closer to home (as demonstrated by the Norman invasion of England in 1066), and in any case few of the knights who left on pilgrimage showed any indication that they planned to settle at the end of their journey; fewer still actually did so.

If the Peace and Truce of God prohibited the killing of Christians, which would mean spilling the blood of Christ himself, it was not a very great step from there to sanctifying violence against heretics and Muslims. This is precisely in fact what happened in the preaching of the Crusades, although violence was Christianized and sanctified earlier, in the midst of the Peace movement itself, at least in its later phases. As Carl Erdmann argues in his classic study of the development of Crusader ideology:

> the Peace of God ... had a positive implication for the warrior profession. The many provisions of the Peace of God resolutions against breakers of peace amounted to nothing less than a new form of war, one provided for this time by the church itself. ([1935] 1977: 63)

Revenge on truce and peace breakers becomes described as an act blessed by God, and in 1038, Archbishop Aimor of Bourges decreed in provincial synod that both the laity and the clergy had the responsibility for using armed force against peace breakers and oppressors of the church ([1935] 1977: 64). An upstanding knight is a defender of the church, the poor and the unarmed, and although he must not spill Christian blood, but Saracens, pagans, Peace breakers and heretics are fair sport.

It is by no means conicidental that Pope Urban II, who instigated the First Crusade, had spent many years at Cluny, the great reforming abbey of southern France, or that he met with his representative in southern France, the bishop of le Puy, before preaching the Crusade at the Council of Clermont (Riley-Smith 2009: 13–30). He then toured the southern and central regions of France to promote crusading. In short, even the geography associated with the call to the Crusade in November 1095 recalled the *pax Dei*, but it is explicit in the accounts of the Pope's speech at Clermont itself. The Pope's preamble to the call to Crusade could have come directly from any of the records of the Peace Councils. In Fulger of Chartres' recounting, the Pope proclaimed:

> You have seen for a long time the great disorder in the world caused by these crimes. It is so bad in some of your provinces, I am told, and you are so weak in the administration of justice, that one can hardly go along the road by day or night without being attacked by robbers; and whether at home or abroad one is in danger of being despoiled either by force or fraud. Therefore it is necessary to reenact the truce, as it is commonly called, which was proclaimed a long time ago by our holy fathers. I exhort and demand that you, each, try hard to have the truce kept in your diocese. And if anyone shall be led by his cupidity or arrogance to break this truce, by the authority of God and with the sanction of this council he shall be anathematized ... Although, O sons of God, you have promised more

firmly than ever to keep the peace among yourselves and to preserve the rights of the church, there remains still an important work for you to do.

Pope Urban proceeds to extend the demands of the truce to include freeing the lands of the Christians from the "Turks and Arabs" promising remission of sins for all who die in this undertaking, singling out the knights both for special need of penance, but also clearly redirecting their energies: "Let those who have been fighting against their brothers and relatives now fight in a proper way against the barbarians" (Thatcher and McNeal 1905: 513–17).

The Peace and the Truce of God had prepared the way for the message of the Crusade by disciplining and circumscribing violence, but also at the same time legitimizing and Christianizing it. Violence becomes more than an occasional necessary evil, as it is in St Augustine, but properly exercised, it becomes an act of piety. This was a revolutionary transformation in the church's conception of violence, and made possible, by the time of the Second Crusade, not just crusading as a means of penance, but the creation of religious-military orders, like the Knights Templar.

The Peace and the Truce of God does seem to have had a positive impact on the taming of violence at home, contrary to Elias' depiction of the unrestrained medieval *habitus*. This is, of course, a matter of degree. To the extent that our witnesses are clergy concerned about the threats to themselves, their churches and monasteries (and the fate of unarmed merchants and peasants), there are always complaints to be made (some, no doubt, exaggerated for effect). Sociologists schooled in Elias' great work, would not expect a change overnight in any case: the civilizing process is slow, uneven and even contradictory. Nonetheless, there does seem to be every evidence that the movement, especially as it was appropriated by the lords themselves, had an effect.

The violent actions of the nobilitiy were slowly and increasingly constrained. Excommunications were levelled against those who committed violence (including theft) against, or even near, a church (Cowdrey 1970; Gergen 2002). Thus certain persons and places were increasingly defined as zones exempt from violence. Being an excommunicate may have involved a danger to a noble's immortal soul, but it was no less of a concern for the mortal body: being labelled a heretic made a noble more vulnerable to attacks from 'legitimate' Lords. Even if the Truces were not consistently maintained, warriors were becoming increasingly concerned about committing acts of violence and engaging in warfare at holy times. This is not to say that the dispositions of the knighthood do not continue to be profoundly contradictory, but neither it be said that religious pressures play no part in the ongoing development of their dispositions (Kaeuper 2009).

It is by no means accidental that the dukes, and increasingly the lesser lords, began to appropriate the demands of the Peace and the Truce of God. As Adrian Bredero (1995) argues, it constrained their action in some respects, but it also granted them more responsibility, or in other words, legitimate power. In structuring the options for competition entailed in the monopoly mechanism, and ultimately feeding into the royal mechanism, the sacramental mechanism contributed to a situation of 'bounded competition' between elites within a state that different quite fundamentally from the relatively unbounded competition between elites in different emerging states. Summarizing the way that Christian beliefs and practices structured competitive struggles in this period, Michael Mann rightly characterizes it as:

> Not anarchy or anomie but normative regulation was provided by Christendom. Political and class struggles, economic life and even wars were to a degree regulated by an unseen hand, not Adam Smith's but Jesus Christ's. By joining the two men's theories in this metaphor we can observe that Christian hands were piously clasped in the prayers of a whole normative community and were actively employed in rational improvement of an imperfect world. (1986: 398)

That is to say, that what I am calling the sacramental mechanism constrained and shaped competition in the monopoly mechanism, as well as shaping the development of the royal mechanism – the monarchy itself being far from a purely secular construct (Kantorowicz 1957) – in which collections of holy relics became a source of royal, as well as ecclesiastical, power (Freeman 2011), necessitating important building campaigns to hold the relics (most famously Sainte Chapelle). While the complex interweaving of these three mechanisms requires further research, and is well beyond the reach of this chapter, the sacramental mechanism itself needs to be explicated further at this point.

The Sacramental Mechanism and the Prohibition of Violence

In *The Elementary Forms of the Religious Life* Durkheim ([1912] 1995) recognized that certain places and certain times are consecrated (designated as 'sacred') and therefore radically opposed to all that which is profane. Since, by definition, 'elementary' religion has no division of labour by which consecrated persons would be consecrated except only temporarily. Insofar as we are talking about medieval Europe, however, with a well-established division of religious labour, we need also to talk about consecrated persons, in addition to places and times.

There is a more fundamental difficulty with Durkheim's conception of sacred and profane, at least as it applies to the sacramental delimitation of violence. That is, while in Durkheim's conception, the sacred may change (some things may become sacred that were previously profane and vice versa), or simply grow, the distinction between sacred and profane is nonetheless absolute ([1912] 1995: 34ff.). What we find by looking at the delimitation of violence by the sacramental mechanism is that it distinguished sacredness by matter of degree. This is important, because it allows for the gradual expansion of persons, places and times in which violence is prohibited by the sacramental mechanism; it thereby provides increasing pressure towards civilized dispositions in tangent with the increasing royal monopolization of the use of force.

It is worth considering at this point one of the most famous examples of medieval violence with respect to the sacramental mechanism and its violation. In the five more or less eyewitness accounts of the murder of Thomas Becket (as well as in later hagiographies), we find repeated references to the seriousness of the crime committed by four of King Henry's knights, not just as an act of murder, but because of the way that it violated the sacred. The sinfulness of the murder was 'compounded' by 'violating a sacred trinity of time, space and body' (Hayes 2004: 198). This was not only the murder of a consecrated priest, but the anointed Archbishop of Canterbury. This was not only a murder within a church, but the most important cathedral in the land. The violation of the sacred could only have been made worse by measure of time: the violence took place at a side altar in the north aisle, and not at the main altar, and during the Octave of Christmas (29 December 1070), not during the Easter season (Barlow 1986).

The violation of the sacred had the paradoxical effect of 'polluting' (or profaning) the cathedral, and also increasing the sacredness of the corpse of Thomas Becket. Sacraments were suspended at the cathedral for the better part of a year until the cathedral could be reconciled; at the same time, the late archbishop, who, during his lifetime was a somewhat unlikely candidate for beatification, had quite spontaneously been sainted by the people, with only slow and reluctant acquiescence from his own monks, and the belatedly approval of the Pope (Barlow 1986). Becket's remains and the site of his murder quickly became one of the most popular pilgrimage destinations in Europe.

Sometimes, as in the case of Becket, the saints are made holier by suffering violence and martyrdom. There was a long-standing prohibition (even when it was observed in the breech) against consecrated persons committing acts of violence and warfare. When the bishops and Peace Councils stepped into the Carolingian defenders of the church's shoes, they affirmed what had long been an implicit rule; the steps that they took to reinforce it set into motion a new set of dynamics. The Peace Councils' initial concern was to 'set apart' consecrated persons from acts of violence, and to protect the sacred with anathemas, and by extracting vows sworn in the presence of relics of the saints (themselves often sanctified by violence).

The peasantry were initially protected from violence since they fell under the care and responsibility of the bishops, along with their livestock, a sort of contagion of the sacred that did not quite provide quite the same protection as religious orders. The peasants are included from the very beginning of the Peace Councils, but typically without much by way of rationalization beyond their bishops' protection, and their status as unarmed persons. From the Council of Narbonne (1054), however, the category of sacred person comes to include all Christians, including not only the peasants, but also the warrior class itself (Head and Landes 1992: 8). This is not to say that all Christians become of equivalent sacredness, and indeed violent offences against the clergy continue to be taken as much more serious offences than violence against lay persons – there is a degree of sacredness conferred on each, but they are considered quite distinct from the Saracen, the pagan or the heretic, against whom violence becomes not only licit but an act of piety.

The early Peace Councils clearly identify monasteries and churches as institutions to be preserved from violence, or against whom violence may not be directed, including buildings, property and people. Rituals of consecration designate them as such, and should violence occur in the sacred space, the celebration of the Eucharist would be suspended until the building could be cleaned of its pollution by means of a ritual of reconciliation – effectively needing to be re-consecrated. The occurrence of violence in sacred space had the capacity to pollute and render it unfit for the celebration of the Eucharist. Given the importance of the Eucharist for medieval Christian spirituality, extensive efforts were taken to prevent people from exercising violence in sacred space. Daniel Thiery tells an amusing story about two men who get into a fight in the parish church, end up assaulting and bloodying the priest who warns them against committing violence in the church; thereafter they try to force him to continue to say the Mass, so as to un-pollute (or prove that they have not polluted) the parish church, and to thereby escape the social consequences that their violation would inevitably entail (Thiery 2009).

The parish church was one of the few indoor public spaces in most medieval communities. However, sanctuary from violence did not end at the door to the church. Varying degrees of sacredness surround the church, certainly encompassing the graveyard and perhaps also a perimeter of up to 50 meters, including the buildings nearby. Abbeys and cathedrals might have a larger surrounding area designated as free from violence. Durham Cathedral, which had a charter of sanctuary making it a place of refuge from the law (though with conditions), had a zone of sanctuary that extended a mile from the cathedral doors. Within the building, not all spaces are equally sacred. Thus, the porch, where relatively secular business could be conducted, disputes settled and marriage contracts made, is considered less sacred than the nave. This was in turn marked off from the quire and presbytery as less sacred space.

The first declaration of the Truce of God a the Council of Toulouges (1027) was designed to protect the Sabbath from being desecrated by violence and hence extended from Saturday night to Sunday morning, offering some hours that insulated the Sabbath on either side. Through the 1030s and 1040s, the days of the Truce tended to expand, not just to other days of the week, but to other high days and holy days, including a significant season at Christmas and Easter.[1] The Council of Narbonne (1054) made violence and warfare licit on just 80 days out of the calendar year (Cowdrey 1970).

In short, in the period from the Peace Councils through the Middle Ages, we find increasing areas consecrated and (at least in designation) free from violence, an expansion of consecrated time, and an increasing range of people against whom violence ought not to be directed by virtue of their sacred protection. Violence is increasingly constrained by the threat of excommunication, anathema and the consequences of polluted religious space. The sacramental mechanism determines where, when and against whom violence may be legitimately directed without profaning those who commit the violence, or the space in which it is committed.

Conclusion

Norbert Elias' *Civilizing Process* is one of the most important works of macro-historical sociology, and it provides a powerful analysis of the trajectory of Western Europe, particularly in the increasing constraint against the use of violence, and its concomitant changes to the *habitus*. It is, however, the poorer

---

[1] I have often thought it should be noted, but have not seen anyone do so, that both of these seasons tend to fall outside the summer months, which were much preferred for long distance travel and warfare, as roads were passable, and fields provided sufficient grazing for the many horses a military action entailed.

for its neglect of religious beliefs and institutions. Although the Peace of God movement is by no means the only example of how the church has acted to shape the trajectory of the civilizing process within the very time frame and geographical area with which Elias was primarily concerned, it is an instructive one. The sacramental mechanism does not simply (or even primarily) shape behaviour of the warrior elite with promises of eternal rewards and punishments, but by the concrete and this-worldly effect of anathemas and threats of excommunication. The effects of the sacramental mechanism are also far from straightforward – as I have suggested, the very means that contributed to the constraining of violence in Western Francia also contributed, and for similar reasons, to the exercise of violence against heretics and Saracens. The sacramental mechanism provides a means of both consecrating violence under certain circumstances, and prohibiting under others – protection from violence being provided for sacred persons, in sacred times, and at sacred locations.

The argument presented here points to the need for further research. Since we have no reason to assume that the sacramental mechanism would always work in the same manner, even in the geographical area and time frame covered by *The Civilizing Process* (2000). Rather, Elias' general principles of historical sociology would incline us to suspect that the particular mechanisms and their effects would be highly dependent on the web of interactions with other mechanisms, and depending on the previous shaping of the civilized *habitus*, and shaped in the context of increasingly differentiated social relations. These differences need to be identified and theorized. Furthermore, I have not attempted to theorize interrelations of the sacramental mechanism with the monopoly mechanism and the royal mechanism; a fuller understanding of the civilizing process and the role of religious institutions demands such an examination of these articulations.

Religion has long been intertwined with relations of violence and practices of peacemaking. Adding the concept of the sacramental mechanism to Elias' theory of the civilizing process allows us to better understand the roles of religion in the *longue durée* of the increasing constraints on the use of violence and the civilization of human dispositions. The case of the *pax Dei* shows, however, that although religious beliefs and practices are far from insignificant (at least at that point in time), it is far from a matter of peaceful religious values inculcating peaceful dispositions. Through the sacramental mechanism, the sacred had 'teeth' with which to enforce increasingly civilized dispositions on often unwilling and uncooperative warrior elites. The capacity, and interest, of religious elites in different times and places to use their powers of consecration and deconsecration to shape, channel or constrain the use of violence will differ dramatically. More research remains to be done in order to understand these differing contexts and the relative role of religious power in them.

Acknowledgments

I am grateful to Professors Steve Bruce, Stephen Mennell, John Brewer and David Inglis for their comments and criticisms of an earlier version of this chapter.

References

Appleby, R.S. (2000). *The Ambivalence of the Sacred: Religion, Violence, and Reconciliation, Carnegie Commission on Preventing Deadly Conflict*. Lanham: Rowman & Littlefield.

Arnason, J.P. (1989). Civilization, Culture And Power: Reflections On Norbert Elias' Genealogy Of The West. *Thesis Eleven*, 24, 44–70.

Barlow, F. (1986). *Thomas Becket*. London: Weidenfeld & Nicolson.

Bast, R.J. (1995). Honour Your Fathers: Reform Movements, Catechisms, and the 'Civilizing Process' in Late Medieval and Early Modern Germany. *Amsterdams Sociologisch Tijdschrift*, 21, 116–25.

Bax, M. (1987). Religious Regimes and State Formation: Towards a Research Perspective. *Anthropological Quarterly*, 60, 1–11.

Bisson, T.N. (1977). The Organized Peace in Southern France and Catalonia, ca. 1140-ca. 1233. *The American Historical Review*, 290–311.

Borkenau, F. (1938). Book Review of Norbert Elias, Ueber den Prozess der Zivilisation, Vol. 1. *The Sociological Review*, 30, 308–311.

Borkenau, F. (1939). Book Review of Norbert Elias, Ueber den Prozess der Zivilisation, Vol. 2. *The Sociological Review*, 31, 450–452.

Bredero, A. (1995). *Christendom and Christianity in the Middle Ages*. Grand Rapids: Wm B Eerdmans.

Brewer, J.D. (2010). *Peace Processes: A Sociological Approach*. Cambridge, MA: Polity Press.

Cowdrey, H.E.J. (1970). The Peace and the Truce of God in the Eleventh Century. *Past & Present*, 46, 42–67.

Debord, A. (1992). The Castellan Revolution and the Peace of God in Aquitaine, in *The Peace of God: Social Violence and Religious Response around the Year 1000*, ed. Thomas Head and Richard Landes. Ithaca: Cornell University Press, pp. 135–64.

Des Vaux-de-Cernay, P. (1998). *Historia Albigensium*. Woodbridge, UK and Rochester, NY: Boydell Press.

Duby, G. (1953). *La societe aux XIe et XIIe siecles dans la region mâconnaise*. Paris: Éditions de l'École des Hautes Études en Sciences Sociales.

Duby, G. (1980). *The Three Orders: Feudal Society Imagined*. Chicago: University of Chicago Press.

Durkheim, E. [1912] (1995). *The Elementary Forms of the Religious Life*. New York: The Free Press.

Elias, N. (1987). The Retreat of Sociologists into the Present. *Theory, Culture & Society*, 4, 223–47.

Elias, N. (2000). *The Civilizing Process*, 2nd revised edn. Oxford: Blackwell.

Erdmann, C. [1935] (1977). *The Origin of the Idea of the Crusade*. Princeton: Princeton University Press.

Freeman, C. (2011). *Holy Bones, Holy Dust: How Relics Shaped the History of Medieval Europe*. New Haven: Yale University Press.

Gergen, T. (2002). The Peace of God and its Legal Practice in the Eleventh Century. *Cuadernos de Historia del Derecho*, 9, 11–27.

Gorski, P.S. (2003). *The Disciplinary Revolution: Calvinism and the Rise of the State in Early Modern Europe*. Chicago: University of Chicago Press.

Goudsblom, J. (2004). Christian Religion and the European Civilizing Process: The Views of Norbert Elias and Max Weber Compared in the Context of the Augustinian and Lucretian Traditions, in *The Sociology of Norbert Elias*, ed. Steven Loyal and Stephen Quilley. Cambridge: Cambridge University Press, pp. 265–80.

Graham, M.F. (1996). *The Uses of Reform: 'Godly Discipline' and Popular Behavior in Scotland and Beyond, 1560–1610*. Leiden: E.J. Brill.

Hayes, D.M. (2004). Body as Champion of Church Authority and Sacred Place: The Murder of Thomas Becket, in *A Great Effusion of Blood? Interpreting Medieval Violence*, ed. Mark D. Meyerson, Daniel Thiery and Oren Falk. Toronto: University of Toronto Press, pp. 190–215.

Head, T. and Landes, R. (1992). *The Peace of God: Social Violence and Religious Response around the Year 1000*. Ithaca: Cornell University Press.

Huizinga, J. (1924). *The Waning of the Middle Ages: A Study of the Forms of Life, Thought and Art in France and the Netherlands in the XIVth and XVth Centuries*. London: Arnold.

Jaeger, C.S. (1985). *The Origins of Courtliness: Civilizing Trends and the Formation of Courtly Ideals, 939–1210*. Philadelphia: University of Pennsylvania Press.

Juergensmeyer, M. (2003). *Terror in the Mind of God: The Global Rise of Religious Violence*. Berkeley: University of California Press.

Kaeuper, R.W. (2009). *Holy Warriors: The Religious Ideology of Chivalry*. Philadelphia: University of Pennsylvania Press.

Kantorowicz, E.H. (1957). *The King's Two Bodies: A Study in Mediaeval Political Theology*. Princeton: Princeton University Press.

Knox, D. (1995). Erasmus' De Civilitate and the Religious Origins of Civility in Protestant Europe. *Archiv für Reformationsgeschichte*, 86, 7–55.

Lauranson-Rosaz, C. (1992). Peace from the Mountains: The Auvergnat Origins of the Peace of God, in *The Peace of God: Social Violence and Religious Response around the Year 1000*, ed. Thomas Head and Richard Landes. Ithaca: Cornell University Press, pp. 104–34.

Le Goff, J. (2005). *The Birth of Europe*. Oxford: Blackwell.

Lincoln, B. (2006). *Holy Terrors: Thinking about Religion after September 11*. Chicago: University of Chicago Press.

Mann, M. (1986). *The Sources of Social Power: A History of Power from the Beginning to A.D. 1760*. Cambridge: Cambridge University Press

Mennell, S. (1992). *Norbert Elias: An Introduction*. Oxford: Blackwell.

Meyerson, M., Thiery, D. and Falk, O. (2004) *A Great Effusion of Blood? Interpreting Medieval Violence*. Toronto: University of Toronto Press.

Riley-Smith, J. (2009). *The First Crusade and the Idea of Crusading*. London: Continuum.

Rosenwein, B. (1998). *Anger's Past: The Social Uses of an Emotion in the Middle Ages*. Ithaca: Cornell University Press.

Thatcher, O.J. and McNeal, E.H. (1905). *A Source Book for Medieval History*. New York: Scribners. Available online at the *Fordham Internet Medieval Sourcebook*: www.fordham.edu/halsall/source/urban2-5vers.html [last consulted June 2011].

Thiery, D. (2009). *Polluting the Sacred Violence, Faith, and the 'Civilizing' of Parishioners in Late Medieval England*. Leiden: Brill.

Turner, B.S. (2004). Weber and Elias on Religion and Violence: Warrior Charisma and the Civilizing Process, in *The Sociology of Norbert Elias*, ed. Steven Loyal and Stephen Quilley. Cambridge: Cambridge University Press, pp. 245–64.

Van Krieken, R. (1989). Violence, Self-Discipline and Modernity: Beyond the Civilizing Process. *Sociological Review*, 37(2), 193–218.

Van Krieken, R. (1998). *Norbert Elias*. London and New York: Routledge.

Van Krieken, R. 2011. Three Faces of Civilization: In the Beginning all the World was Ireland. *The Sociological Review*, 59(S1), 24–47

Wood, S. (2006). *The Proprietary Church in the Medieval West*. Oxford: Oxford University Press.

PART III
Religion and Modernity

Chapter 6
Religion and Monetary Culture in the Sociology of Georg Simmel

Dominika Motak

Introduction

Georg Simmel is widely recognised as a prominent turn-of-the-century German philosopher of culture and one of the founding fathers of sociology, but he could quite properly also be described as a classical theorist of religion. Despite his eminent position in the history of Western thought, Simmel's work on religion continues to be neglected – especially by comparison with that of Durkheim and Weber (Lechner 1990: 169). His concept of religion was not yet reflected in its full complexity, but was only occasionally referred to in the discussions concerning particular topics (Krech 1998: 1), and the task of incorporating it into the contemporary academic discourse remains unfulfilled. I will try to demonstrate that this still not properly appreciated part of Simmel's legacy is most intimately connected with the two much better known areas of his research: monetary culture and general sociology. A rough sketch of Simmel's concept of religion sheds light on Simmel's theory of society and allows to question the prevailing view that the Simmelian 'impressionist' sociology stands in sharp contrast to the classical French 'positivist' tradition of sociological inquiry, as epitomised by Émile Durkheim. The main subject of this chapter – Simmel's thesis on homology of money, society and the idea of God – provides a good argument that, even many decades later, Robert A. Nisbet's (1959: 81) appraisal of Simmel as the most relevant of all the pioneers of sociological reflexion still holds true.

Money/Religion Complex

The thesis on homology of money and the idea of God is a recurrent theme in Simmel's writings. In his philosophically informed sociology money serves as a symbol of modernity, expressing its contradictory character. Moreover, being a symbol of unity, money has remarkable affinity with the Judeo-Christian concept of God. At the same time, God constitutes a conceptual equivalent of society; and a notion of society shares certain characteristics with money. All these terms – money, God, society and modernity – are thus inextricably intertwined. It should come as no surprise, then, that in Simmel's eyes there is at least a kernel of truth in the lament that 'money has become the God of our time'. As we shall see, Alain Deneault was right in saying that 'Simmel does more than just reproduce the worn-out money-God metaphor' (Deneault 2006: 164).

Simmel's serious academic interest in monetary culture lasted more than a decade and may be tracked back to his essay of 1889 entitled *On the Psychology of Money* (see Simmel 1997b). The next evidence of his comittment to the study of money was *Money in Modern Culture* (*Das Geld in der modernen Kultur*), published in 1896 (see Simmel 1997a). This text introduced some of the central themes of *Philosophy of Money* (1900) – Simmel's *opus magnum* which, according to Hans Blumenberg (1976: 130), ranks among the very few books written after Nietzsche that belong to the Western canon. In the beginning of the twentieth century Simmel was shaping the foundations of an emerging discipline of sociology, at the same time developing a very distinctive framework for the analysis of religion. His explorations into religion, which transcended disciplinary borders of at least three disciplines: philosophy, sociology and psychology, continued for 20 years: from 1898 (when he published the first text devoted explicitly to religion: *A Contribution to the Sociology of Religion*) until his death in 1918. Religion constituted the main subject of several essays written in this period (Simmel 1997). In 1906 he published his main work on religion – a slim book with a simple title, *Religion* (an extended edition appeared in 1912). There is also a clear evidence of Simmel's continued commitment to the study of religion in many other writings, including his seminal *Philosophy of Money*. What is particularly important in our context, every single one of his texts which deals with money discusses its relationship to religion. Religion appears in numerous contexts in *Philosophy of Money*, wherein also a relationship of money, society and modernity has been elaborated, so this text will be our point of departure.

According to Simmel's own remark in the preface to *Philosophy of Money*, not a single line of his investigations was meant to be a statement about economics (Simmel 2004: 54). He claimed that 'just as the appearance of a founder of a religion is not simply a religious phenomenon, so the fact that two people exchange their products is not simply an economic fact' (Simmel 2004: 55). Simmel described his intention as an attempt to underpin the historical materialism in such a way that the explanation of culture in terms of economic forms remains preserved, 'while these economic forms themselves are recognised as the result of more profound valuations and psychological or even metaphysical pre-conditions'. He stated that such explanation 'must develop in infinite reciprocity' (Simmel 2004: 56). It is, as we may add, a hermeneutical procedure; it generates a specific circular style of reasoning, consequently applied in his discussion of our main topic (money=society=God=money ... ad infinitum).

Money/Society Equation

Before we can turn to a description of the money/society equation we need to clarify Simmel's understanding of society. As David Frisby (1992: 5) reminds us, Simmel maintained that 'only by abandoning society as a hypostatized and totalized object could sociology develop succesfully as an independent academic discipline'. This remark supports the established view that Simmel's theoretical perspective presents a model version of the German anti-Positivist paradigm of social research: 'methodological individualism', which stands in sharp contrast to 'methodological holism' of French school of sociology (as epitomised by Durkheim), which focuses on society understood as a specific entity of total character. This vision, however, needs to be corrected. It is true that Simmel postulated the shift in focus of sociological research from the society as a whole and from the great organs and systems to 'minor forms of interaction (*Wechselwirkung*) ... the less obvious and visible interactions which tie people together', because these 'fluctuating unpretentious interactions constitute the principle of social unity, a unity which in the empirical sense is nothing but the interactions of elements' (Featherstone 1991: 6). Nevertheless, Simmel was also convinced that, being a product of interactions between its members, the 'society of individuals' is itself an individual entity, a specific synthetic unit ('eine besondere Einheit') which calls for a separate analysis. Moreover, it seems that Durkheim's famous definition of society as 'une unité *sui generis*' is in fact a translation of Simmel's formulation (Levine 1984: 319). We shall later discuss theoretical interdependencies between Simmel and Durkheim which can be observed in the field of sociology of religion.

Simmel's general notion of society is not easy to define. Frisby, who stresses the diversity of Simmel's conceptions of society, distinguished four understandings of society which might be inferred from Simmel's writings: society as a totality (*Gesellschaft*), society as sociation (*Vergesellschaftung*), society as experience and society as aesthetic object (Frisby 1992: 6ff.). Nevertheless, all these conceptualisations are not mutually exclusive but rather complementary. In fact, they are all based on the general premise that the idea of society is closely related to – or is a conceptual version of – the idea of 'the whole' understood as unity (*Einheit*). Frisby often translates the polysemic German word *Einheit* as 'totality', but there are good reasons to translate it as 'unity'. 'Totality' suggests understanding of 'the whole' as an aggregate formed by collections of particulars, whereas 'unity' suggests a synthesis, oneness, concord. The shift in meaning seems to be small, but it is important for at least two reasons. First, if we assume – as Simmel did – that the society as a whole (*Gesellschaft*) *is* nothing but the unity of reciprocal actions (*Wechselwirkung*) – in today's sociological idiolect: interactions – then we see that Simmel never imagined society as a rigid, hypostasised entity, but saw it as a dynamic, 'living' unity of processes of sociation (*Vergesellschaftung*). Frisby himself noted rightly that 'unity' by Simmel cannot be understood as a monolith, but is conceptualised in terms of reciprocal relations (interactions) between elements. This 'unifying' quality is somehow lost in translation if we use the word 'totality'. Secondly, 'unity' is an absolutely underlying category of Simmel's thought: one constantly comes across this term throughout Simmel's writings (Featherstone 1991: 5). It is widely acknowledged that Simmel's main heuristic device was the dialectic of form and content. Nevertheless, at least equally important is dialectic of the part and the whole, of the idividual and the unity. One can even say that the mutual relation of part and the whole constitutes the underlying theorem of Simmel's philosophy and sociology. In consequence, it also constitutes the matrix of sociological conceptualisation of the relationship between the individual and the society: both the part (individual) and the whole (society) were conceived as singular 'individuals'. The idea of unity, understood not as monolith but as the entirety of interconnected and interacting elements, constitutes a common matrix of the three discussed concepts: money, society and God, which can be all characterised as unifying agents and metaphors for unity.

The main common feature of money and society lies in fact that they both are transindividual constructs of universal and yet not abstract character. What is even more important, both money and society are based on acts of exchange. In *Philosophy of Money* Simmel argues that exchange does not simply promote sociation, but exchange itself is a form of sociation: a relationship which transforms a sum of individuals into a social group (Simmel 2004: 175). As Frisby (1992: 12) observed, Simmel took exchange to be 'both paradigmatic and symbolic of society as a whole'. Being a form of sociation, exchange reduces 'the human tragedy of competition' (Simmel 2004: 291). Money serves as a universal medium of exchange. It can be said that money (as a petrified form) is equivalent to exchange (as an action); in his own words: 'money belongs to the category of reified social functions. Like a flag incarnates the unity of a regiment, so money incarnates the function of exchange as a direct interaction between individuals' (Simmel 2004: 175). Already in *Money in Modern Culture* (1896) Simmel stated that 'money ties people together, for now everyone is working for the other'; 'money provides a common basis of direct mutual understanding'; it also 'serves as an ideal adhesive' in a certain type of social organisations, which 'represent one of the most enormous advances of culture' because 'it offers the only opportunity for a unity which eliminates everything personal' (for instance, trade union has only become possible by virtue of money). Therefore he concludes that 'money creates an extremely strong bond among the members of an economic circle. Precisely because it cannot be consumed directly, it refers people to others' (Simmel 1997a: 246ff.). To sum up: for Simmel, money is 'entirely a sociological phenomenon, a form of human interaction' (Simmel 2004: 172) and 'a claim upon society' (Frisby 1981: 96), whereas society (*Gesellschaft*) is understood as 'a synthesis or the general term for the totality of ... interactions' (Simmel 2004: 175). The next important equation of Simmel's conceptualisation of the mutual relationship between religion and monetary culture is the thesis on homology of society with the idea of God. To sketch this relationship properly we have to briefly address Simmel's general understanding of religion.

Simmel's Concept of Religion

Bryan S. Turner's answer to the question why the sociology of religion would matter from the point of view of sociology as a whole is: because it is the very nature of the social itself which is at stake here, and 'sociologists have been interested in religion because it is assumed to contain the seeds of social life as such' (Turner 2010: 20). Although Turner illustrates this point by the example of Émile Durkheim, his statement applies equally to Georg Simmel. It would be difficult to find another classical sociologist whose understanding of society would be so inextricably interwoven with their theory of religion as it is the case in Simmel.

An attempt to present Simmel's complex theory of religion in a short article would be doomed to fail. I have undertaken this task in other places (Motak 2012, Motak 2013), but for the sake of our argument it is necessary to sketch briefly its crucial points. Simmel uses the word 'religion' (*die Religion*) sometimes in the wider, and sometimes in the stricter, sense. 'Religion in the wider sense' means *a priori* form – in contradistinction to religious content, and it refers to a phenomenon which does not necessarily amount to a historical institution. This *a priori* form is capable of creating the special 'world of religion', therefore Simmel calls it also a 'world-form'. In this wider sense, the term 'religion' is used interchangeably with many other expressions, like 'religiosity', 'a subjective human process', 'religious state of the soul', 'religious attitude', 'religious tone' and – last but not least – 'religious mood'. All these words describe emotional 'origins' of religion or a kind of pre-stage of religion. Individual religious attitude (especially towards the natural world, towards fate and towards other people) 'creates' the finished product of religion: religion in the stricter sense. 'Religion in the stricter sense' might be identified with the 'objective religion' – any historical religion or its 'content' (transcendent beliefs). Moreover, objective religion is clearly contrasted with subjective 'religiosity' (*die Religiösität*).

Simmel contrasts religion understood in terms of content ('religion in the stricter sense') with religion understood in terms of subjective process ('religion in the wider sense') – or religiosity. In the essay *Contributions to the Epistemology of Religion* (*Beiträge zur Erkenntnistheorie der Religion*, 1902 – see Simmel 1997: 121–33) he clarified this distinction as an opposition between religion (religious content) and religiosity (religious form). In Simmel's own words: 'neither does the religious state of the soul logically require any specific content nor does any such content bear within itself the logical necessity to become religion' (Simmel 1997: 125). Religiosity as a fundamental *a priori* category, as one of the 'great forms' (among others, like science or art) can accept as its content the entire wealth of reality. Every such form gathers the fragments of existence into a unified totality. None of them can be privileged over any other; and none is ever able to substitute for another.

Seen as a 'great form', religiosity is a way of life, or life process, of the religious person. When we are in a religious mood, we experience all possible spheres of life as religious. Then, 'from this general religious mood of life, the process of religion acquires a physical, objective form' (Simmel 1997: 144). Religious attitude (especially towards the natural world, towards fate and towards other people) 'creates' the finished product of religion, in which the religious quality has acquired concrete shape and content. Therefore Simmel concludes: 'religion does not create religiosity, but religiosity creates religion' (Simmel 1997: 150).

Religiosity – as a 'particular spiritual quality' or 'attitude of the soul', a way of looking at the world as a whole – constitutes a kind of pre-stage of religion. This particular perspective of religion-like (*religioid*) character prepares an individual foundation for religion, but it can also express itself in other cultural pursuits (like science or art). Religiosity becomes religion when it assumes a specific form in human interaction. Still, not every product of a religious attitude can be termed 'religion'. We should not forget that for Simmel the idea of God remains constitutive for religion in the stricter sense. His observation concerning the modern transformations of the idea of God is worth noting in this context. In *The Personality of God* (*Die Persönlichkeit Gottes*, 1911 – see Simmel 1997: 45–62), he claimed that 'the concept of God has passed through so much heterogeneous historical content and so many possibilities of interpretation that all that remains is a feeling that cannot be fixed in any precise form' (Simmel 1997: 45).

In one of his last texts, *The Conflict of Modern Culture* (*Der Konflikt der moderner Kultur*, 1918 – see Simmel 1997: 20–25), he noticed that the eternal struggle between life and form has entered a new stage: it is no longer a struggle of a new form against an old, lifeless one, 'but the struggle against form itself, against the very principle of form'. As a consequence, 'the fixed content of religious beliefs tends to dissolve into religious life' – understood as a tuning of the inner process of life from which the content of belief originally developed (Simmel 1997: 21). Deena and Michael Weinstein (1995: 137f.) consider the Simmelian theorem of 'liberation of religiosity from religion' to be a 'heroic project' of 'radical reorientation of the religious impulse from transcendentalized objects to the depths of life' and – consequently – a variation of the death-of-God story.

Simmel neither sought to determine the social function of objective religion nor suggested that religion is an integrating force. As a matter of fact, he rather attempted to reveal the common root of both social as well as religious phenomena: a drive for unity which is the most powerful integrating factor. This cohesive force expresses itself in very strong, elementary emotions – 'social feelings', which play the crucial role in creation of social institutions, and – after reaching a certain level of intensity – provide also conditions for emerging of a special social institution: the objective religion. For Simmel, the objective religion understood as a concrete social and historical reality is – like society – a result of reciprocal actions and it is structured around the idea of God.

God as a Symbol of Society

In Simmel's sociology God constitutes a conceptual equivalent of society. The main common features of these two notions are found in the phenomenon of faith and in the idea of unity. In *A Contribution to the Sociology of Religion*, and later in *Religion*, Simmel stated that many human relations – social conditions or interpersonal relationships – like the relation of a child to its parents, of a patriot to their country, of a worker to their class, of a subject to their sovereign, etc., may have a common tone which has to be described as religious. This 'religious tone' constitutes a mixture of specific feelings: 'of unselfish devotion and eudaimonic desire, of humility and exaltation, of sensual concreteness and spiritual abstraction' (Simmel 1997: 104). Even faith, which is commonly held to be the essence of religion, is first a relation between individuals:

> We illustrate a specific psychological reality, hard to define, when we [say that we] 'believe in someone' – the child in its parents, the subordinate in his superior, the friend in a friend ... The social role of this faith has never been investigated, but this much is certain: without it, society would disintegrate. (Simmel 1997: 109)

Our primary confidence or trust in other people – which Simmel calls 'practical faith' – is one of the strongest of the ties that bind society, an *a priori* condition which makes society possible. What is particularly interesting in our context, Simmel also stressed the crucial role of trust for monetary economy: without it, the circulation of money would collapse. As Patrick Watier reminds us, Simmel was convinced that the modern society in which we live is grounded on 'a "credit economy" in a much broader than a strictly economic sense' (Watier 2009: 211).

For Simmel, practical faith (or: trustfulness – 'Gläubigkeit') is a specific 'emotional factor' of social origin which serves as a mediating element between subjective religiousness and objective religion. It is exactly this feeling that lies at the heart of many social relations: not only these listed above (the relation of a child to its parents, etc.), but also of every act of exchange (Simmel 1997: 158). The very form of these relations makes them an ideal foundation for the objective religion. As Watier comments, 'Social forms of confidence ... always contain a bit of this sentimental, even mystical "faith" of man in man' (Watier 2009: 205). One can also say that there are some forms of social relations whose structure predestines them to be an ideal raw material for development of religious life. Simmel characterises these relations as 'semireligious in form' (or as the 'religious semi-products': *religiöse Halbprodukte*; he also uses the term 'religioid factors'). If they reach a certain level of intensity, they may condense or refine themselves into a system of religious ideas, and 'form religion – that is, the world of the objects of faith' (Simmel 1997: 150). Religious faith emerges when the practical faith loosens its bonds with social partner and enters the transcendental plane. In other words: on the basis of social relations there develops a 'religious function', which creates itself a new object: 'gods'. For Simmel, a god is a 'general object of faith', in which religious function crystallises ('precipitates'). This statement also calls to mind Luther's words from his *Large Catechism*: 'to have a god is to have something in which the heart entirely trusts.'

The transcendent idea of God constitutes an absolute object of faith (Simmel 1997: 171). It also constitutes an ultimate answer to the 'desire' for 'unity', the need to be unified with the whole, which is rooted in the social nature of humans. This 'drive for unity', as Simmel also calls it, finds its expression in the desire for resolving inner conflicts and being united (or reconciliated) with social partners. Simmel identifies this drive as a kind of general 'religious drive' (Simmel 1997: 111ff.). The idea of unity constitutes for Simmel another basic common feature of the notion of God and the notion of society. He claimed that 'the unity of things and interests which first impresses us in the social realm finds its highest representation ... in the idea of the divine' (Simmel 1997: 112). Simmel suggested that God was a name given to the social unit: the interactive processes within the group 'have taken on their own distinct existence as the god' (Simmel 1997: 208).

In Simmel's opinion, the idea of unity originated in the social group. It developed from a twofold contrast: firstly, from the hostile demarcation from other groups; and secondly, from the relation of the group to its individual elements. Since all social life is interaction, it is also unity (Simmel 1997: 174). Synthesis of individuals in the form of group unity is often perceived by the individual as some kind of miracle. Simmel stated that the process of social unification causes a religious reaction: the individual experiences at first-hand their dependency upon mysterious, incomprehensible forces. The point is that such a feeling does not result from a simple recognition of numerical advantage of the other group members over a given individual, but exactly from the fact that the group is more than a sum of its elements: it develops powers which cannot be detected in individuals themselves (Simmel 1997: 165, 181).

The consequence of the thesis that the idea of God is a representation of the group forces is the statement that God might be conceived of as the unity of existence. This unity is not a pantheistic monolith, nor a simple aggregate, but rather a cohesive whole: a network of reciprocal bonds, of relations tying together all the elements of the world. The idea of unity, elevated to the transcendental plane, is somehow personified in God – a specific entity who emerges at the intersection of all these relations. Only such construction of the idea of God as a cohesive unity (in contrast to monolithic, pantheistic conception of God) makes it suitable for an object of faith and religion, because only in this case God is placed vis-à-vis of an individual as a partner of relation. It is clear, though, that emotions associated with the idea of God can be traced back to the relation of individuals to the social unit.

Simmel and Durkheim

One can easily notice the parallels between Simmel's theory of social origin of religion and that of Émile Durkheim. The Simmelian scholars (see for instance Levine 1984; Lechner 1998) have recently started to stress the connections between his perspective and that of Durkheim. As Frank Lechner observed: 'like Durkheim, Simmel offered a kind of sociological projection theory. Religion emerges in social relations of special intensity. In his relation with God, the individual repeats and transcends his relation to the collectivity. The unity of the group is expressed in religious terms; the deity is the name for that unity' (Lechner 1998).

At the same time, Durkheimian scholars do not seem to notice this theoretical interdependency (see for instant Pickering 1984: 7; Lukes 1973: 237ff.) – with a notable exception of Stjepan G. Meštrović (1991: 55ff.) and, to a lesser extent, Donald A. Nielsen (1999: 233f.). Unfortunately, Nielsen, who gave an excellent philosophical analysis of Durkheim's underlying conceptual 'trinity' – society, deity and unity – did not notice that the 'three faces of God' which he identified in Durkheim's work are almost identical with Simmel's 'trinity': society, deity and money (with – as we may add – an underlying category of unity). The only common point of Simmelian and Durkheimian sociology lies for Nielsen in 'methodological monism' based on Spinoza's philosophy, which is particularly manifest in Simmel's *Philosophy of Money*: 'Everything in culture and society is related to the problem of money, like parts to a whole, ones comprehensible only in relationship to the whole' (Nielsen 1999: 233).

There are many more points of convergence between the two classics. We have already pointed above at the similarity between the Simmelian and Durkheimian concept of society. The careful point-to-point comparison of both theoretical frameworks would require a separate, extensive study. Therefore I would like to briefly refer to only two – closely intertwined – common aspects of Simmel's and Durkheim's sociologies of religion: the thesis on the social and emotional origin of religion.

It is important to bear in mind that exactly like Durkheim, Simmel also started his sociological investigations as a social psychologist. He was then – on the one hand – often reproached for his 'psychologism' – and on the other hand praised for being 'a Freud of the society' (Everett Hughes). The reason for this attribution lies in the fact that Simmel firmly held that understanding a society requires a psychological knowledge – a knowledge about human needs and motivations, but most of all a knowledge about emotions that binds people together. These emotions, which play a crucial role in socialisation and in establishing reciprocal bonds, might be called – according to Patrick Watier – 'psychosocial feelings'. Mutual trust, a certain belief in a self-presentation of the other, is for Simmel an *a priori* condition which makes society possible. This 'socio-psychological "faith" is strongly related to religious belief, since it is not based on a demonstration' (Watier 2009: 213). In Chris Shilling's opinion, the German classics of sociology (including Simmel, whom Shilling regards also as a pioneer of the sociology of emotions) shared the Nietzscheanian presumption that human beings are driven by the need for self-realisation, and therefore they analysed emotions from the perspective of individual. In contradistinction to them, the French classics (including Durkheim) regarded emotions as a kind of binding agent, indispensable for social order (Shilling 2002: 10ff.). However, this opposition is too simplistic. Simmel's concept of emotions is much more nuanced. It focuses on emotional aspects of 'inner life': a life which strives for the full realisation of individual self but might as well – in form of 'religious life' – strive for the union with the highest principle: God. Therefore, as we have shown, it also takes into consideration 'psychosocial feelings' understood as integrating forces, which ensure social cohesion (the list of such feelings, provided by Watier (2009: 200) includes – apart from 'intuitive trust in other people' characterised above – also sympathy, gratefulness, devotion, fidelity, gratitude, intimacy).

Nevertheless, both founding fathers of sociology of religion also differ in many respects. For Simmel, 'religion is not mere reflection or projection ... The social origins of religion do not fully account for its nature and function' (Lechner 1998). According to Simmel, religion 'is not a finished product, but a vital process which each soul must beget for itself, no matter how stable the traditional content may be'. Religion is able to draw a given content into the flow of the emotions, which continuously renew it: 'in this sense there are really "origins" of religion whose appearance and effectiveness occur long after the [historical] "origin" of religion' (Simmel 1997: 119).

God/Money Equation

In *Religion* Simmel states clearly that 'God conceived of as the unity of existence can be nothing other than the agent of ... interaction between things' (Simmel 1997: 201). This brings us to the third important equation of Simmel's theory, which logically follows from both formulas of homology introduced above (money=society and society=God): that of God with money. To demonstrate the homology of the idea of God and the idea of money Simmel employs two formulations, rooted in the classical theological reflexion. The first one – the term 'unmoved mover' (*akineton kinoun*) – is an Aristotelian notion of the first cause, adopted later by Thomas Aquinas; the second – 'the unity of contradictions' (*coincidentia oppositorum*) is a famous metaphor for God, coined by Nicholas Cusanus.

The first trace of the God–money homology is to be found already in the essay *On the Psychology of Money*, wherein money was described as the 'unmoved mover', which raises itself 'above everything individual' (Simmel 1997b: 243). This ability allowed Simmel to draw a parallel between the idea of God and money: 'just as God in the form of faith, so money in the form of the concrete object is the highest abstraction to which practical reason has risen' (Simmel 1997b: 243). But Simmel stressed also the similarity of psychological effect exerted by the idea of God and the idea of money. He found the *tertium comparationis* in the feeling of peace and security, the trust in omnipotence of the highest principle which is provided by the possession of money and which corresponds psychologically to the emotional state of the pious person who places his or her faith in God. Simmel thus described the idea of God as a tranquilising force (Simmel 1997: 168). He then elaborated this metaphor in *Philosophy of Money*, wherein he noticed that money produces its powerful effects not simply through its material value, but through the hope and fear, the desire and anxiety that are associated with it: 'it radiates economically important sentiments, as heaven and hell radiate them: as pure ideas ... In this instance, money can truly be described as the "unmoved mover"' (Simmel 2004: 171; translation amended by D.M.). Furthermore, the essence of the idea of God lies in the fact that, as an absolute object, God unifies all the divergent elements of reality, which found its perfect articulation in the theological formulation of Nicholas Cusanus: 'the unity of contradictions'. In *Philosophy of Money* Simmel added that exactly from the idea that all conflicts of existence find their unity and equalisation in God 'there arises the feeling of peace and security', and continues:

> Money evokes similar feelings. As money becomes an absolutely adequate expression and equivalent of all values, it rises to abstract heights above the whole diversity of objects. It becomes the centre in which the most opposed, the most estranged and most distant things find their common denominator and come into contact with one another. Thus, money provides a confidence in its omnipotence. (Simmel 2004: 236)

This description of identical psychological effects of the idea of God and that of money closely resembles Luther's comment on the First Commandment from his *Large Catechism* of 1529:

> the confidence and faith of the heart alone make both God and an idol ... Many a one thinks that he has God and everything in abundance when he has money and possessions ... such a man also has a god, Mammon by name, on which he sets all his heart, and which is also the most common idol on earth. He who has money and possessions feels secure, and is joyful and undismayed as though he were sitting in the midst of Paradise. (Luther 1529)

Luther is unambiguously critical towards money, which is presented as a rival deity. Of course, Luther deploys an old trope here. The identification of money (or Mammon) as the (false) God regularly returns – in many versions – in Western history, starting at least with the New Testament (we read in Luke and Matthew: 'No one can serve two masters; you cannot serve both God and Mammon'). Critique of money – although not equally devastating – is also present in Simmel's *Psychology of Money*. Money is 'common, because it is the equivalent for everything and anything; and that which is equivalent to many things is equivalent to the least among them and therefore pulls even the highest thing down to the level of the lowest'. Money is 'seductive – St Francis allowed his order to beg for food and clothing, but never for money' – because 'it can be transformed into everything possible at any time' (Simmel 1997b: 240).

Simmel's characteristics of money as common and seductive bear an uncanny resemblance to Shakespeare's description of money (from *Timon of Athens*) as 'common whore of mankind' and a 'visible God'. This Shakespearian phrase served also Karl Marx as an illustration of his argument. In one of the *Economic and Philosophic Manuscripts of 1844*, entitled *The Power of Money*, he stated that money has divine power: it possesses 'the *property* of buying everything', therefore it is 'regarded as an omnipotent being' and 'the supreme good' (Marx 1959). This last statement might constitute a bridge which allowed Simmel to develop his money/God analogy from a notion of an abstract absolute to a notion of supreme being who has at least some qualities of an animated being. A decade later, in *Philosophy of Money*, Simmel compared money to the bloodstream and stated: 'money is the symbol of the unity of being, out of which the world flows. And this being however empty and abstract its pure notion may be, appears as the warm stream of life ... Of all practical things money comes closest to this power of being' (Simmel 2004: 498).

Mammonism

Nevertheless, as we have shown above, money displays certain decisively negative traits which make it impossible for Simmel to fully identify it with 'the power of being' or Judeo-Christian God. Money – although posessing almost divine powers – is 'a god' – 'but not this true and only God', as Luther would comment. Eventually, Simmel denounces it as a false God, an idol, the golden calf. This thread running within Simmel's work on money found its explicit formulation in one of his war writings, wherein he returned to many of the points made in *The Philosophy of Money* (Watier 1991: 219). The essay *Germany's Inner Transformation* of 1914 (Simmel 2003) contains a vivid description of a recent social phenomenon, observed by Simmel with grave concern: 'mammonism'. For Simmel, mammonism does not mean the fact that money – being the means of satisfying almost every human desire – becomes a final value and an end in itself; but, mammonism is:

> an intensification, a heightening of this [subjective desire], so that it takes on an objective and metaphysical character. It dissociates itself from anything practical and becomes a worship of money and of monetary value of things ... Just as the truly pious pray to their god not only because they want or hope something from him ... so the mammonist venerates money ... The golden calf has become transcendent and the idealism of monetary values is now endemic in our great cities. Even if this phenomenon always appears mingled with actual avarice, thirst for pleasure and profit, I consider it to be a more refined and profound danger than all those more materialistic and more avaricious shadows of the monetary economy.[1]

How shall we understand this warning? Simmel's thesis on homology of money and the idea of God – as well as the broader analogy between religion and

---

[1] Quoted after Leck (2000: 183–4; translation amended by D.M.).

monetary culture – wasn't yet exhaustively commented and seems to be taken into serious consideration only by Ralph M. Leck (2000, 2000a: 181ff.) and Alain Deneault (2006). Deneault (2006: 164) holds that Simmel focuses on the narrative character of the economic culture and defines the monetary economy in terms of its ability to 'promise salutary, conceptual and spiritual unity beyond the proliferation of various empirical phenomena' and to 'convince and seduce'. For Leck, Simmel is first of all a representative of 'avantgarde sociology' or even a counter-cultural thinker; he regards *The Philosophy of Money* as 'one of the great sunken treasures of critical theory' (Leck 2000: 116). In critique of mammonism Leck sees mainly an attempt to justify Simmel's temporary 'militarist' aberration of the Great War period, which stood in a sharp contrast to his liberal political views. Indeed, his ardent calls for military engagement were then – and still are – a source of embarrassment for Simmel's aficionados. If we look for an excuse for Simmel, we should assume – as Patrick Watier did – that war as a 'total social fact', bringing 'the effervescence of beginning', was for Simmel a promise of a new relation between people: 'the birth of a new form of life'; and that 'our moral condemnation of war may prevent us from seeing all sides' (Watier 1991: 231f.).

Coming back to Simmel's judgement of mammonism: in any case, Leck was right in saying that Simmel certainly was not a conservative thinker. He was 'a modernist, not a romantic antimodernist' (Leck 2000a: 20), and – for all we know – he was not nostalgic about the petrified contents of Judeo-Christian religion. Simmel was convinced that the melting of religious content poses a problem only for non-religious or inadequately religious people, for whom 'religious dogma is the only possible way of leading some kind of religious existence'. In contrast to them, a truly religious person simply cannot lose religion: 'A religious person is never left with nothing, for he has a fullness of being' (Simmel 1997: 17). What concerned him, though, was the prospect of replacement of already petrified religion with a new one, organised around a new object – money. The danger lies in the fact that people, instead of turning to sources of their inner life, would start to dance around the golden calf again. If the golden calf has become transcendent, it has become 'a god'; his 'cult' is our 'religion'. Money/God homology leads logically to the claim of isomorphy of religion and modern economic system: in other words, to the claim about the religious character of modern capitalism.

Capitalism as Religion

One of the best-known classical versions of this much discussed claim was formulated by Walter Benjamin in 1921 in a short and cryptic fragment entitled *Capitalism as Religion*. The fragment was not intended for publication and was never fully elaborated; it remains open for different readings. Benjamin's thesis is usually interpreted as a critical inversion of Max Weber's so-called thesis, i.e. his conceptualisation of the relationship between religion and the capitalist system. There is, however, some evidence that the stimulus for this inflection of arguments was given by Weber himself. Moreover, it undoubtedly bears the stamp of the 'underground influence' of Benjamin's mentor and 'intellectual predecessor' (Jameson 1999): Georg Simmel.

Benjamin explicitly refers to Weber by saying that capitalism is 'not only a religiously conditioned construction, as Weber thought', but 'an essentially religious phenomenon'.[2] The fragment opens with a provocative statement: 'one can see in capitalism a religion, that is to say, capitalism essentially serves to satisfy the same worries, anguish, and disquiet formerly answered by so-called religions'. In other words, capitalism became a functional equivalent of established religious systems. However, it did not gain this position simply at the expense of traditional religions, in the consequence of institutional secularisation – but rather, to use an economic expression, as a result of a hostile takeover. In the polemic with Weber Benjamin holds that Western Christianity did not stimulated the emergence of capitalism, but rather transformed into capitalism. Benjamin identified four distinctive characteristics of the religious structure of capitalism. First, capitalism is a religion which consists entirely of cult; it has no specific dogma nor theology. Secondly, capitalism is characterised by the permanent duration of the cult – 'without respite and without mercy'. There is no 'weekday', no day 'that would not be a holiday in the awful sense of exhibiting all sacred pomp'. Thirdly, this is a cult that engenders guilt/debt (the German word *Schuld* has double meaning; Benjamin mentions in this context 'the daemonic ambiguity of the word *Schuld*'): 'capitalism is presumably the first case of a cult that does not bring expiation, but burdens with guilt/debts'. And, finally, the last characteristics of the religious structure of capitalism is that 'its God must become concealed'.

Benjamin has never revealed the name of this hidden deity which has taken the place of the Judeo-Christian God. To identify the God of capitalist religion,

---

[2] All citations from Benjamin's fragment in Chad Kautzer's translation (Benjamin 2005).

and to properly understand Benjamin's capitalism/religion equation, we have to dig into the sources of ideas and images he is deploying. The dependence on Weber is rather obvious. The fragment refers explicitly to Nietzsche, Marx, Freud, Ernst Troeltsch and Gustav Landauer. A general reference to Gustav Landauer's book *A Call for Socialism*, which contains the sentence 'money has become a god, it has become a man-eater' (Landauer 1920: 144), hints at the identity of the anonymous capitalist deity (see Hamacher 2003: 98; Soosten 2003: 134). Troeltsch might have inspired Benjamin by the statement (from *Social Teachings of Christian Churches and Groups*) that with John Calvin capitalism 'has broken into Christianity'. But there are also other possible inspirations never mentioned by Benjamin.

As some critics have pointed out, the title of the fragment is directly borrowed from Ernst Bloch's *Thomas Münzer, Theologian of Revolution* – a book which appeared earlier in the same year (1921). Bloch was a Marxist, a member of Max Weber's circle in the years 1912–14, and a close friend of Walter Benjamin. The expression 'capitalism as religion' appears indeed in Bloch's book, but it is equally possible that it was Bloch who borrowed the phrase from Benjamin (they frequently exchanged ideas and Benjamin later even accused Bloch of stealing his own formulations). Be that as it may, the fragment in which Bloch refers to 'capitalism as religion' is very short, and the concept itself is not elaborated.

The capitalist economy today, says Bloch, is totally liberated from all qualms of Christianity, and the responsibility lay with Calvin. According to Bloch, Calvin deviated from the Christian radicalism by reducing the tension between everyday life and a life hereafter; he 'unleashed the everyday life'. The majesty ascribed to Christian God transferred to bookkeeping, and the sense of divine soon became reduced to 'a paradoxal relaxation of a dead Sunday'. In the end, Calvin's reform 'brought about not just a simple abuse of Christianity, but the total apostasy from Christianity, or even the aspects of a new religion: capitalism as religion and the Church of Mammon' (Bloch 1967: 142f.).

There are some obvious similarities between Bloch's and Benjamin's statements. The phrase 'Church of Mammon', however, leads us to Georg Simmel, who was an intellectual predecessor of both thinkers – and especially of Walter Benjamin, who attended Simmel's seminar in 1912 and forever 'failed to escape the force field of Simmel's thought' – as it was stated by Frederic Jameson (1999) and meticulously documented by Marian Mičko (2010).

The intellectual context of his argument allows us to identify the capitalist God that 'must become concealed' as Mammon – the money. This conclusion finds its justification in Benjamin's own note, saying 'compare the holy iconography of various religions on one hand with the banknotes of various countries on the other'. And further: 'to examine what associations money has formed with myth in the course of history – until it could seize enough mythical elements from Christianity to be able to constitute its own myth'. This myth would not develop an explicit dogma or theology; if there is any 'capitalist doctrine', then probably the gist of it was given by Marx in his *Capital*: 'Accumulate! Accumulate! That is Moses and the prophets!' If capitalism has no specific dogma, then what counts are the actions, which take the form of cult practices. As Michael Löwy (2010) put it: 'Money, in the form of paper-notes, would be the object of a cult similar to the one of saints in "ordinary" religions.' This cult would have to be permanent: Benjamin has probably absorbed Weber's description of the religious value set in Protestant ethics on restless, continuous and systematic work; analogous to it, capitalist practices are also characterised by their permanence; but, ironically, in the reversal of Puritan disregard for religious feasts, now every day is a holiday because it is fully devoted to the celebration of this-worldly deity. And, finally, as to the statement that this cult engenders guilt/debt: according to Burkhard Lindner, 'the historical perspective of the fragment is grounded on the premiss that one cannot separate, in the system of capitalist religion, the "mythical guilt" and the economic debt' (quoted after Löwy 2010).

After almost a century we have to acknowledge Benjamin's foresight: today, even a 'relaxation of a dead Sunday' is abolished. Stock exchange operates continuously and shopping malls are open each and every day until all hours; the worship continues 'without respite and without mercy'. Those who are not convinced should consider Falk Wagner's comment that a consciousness, defined by omnipotence and omnipresence of money, would have to be considered as religious consciousness, although not in its self-understanding (Wagner 1984: 13). And that is exactly the point that Benjamin is making in the closing sentence of his fragment: 'it contributes to the knowledge of capitalism as a religion to imagine that the original paganism certainly grasped religion not as a "higher" "moral" interest, but as the most immediately practical – that, with other words, just as today's capitalism it had not been aware of its "ideal" or "transcendent" nature.'[3]

Acknowledgement

Some aspects of this article first appeared in Georg Simmel's Concept of Religion and Religiosity, *Studia Religiologica* 45 (2012), 109–15, and *Między*

---

[3] Translation amended by D.M.

transcendencją a immanencją. Religia w myśli Georga Simmla (Kraków: Libron, 2013).

References

Benjamin, W. (2005). Fragment 74: Capitalism as Religion, in *Religion as Critique: The Frankfurt School's Critique of Religion*, ed. E. Mendieta. New York: Routledge, pp. 259–62. Available at www.rae.com.pt/Caderno_wb_2010/Benjamin%20Capitalism-as-Religion.pdf [accessed: 4 October 2013].

Bloch, E. (1967). *Thomas Münzer als Theologe der Revolution*. Frankfurt am Main: Suhrkamp.

Blumenberg, H. (1976). Geld oder Leben. Eine metaphorologische Studie zur Konsistenz der Philosophie Georg Simmels, in Ästhetik und Soziologie um die Jahrhundertwende: Georg Simmel, ed. H. Böhringer and K. Gründer. Frankfurt am Main: Vittorio Klostermann, pp. 121–34.

Deneault, A. (2006). How Simmel's *Philosophy of Money* Defines Economy, in *Georg Simmel in Translation: Interdisciplinary Border-Crossings in Culture and Modernity*, ed. D.D. Kim. Newcastle: Cambridge Scholars Press, pp. 158–72.

Featherstone, M. (1991). Georg Simmel: An Introduction. *Theory Culture and Society*, 8(3), 1–16.

Frisby, D. (1981). *Sociological Impressionism: A Reassessment of Georg Simmel's Social Theory*. London: Heinemann.

Frisby, D. (1992). *Simmel and Since: Essays on Simmel's Social Theory*. London and New York: Routledge.

Hamacher, W. (2003). Schuldgeschichte. Benjamins Skizze 'Kapitalismus als Religion', in *Kapitalismus als Religion*, ed. D. Baecker. Berlin: Kulturverlag Kadmos, pp. 77–119.

Jameson, F. (1999). The Theoretical Hesitation: Benjamin's Sociological Predecessor. *Critical Inquiry*, 25(2), 267–88.

Krech, V. (1998). *Georg Simmels Religionstheorie*. Tübingen: Mohr Siebeck.

Landauer, G. (1920). *Aufruf zum Sozialismus*. Berlin: Paul Cassirer.

Lechner, Frank J. (1990). Social Differentiation and Modernity: On Simmel's Macrosociology, in *Georg Simmel and Contemporary Sociology*, ed. M. Kaern, B.S. Phillips and R.S. Cohen. Dordrecht, Boston and London: Kluwer Academic Publishers, pp. 155–80.

Lechner, F.J. (1998). Simmel, Georg, in *Encyclopedia of Religion and Society*, ed. W.H. Swatos, Jr. Walnut Creek: Altamira Press. Available at http://hirr.hartsem.edu/ency/Simmel.htm [accessed: 20 November 2011].

Leck, Ralph M. (2000). Americanization as a Symbol of Money: Simmel as Critical Theorist, in *Georg Simmel's Philosophy of Money: A Centenary Appraisal*, ed. J.G. Backhaus and H.-J. Stadermann. Marburg: Metropolis Verlag, pp. 115–47.

Leck, Ralph M. (2000a). *Georg Simmel and Avant-Garde Sociology: The Birth of Modernity, 1880–1920*. New York: Humanity Books.

Levine, D.N. (1984). Ambivalente Begegnungen: 'Negationen' Simmels durch Durkheim, Weber, Lukács, Park und Parsons, in *Georg Simmel und die Moderne*, ed. H.-J. Dahme and O. Rammstedt. Frankfurt am Main: Suhrkamp, pp. 318–87.

Löwy, M. (2010). Anticapitalist Readings of Weber's *Protestant Ethic*: Ernst Bloch, Walter Benjamin, György Lukacs, Erich Fromm. *Logos*, 9(1). Available at www.logosjournal.com/anticapitalist-readings-of-webers-protestant-ethic.php [accessed: 1 December 2003].

Lukes, S. (1973). Émile Durkheim: *His Life and Work*. Middlesex: Penguin.

Luther, M. (1529). *Large Catechism*. Available at www.sacredtexts.com/chr/luther/largecat.htm#Heading3 [accessed: 26 September 2013].

Marx, K. (1959). The Power of Money, in *Economic and Philosophic Manuscripts of 1844*. Moscow: Progress Publishers. Available at www.marxists.org/archive/marx/works/1844/manuscripts/power.htm [accessed: 26 September 2013].

Meštrović, S.G. (1991). *The Coming Fin de Siècle: An Application of Durkheim's Sociology to Modernity and Postmodernism*. London: Routledge.

Mičko, M. (2010). *Walter Benjamin und Georg Simmel*. Wiesbaden: Harrassowitz.

Motak, D. (2012). Georg Simmel's Concept of Religion and Religiosity. *Studia Religiologica*, 45, 109–15.

Motak, D. (2013). *Między transcendencją a immanencją. Religia w myśli Georga Simmla*. Kraków: Libron.

Nielsen, D.A. (1999). *Three Faces of God: Society, Religion, and the Categories of Totality in the Philosophy of Émile Durkheim*. Albany: State University of New York Press.

Nisbet, R.A. (1959). Comment. *American Sociological Review*, 24(2), 479–81.

Pickering, W.S.F. (1984). *Durkheim's Sociology of Religion: Themes and Theories*. London: Routledge & Kegan Paul.

Shilling, C. (2002). The Two Traditions in the Sociology of Emotions, in *Emotions and Sociology*, ed. J. Barbalet. Oxford: Blackwell Publishing, pp. 10–32.
Simmel, G. (1997). *Essays on Religion*, ed. and trans. H.J. Helle. New Haven: Yale University Press.
Simmel, G. (1997a). Money in Modern Culture, in *Simmel On Culture: Selected Writings*, ed. D. Frisby and M. Featherstone. London: SAGE Publications, pp. 243–55.
Simmel, G. (1997b). On the Psychology of Money, in *Simmel On Culture: Selected Writings*, ed. D. Frisby and M. Featherstone. London: SAGE Publications, pp. 233–43.
Simmel, G. (2003). Deutschlands innere Wandlung, in *Georg Simmel Gesamtausgabe*, vol. 15, ed. U. Kösser, H.-M. Kruckis and O. Rammstedt. Frankfurt am Main: Suhrkamp, pp. 271–86.
Simmel, G. (2004). *The Philosophy of Money*, trans. T. Bottomore and D. Frisby. London: Routledge.
Soosten, von J. (2003). Schwarzer Freitag: Die Diabolik der Erlösung und die Symbolik des Geldes, in *Kapitalismus als Religion*, ed. D. Baecker. Berlin: Kulturverlag Kadmos, pp. 121–44.
Turner, B.S. (2010). Introduction: Mapping the Sociology of Religion, in *The New Blackwell Companion to the Sociology of Religion*, ed. B.S. Turner. Oxford: Wiley-Blackwell, pp. 1–29.
Wagner, F. (1984). *Geld oder Gott? Zur Geldbestimmtheit der kulturellen und religiösen Lebenswelt*. Stuttgart: Klett-Cotta.
Watier, P. (1991). The War Writings of Georg Simmel. *Theory Culture and Society*, 8(3), 219–33.
Watier, P. (2009). Psychosocial Feelings within Simmel's Sociology, in *Soziologie als Möglichkeit: 100 Jahre Georg Simmels Untersuchungen über die Formen der Vergesellschaftung*, ed. C. Rol and C. Papilloud. Wiesbaden: VS Verlag für Sozialwissenschaften, pp. 199–216.
Weinstein, D. and Weinstein, M.A. (1995). The Liberation of Religiosity from Religion, in *Georg Simmel between Modernity and Postmodernity*, ed. F. Dörr-Backes and L. Nieder. Würzburg: Königshausen&Neumann, pp. 129–41.

Chapter 7

Putting Baby Back in the Bath: Theorising Modernity for the Contemporary Sociology of Religion

Andrew Dawson

The Problem at Hand

The concerns and issues addressed in this chapter arise from a number of areas. First, they arise from my own work on contemporary religious developments in Europe, South America and the United States (e.g. Dawson 2007, 2011, 2013). Though mindful of the variegated socio-cultural terrain and varied geographical contexts in which research occurs, I nevertheless seek to articulate an understanding of contemporary religious change against the overarching theoretical backdrop of modern societal transformation. In short, the concept of 'modernity' provides a unifying analytical theme to my attempts to explicate the character and implications of ongoing transformations in religious belief and practice across a range of socio-cultural contexts. Perhaps precisely because of the modernity-oriented and transnational aspirations of my research, I have been struck by the growing popularity of academic discourse which both problematises modernity as a viable theoretical tool and eschews any meaningful attempt to relate an otherwise local or regional analysis with wider processes and dynamics of a cross-border or global nature (see below).

Second, the concerns and issues addressed below arise from personal interactions with academics and colleagues who, imbued by an increasingly fashionable theoretical provincialism, criticise my use of modernity as a transnational heuristic as both ideologically corrupt (because of its Western provenance) and analytically naive (in view of its international aspirations). In one exchange, for example, my interlocutor baulked at my qualified use of late-modern theory (à la Bauman, Beck, Giddens, et al.) to engage the nonmainstream religiosity of urban-professional practitioners in Brazilian cities such as Brasília, Rio de Janeiro and São Paulo. My reply that new middle-class members of Brazil's alternative religious scene frequently have more in common with nonmainstream adepts in the big cities of Australasia, Europe and North America than they do with many of their fellow citizens nevertheless failed to mitigate an evident discomfort with the purportedly unwarranted application of 'foreign' concepts to Brazil's domestic religious field. Offering absolutely no engagement with the theories being applied, my critic's discomfort rested solely upon an ostensible violation of Brazil's regional particularity. In the same vein, an academic colleague commonly rejects all attempts to explain the sociocultural transformations currently underway in her/his geographical area of specialisation which mobilise established sociological theories and concepts. Drawing a clear distinction between 'East' and 'West', my colleague refutes the relevance of concepts like 'modernity' on the grounds that they apply only to the socio-cultural cradle (i.e. the West) of their birth. Likewise offering no substantive critique of the sociological theories mobilised, my colleague's intellectual distress is provoked solely by the purported violation of regional integrity caused by the transnational application of social theories of modernity.

What follows opens by situating the suspicions of my interlocutors within the broader theoretical backdrop of recent problematisations of modernity as an ahistorical evolutionary model which is both overly homogenising and regionally biased. Given its progressively fashionable status within the sociology of religion, the multiple modernities paradigm is subsequently treated as a working example of such a critique. The remainder of the chapter then addresses the contemporary problematisation of modernity by doing two things. First, it argues that the problematisation of modernity currently in vogue within the sociology of religion actually loses as much as it gains in respect of its theoretical grasp of contemporary belief and religious practice. In effect, the views expressed by aforementioned interlocutors and exemplified by the multiple modernities paradigm serve only to swap one faulty conceptualisation of modernity (and thereby religion's place in it) for another. Though ideologically more 'right-on' than traditional representations, the conceptualisation of modernity currently fashionable among many sociologists of religion is as equally problematic in respect of its analytical limitations. Second, the chapter argues for the theoretical indispensability of modernity as a means of construing and interpreting contemporary societal and religious developments as both locally instantiated and transnationally accomplished. Serving both as a *cri de coeur* and rudimentary prolegomenon, the latter part of what follows identifies a number of requirements which any conceptualisation of modernity must meet in order to be of use to sociological engagement with contemporary religion.

Modernity in the Dock

The problematisation of modernity as a transnational heuristic owes much to the relatively recent demise of the 'modernisation' paradigm, the central pillar of which Gaonkar identifies as:

> The proposition that societal modernisation, once activated, moves inexorably toward establishing a certain type of mental outlook (scientific rationalism, pragmatic instrumentalism, secularism) and a certain type of institutional order (popular government, bureaucratic administration, market-driven industrial economy) irrespective of the culture and politics of a given place. (2001: 16)

According to Elsje Fourie, the demise of and theoretical backlash against the modernisation paradigm has left its portrayal 'disowned', 'deconstructed' and 'unfashionable' to the 'extent that no formal discussion of' modernity 'seems complete without a distancing of author from subject' (2012: 53). Part of the postmodern turn, Jean-François Lyotard did much to set the tone for those eager to disown and deconstruct prevalent understandings of modernity as ineluctably associated with historical convergence and socio-cultural homogenisation. Lyotard allies Wittgenstein's notion of 'language games' with the assertion that the rise of the 'postindustrial age' and 'postmodern culture' of the late-twentieth century involves a loss of 'credulity' in respect of traditional modes of 'legitimation' and established 'grand narratives' by which modernity has customarily been underwritten. The postmodern 'incredulity toward metanarratives', he argues, both rejects notions of 'totality', 'unicity' and 'system' and 'refines our sensitivity to differences and reinforces our ability to tolerate the incommensurable'. In marked contrast to modernising narratives of homogeneity and convergence, Lyotard posits 'local determinism' and 'temporal disjunction' as characteristic of postmodernity's 'breaking up of grand Narratives' (1984: xxiii–xxv, 3–37). Though of a principally philosophical nature, the postmodern problematisation of 'metadiscourse' exemplified by Lyotard has enjoyed continued popularity among social scientists uncomfortable with the concept of modernity as a 'Great Unifier' (Therborn 1995) or seeking to articulate a 'culturalist approach' to regional dynamics free from 'a larger narrative explaining how everything is ordered in a universally valid theoretical system which subjects them to a teleological necessity or causation' (Baykan 1990: 139).

The disowning and deconstruction of established portrayals of modernity is likewise undertaken by scholars championing postcolonial and subaltern narratives rooted in regional identity-politics. Walter Mignolo, for example, espouses a 'geopolitics of knowledge' which rejects the 'colonial imaginary' underwriting Western theories of modernity in favour of the 'reinstitution of *location* as a geopolitical and epistemological configuration of knowledge production' (2000: 305). As 'there is no modernity without coloniality', he argues, there can be no 'critique of modernity from the perspective of modernity itself'. Forged through the 'desubalternization of local knowledge', the reconstruction of 'local histories' as 'pluritopic' critiques of modernity offers the only viable means of escaping the 'coloniality of power' implicit within the 'overarching metaphor' of 'Occidentalism' (2000: 13, 43, 87). In the same vein, Gurminder Bhambra eschews prevailing 'sociological constructions of modernity' because of their dependence upon 'a particular historical understanding' which 'privileges' one regional perspective over others. Formulated amidst the 'institutions', 'practices' and 'structures' of Europe, he maintains, the '"facts" of modernity' articulated by dominant 'analytical categories' are nothing more than 'hermeneutical fabrications' unavoidably peddling 'a form of Eurocentrism' (2007: 145–7).

Avoiding the wholesale disownment and scorched-earth deconstructionism championed by Mignolo and Bhambra, Arjun Appadurai nevertheless performs an act of authorial distancing from established theorisations of modernity by calling for more pluriform representations which account for 'the *multiple* worlds that are constituted by the historically situated imaginations of persons and groups spread around the globe' (1996: 33). Articulated by complementary qualifications of modernity (or modernities) as, for example, 'alternative' (Goankar 2001), 'hybrid' (Canclini 1995), 'later' (Kaya 2004), 'local' (Rosati 2012), 'mixed' (Ortiz 1994), 'organised' (Carleheden 2007), 'successive' (Wagner 2012) and 'varied' (Schmidt 2006), the most popular form of terminological distancing from traditional notions of modernity has been effected by appending the prefix 'multiple' (e.g. Eisenstadt 2000; Arnason 2002). Indeed, both across the sociological community in general and within the sociology of religion in particular, the 'multiple modernities' paradigm has enjoyed something akin to hermeneutical dominance subsequent to its formative popularisation by Shmuel Eisenstadt.

Multiple Modernities

According to Eisenstadt, the argument for 'multiple modernities' rejects the presumed 'convergence of industrial societies' implicit within 'classical theories of modernization' and Western modes of 'sociological analysis' (2000: 1–29). 'Even if implicitly', he asserts, classical sociological approaches 'all assumed' that the cultural program of modernity as it developed in modern Europe and the basic institutional constellation that emerged there would ultimately take over in all modernizing and modern societies; with the expansion of modernity, they would prevail throughout the world. (2000: 1)

The historically recent globalisation of modern processes and dynamics, Eisenstadt maintains, has engendered 'multiple institutional and ideological patterns' which both refute 'the homogenizing and hegemonic assumptions' of classical approaches and negate the theoretical association of modernisation with Westernisation. Although Western modes of modernity continue to 'enjoy historical precedence' and serve as 'a basic reference point for others', an important consequence of recent developments is the growing realisation that 'Western patterns of modernity are not the only "authentic" modernities' available for concrete societal expression.

Eisenstadt's multiplication of modernity is founded on the socio-cultural variegation generated by 'the ongoing dialogue' between globalising forces of 'modern reconstruction' and regional 'cultural resources' embodied by 'respective civilizational traditions'. By virtue of the ongoing interaction of established civilizational contexts and transnational modern dynamics, not only are multiple modernities engendered but 'within all societies, new questionings and reinterpretations of different dimensions of modernity are emerging'. An 'undeniable trend' arising from this interaction is thereby 'the growing diversification of the understanding of modernity', along with that 'of the basic cultural agendas of different modern societies'. Consequently, and 'while the common starting point was once the cultural program of modernity as it developed in the West':

> more recent developments have seen a multiplicity of cultural and social formations going far beyond the very homogenizing aspects of the original version. All these developments do indeed attest to the continual development of multiple modernities, or of multiple interpretations of modernity – and, above all, to attempts at 'de-Westernization', depriving the West of its monopoly on modernity. (2000: 24)

Engendered by the interaction of the 'cultural program of modernity' and the 'specific cultural patterns, traditions, and historical experiences' of regional contexts, contemporary 'trends of globalization' are regarded by Eisenstadt as 'a story of continual constitution and reconstitution of a multiplicity of [modern] cultural programs'.

Parallel with its growing fashionableness within the sociological community at large (see Fourie 2012), the multiple modernities paradigm has come increasingly into vogue among sociologists of religion (e.g. Spohn 2003; Mardin 2006; Katzenstein 2006; Possamai and Lee 2010). Providing a progressively popular means of critiquing established understandings of the religion–modernity relationship, the multiple modernities thesis has most commonly been employed to problematise traditionally dominant associations of modern society with religious decline. Contrasting 'religious America' with 'secular Europe', for example, Berger et al. argue that 'secularization theory' is shot 'out of the water' by the realisation that 'there is no single paradigm of modernity' (2008: 16). Asserting the 'exceptional' status of European modernity as a distorting lens through which dominant portrayals of religious decline have traditionally been refracted, the authors maintain that:

> Advocates of multiple modernities recognize two very simple things: first that there is more than one way of being modern, and second that not all modernities are necessarily secular – indeed on present showing relatively few are. (2008: 44)

Arguing that formerly dominant theories of modernisation believe modernity to engender 'the necessary and inevitable decline or even abandonment of religion', Smith and Vaidyanathan likewise laud the multiple modernities paradigm for opening up 'an opportunity for rethinking, retheorizing, and reframing our empirical analyses in the social sciences, particularly with regard to religion'. In view of 'the new perspective' furnished by the multiple modernities approach, Smith and Vaidyanathan maintain that traditional associations between modernity and the 'inevitable-secularization thesis, are suspended, if not rejected' (2011: 251–2). In the same vein, Rosati and Stoeckl champion the multiple modernities paradigm as a blessed release from the strict entwining of 'theories of modernity ... with theories of secularization' (2012: 8). Believing 'the Western program of modernity' to include secularisation 'at least ideologically, as one of its principal components', Rosati and Stoeckl reject traditional theories of modernity in favour of 'a multiplicity of continually evolving modernities, each of which realizes a particular institutional and ideological interpretation of the modern program according to specific cultural prerequisites' (2012: 2).

In common with their theoretical benefactor, appropriations by sociologists of religion of the multiple modernities thesis embody a welcome corrective to the uncritically universalising excesses of the once dominant modernisation paradigm, along with its secularising assumptions. Those basking in this corrective glow, however, likewise share the conceptual weaknesses and analytical failings incrementally identified subsequent to the theoretical popularisation of the multiple modernities approach (see Featherstone 2007: 171–4; Fourie 2012: 59–61; Wagner 2012: 24–5). The criticisms are various and apply in equal measure to articulations of the multiple modernities thesis both within and outwith the sociological study of religion.[1] Passing over most of these failings, the following focuses upon the frequently aired criticism that the multiple modernities approach unduly inhibits overarching theorisations of modernity which, by their nature and intent, employ comparative frames and/or transnational perspectives. Wagner, for example, maintains that because the multiple modernities paradigm 'limits the possibility of comparison' it fails to furnish a sufficiently inclusive theoretical focus appropriate to providing a much needed 'world sociology' by which the contemporary 'global social configuration' might be understood (2012: 25, 120). In the same vein, Schmidt regards the emphasis upon diversity made by the multiple modernities paradigm as adding nothing by way of substance for those interested in making transnational comparisons. Referring to the paradigm's assertion that the world 'exhibits a great deal of cultural and institutional diversity', Schmidt asks:

> But is that a really new insight – and are (or were) modernization theorists not aware of it themselves? The question is not, at least cannot seriously be, whether there is diversity in the world. There certainly is. But what do we make of it? How *much* diversity is there? What *kinds* of diversity exist between different modern societies? How *profound* are the existing differences? What is their social theoretical *significance*? And what are their future prospects? (2006: 78)

Fourie likewise criticises the multiple modernities approach for a lack of 'cross-cultural theorizing' which obstructs 'a clearer understanding of the ... collective values and cultural practices of people affected by modernity around the world' that not only 'diverge' but also 'intertwine' (2012: 62).

---

[1] The major criticisms levelled against the multiple modernities paradigm relate to: the reification of cultural or civilisational domains which drastically underplays historical change and socio-cultural diversity while overemphasising regional difference and transcontextual incommensurability; a theoretical reductionism in which contemporary social transformation is attributed solely to the interface of culture and modernisation; the failure to articulate its approach relative to theoretical alternatives (e.g. new modernisation theory and postmodernism); confusion in respect of its particular unit of analysis; a dearth of empirical research and actual case studies; limited theorisation of modernity and its constituent components.

Central to the criticisms levelled against the multiple modernities paradigm is the belief that the conceptualisation of modernity it employs lacks the theoretical depth and analytical breadth necessary to countering the uncritical universalism of established modernisation theory with anything other than an equally unsatisfactory granular provincialism. As it applies to those within the sociology of religion espousing a multiple modernities approach, this failing manifests itself in both an analytical preoccupation with regional particularity and a conceptual disregard for broader questions of a cross-cultural and meta-theoretical nature. In effect, sociologists of religion working within a multiple modernities framework place too much emphasis upon the *multiple* and pay too little attention to the *modern*. Believing this imbalanced emphasis to have thrown out the 'baby' of modernity with the 'bathwater' of traditional modernisation theory, this chapter seeks to open a conversation through which this lopsided focus and its attendant critical lacunae might begin to be corrected.

Deproblematising Modernity

The enervated theory of modernity employed by sociologists of religion working within the multiple modernities paradigm lacks the analytical purchase necessary for a meaningful understanding of contemporary religious transformation. Such is the case, I argue, because their limited conceptualisation of modernity ultimately fails to understand contemporary religious developments as both regionally instantiated and transnationally accomplished relative to processes and dynamics which are, by their origin, character and impact, typically modern. As will be seen below, the fundamental validity of this assertion rests squarely upon the progressively global diffusion of forces and structures intimately associated with modernity as a historically novel social formation and epochally distinct mode of being in the world. As Gaonkar maintains, 'modernity has gone global' to the extent that 'the present announces itself as the modern at every national and cultural site today' (2001: 14). 'Now everywhere', and thereby empirically and theoretically 'inescapable', modernity:

> has arrived not suddenly but slowly, bit by bit, over the longue durée – awakened by contact; transported through commerce; administered by empires, bearing colonial inscriptions; propelled by nationalism; and now increasingly steered by global media, migration, and capital. And it continues to 'arrive and emerge' ... but no longer from the West alone, although the West remains the major clearinghouse of global modernity. (2001: 1)

In tandem with the multiple modernities paradigm, Gaonkar is at pains to distance himself from the 'universalist idioms' and 'convergence' narratives of traditional modernisation theory. At the same time, however, such is the all-pervasive presence of modernity 'as a form of discourse that interrogates the present', Gaonkar argues, that due consideration must be given to the 'strings of similarities' (e.g. 'cultural forms, social practices, and institutional arrangements') which 'surface in most places in the wake of modernity'. As he concludes by way of implicit reference to the multiple modernities approach, 'though cultural modernity is conventionally seen as both the machinery and optic for the limitless production of differences, such difference always functions within a penumbra of similarities … all ineffable yet recognizable [as modern] across the noise of difference' (2001: 16–23). Though working within a different theoretical frame to that of Gaonkar, Schmidt's declaration that 'modernity is now a genuinely global phenomenon' employs a remarkably similar tone. Having 'fascinated generations of sociologists' from 'the beginnings of sociology as an academic discipline', the global spread of modernity has placed it squarely 'back on sociology's agenda'. As Schmidt maintains, 'in the past half-century, modernity has not only penetrated its Western birthplace much more deeply; it has also spread to other regions at a historically unprecedented pace' (2007a: 1, 3). While the global outworking of modernity will inevitably involve elements of regional variation, the 'substantial similarities that exist among modern societies' demands nevertheless, he argues, 'a theory of modernity' capable of analysing and capturing 'what is unique to modernity as against other societal formations' (2007a: 8–9).

In light of aforementioned discussions and views such as those of Gaonkar and Schmidt, the theoretical recuperation of modernity involves, at the very least, meeting the twofold challenge of making it:

1. sufficiently robust to engage the contemporary global scene in a manner which avoids the analytical provincialism exemplified above through reference to the multiple modernities paradigm; and
2. appropriately nuanced to the extent that it eschews the thoroughgoing universalism associated above with traditional modernisation theory.

In contrast to Schmidt, however, I do not believe that the perils of analytical provincialism are best avoided through the conceptualisation of modernity as an albeit reflexively self-critical form of grand theory such as that articulated by the differentiation theory of Niklas Luhmann (2007b: 205–28). Nor do I go along with the discursive indeterminacy of Gaonkar which achieves its hermeneutical nuancing of global modernity at the cost of failing to substantiate its 'band of similarities' through reference to anything as concrete as a defining attribute or typological characteristic (2001: 1–23). As Fourie argues in respect of contemporary discussions and their qualified approaches, 'it is less important to determine whether modernity is singular or multiple than it is to understand what comprises the defining features of modernity, and to what extent variation on these features exists around the world' (2012: 66).

Although neither Gaonkar nor Schmidt offers a particularly satisfactory theorisation of modernity, each stands as a useful reference point on the respective margins of an otherwise viable *via media* between the overly determinative universalism of modernisation theory (with which Schmidt remains too close) and the unduly equivocal provincialism of the multiple modernities paradigm (by which Gaonkar stays too near). As such, the respective positions of Gaonkar and Schmidt stand as the Scylla and Charybdis between which a viable conceptualisation of modernity must steer. Taking Gaonkar and Schmidt as key reference points, I propose that a theorisation of modernity conducive to understanding contemporary religious developments should involve its conceptualisation as:

1. instantiating a particular type of social formation which represents a historically novel constellation of intersecting societal structures and cultural dynamics;
2. susceptible to academic investigation relative to an associated set of empirically analysable practical-symbolic structures and processes; and
3. comprising a range of socio-cultural variegation which plays out across the macro-structural, mid-range institutional and micro-social dimensions of any given society.

Let me address each of these points in turn.

In respect of the first point, Yack makes a salutary contribution to understanding modernity as a particular type of social formation comprising a historically novel constellation of intersecting societal structures and cultural dynamics. Despite becoming 'the leading character in the [academic] drama of our time', he argues, 'there has been relatively little discussion of the viability of the concept of modernity itself' (1997: 1, 11). Addressing what he regards as the contemporary 'fetishism of modernities', Yack criticises those who regard modernity as a 'harmonious unity' or 'coherent and integrated whole' and thereby treat all phenomena appearing in modern times as typical characteristics of the modern experience. Rather, he maintains, because the 'modern era' (*die Neuzeit*) comprises a mixture of old/pre-modern and new/modern features, all that exists or arises in the modern period does not necessarily contribute to what is characteristically unique about 'modernity' (*die Modernität*) as an existentially distinctive mode of 'being in the world' (1997: 7, 19, 37). More than a straightforward inventory of the phenomena and features existing in the current (i.e. modern) epoch, a viable definition of modernity must thereby include those characteristics identified, individually or in combination, as constitutive of both an historically novel social configuration and existentially distinctive mode of human signification.[2] Taking our lead from Yack, a definition of modernity of sufficient analytical purchase for the sociology of religion must therefore, at the very least, be able to make a meaningful distinction between features of the modern landscape which are, de facto, temporally present and characteristics which are, hermeneutically speaking, of epochal significance.

Regarding the second point, and bearing in the mind the need to focus upon matters of epochal significance, a number of approaches may be taken in respect of investigating modernity by way of analysing its constituent set of practical-symbolic structures and dynamics. Treating 'the Western program of modernity', for example, Eisenstadt typically focuses upon its 'cultural' domain, not least its particular conceptualisations of 'human agency', along with 'the possibility of different interpretations of core transcendental visions and ... the institutional patterns related to them'. Among the most significant of the West's typically modern conceptions, Eisenstadt identifies: 'the awareness of a great variety of roles existing beyond narrow, fixed, local, and familial ones'; 'the possibility of belonging to wider translocal, possibly changing, communities'; 'an emphasis on the autonomy of man' and 'his or her ... emancipation from the fetters of traditional political and cultural authority'; and 'belief in the possibility that society could be actively formed by conscious human activity'. In combination, he says, these characteristically Western conceptions give rise to its 'modern program' of 'radical transformation' from which a new 'political order' emerges (2000: 3–5). In addition to his aforementioned framing of Western modernity as one among a number of regional manifestations, Eisenstadt here portrays modernity as a 'cultural program' (constituted by 'new self-conceptions and new forms of collective consciousness') born of 'arguments', 'premises' and 'interpretations' which narrate a typically new mode of being in the world. What he does not do, however, is relate these developments to the practical-

---

[2] Yack identifies, for example, the 'emphasis on innovation', 'continual challenge to traditional authority' and 'the explosion and ever-increasing differentiation of knowledge' as three such instances of characteristically distinctive features of modernity (1997: 35, 133).

symbolic structures and dynamics which have customarily stood at the heart of sociological studies of modernity as a typically novel and empirically realised socio-cultural formation. By overly focussing upon modernity as a cultural programme, Eisenstadt offers a lopsided theorisation that fails to pay due attention to the broader societal context within which 'new self-conceptions and new forms of collective consciousness' emerge.

In contrast to Eisenstadt, for example, Giddens and Wagner offer more rounded theorisations of modernity, each of which understands it as constituted by the triangular intersection of a range of epistemic, economic and political structures and dynamics. According to Giddens, modernity is 'associated with (1) a certain set of attitudes towards the world, the idea of the world as open to transformation by human intervention; (2) a complex of economic institutions, especially industrial production and a market economy; (3) a certain range of political institutions, including the nation-state and mass democracy'. 'Largely as a result of these characteristics', Giddens maintains, 'modernity is vastly more dynamic than any previous type of social order' and 'unlike any preceding culture lives in the future rather than the past' (Giddens and Pierson 1998: 94). In similar vein, Wagner associates modernity with a particular way of understanding (e.g. individual autonomy), instantiating (e.g. nation-state) and addressing (e.g. market economy) three '*basic problématiques*' pertaining to 'the epistemic, the political and the economic' (2012: 74). Whereas Giddens and Wagner differ somewhat in respect of the processes and mechanisms through which modernity obtains its progressively global profile, their corresponding treatments of both its institutional and cultural aspects identify some of the most distinctive practical-symbolic features by which the typically modern social configuration may be subjected to sociological analysis.

By way of complementing the foci of Giddens and Wagner, and perhaps furnishing a more dynamic reading of modernity's empirically analysable practical-symbolic characteristics, mention might also be made of typically modern, and mutually implicating, processes such as, for example, differentiation, transformation, detraditionalisation, de-collectivisation and transnational integration. First, the typically modern characteristic of societal differentiation occurs principally through the combined processes of structural variegation and socio-cultural pluralisation. In structural terms, modernity is characterised by a dizzyingly diverse number of variegated mechanisms and specialised institutions through which the day-to-day activities of humankind occurs. At the same time, modernity exhibits a socio-cultural variety unprecedented in human history. Related in no small measure with structural differentiation, socio-cultural pluralisation occurs as the variegation of practical-symbolic structures engenders progressively diverse life-experiences for the different groups, categories or classes populating the increasingly varied terrain of modern society. Sociocultural pluralisation also results from domestic and transnational migration and the resulting interaction and miscegenation of different social, racial, ethnic and linguistic groups. Second, modernity comprises a thoroughgoingly transformative environment characterised by the rapid, widespread and ongoing reconfiguration of macro-structural, mid-range institutional and micro-social dimensions of societal existence. Exemplified by the transformational dynamics of urban-industrialisation, the modern societal environment is constantly mutating through the ceaseless modification or wholesale replacement of, for instance, infrastructural networks (e.g. state, transport and communication), interactive contexts (e.g. education, work and leisure) and extended webs of dependency (e.g. food, health and technology). Third, and catalysed in large part by the combined dynamics of differentiation and transformation, modernity weakens the influence and implications of both traditional modes of authority and signification and established means of collective determination (e.g. family, class, religion, sex and race). Detraditionalisation unfolds through the practical-symbolic disembedding of individuals, communities and cultures from the material processes and significatory structures bequeathed by past generations. Conventional authority and automatic appeals to tradition are thereby eroded, along with the disruption of established modes of reproduction which have customarily underwritten the continued force, significance and salience of inherited routines, habits, values, beliefs and rituals. The distancing of contemporary generations from received traditions and the authority structures through which they are operationalised incrementally undermines the degree of socio-cultural determinacy exerted by inherited forms of practical-knowledge.

Fourth, and though by no means eradicating communal forms of belonging and identity formation, modernity nevertheless recalibrates collective–individual dynamics in a manner which both enervates the former and empowers the latter. As such, and in comparison with what has gone before, the modern individual enjoys historically unrivalled degrees of self-determination (re: education, employment, leisure and relationships) and subjective expression (re: sexuality, belief and lifestyle). Fifth, scientific developments impacting travel, communications and information technology combine to characterise modernity as a time/place of increasingly rapid and progressively large-scale circulation of material goods, people, information, tastes, values and beliefs. Such is the nature of this worldwide circulation, and so powerful are the market-driven forces implicated within it, that domestic structures and local dynamics are, like it or not, ineluctably interwoven within a highly integrated network of transnational processes and flows. Modernity, then, is typified by an incrementally global network of economic, political, legal and aesthetic dynamics and structures which connect localities and regions to a seemingly limitless number of otherwise disparate locations. Enmeshed within this worldwide network, modern society is constituted by the transnational flow of goods, people, information, power and values occurring at a seemingly unfathomable scale and vertiginous speed.

Having explored the first two aspects of the aforementioned conceptualisation of modernity (as comprising a historically novel social formation embodying a range of practical-symbolic structures and dynamics susceptible to sociological scrutiny), it is now time to examine the third aspect; i.e. the socio-cultural variegation of modernity which plays out across the macro-structural, mid-range institutional and micro-social dimensions of any given society. Again taking Gaonkar and Schmidt as the reference points by which we steer towards an understanding of modernity of use to the sociological study of contemporary religion, the explication of modernity's socio-cultural variegation must navigate between the Scylla and Charybdis of uncritical universalism and granular provincialism. Among those seeking to chart a navigable course between these twin extremes, the self-styled 'cosmopolitan sociology' offers academics of contemporary religion a potentially viable theoretical route-map by which modernity's socio-cultural variegation may fruitfully be explored. According to some of its earliest proponents, cosmopolitan sociology arises in response to the 'global transformation of modernity' and the resulting need 'for a re-thinking of the humanities and the social sciences'. Radicalised by its historically recent constitution as a 'cosmopolitan constellation' of 'border-transcending dynamics, dependencies, interdependencies and intermingling', global modernity requires 'a new conceptual architecture' better suited to understanding the contemporary 'growth of many transnational forms of life', along with 'the emergence of corresponding supra- and transnational organizations and regimes'. Presenting itself as one such example of this new conceptual architecture, cosmopolitan sociology responds to the challenge that 'social and political theory be opened up, theoretically as well as methodologically and normatively, to a historically new, entangled Modernity' (Beck and Sznaider 2006; Beck and Grande 2010).[3]

By way of meeting this challenge, cosmopolitan sociology formulates a 'normative and empirical' package of (analytically discrete but theoretically complementary) approaches which address the moral and methodological

---

[3] Unless otherwise stated, all of the following quotes pertaining to cosmopolitan sociology are taken from these two articles.

issues raised by the emergence of 'Second [i.e. global] modernity'. Understood as a 'normative-political'/'philosophical' project, cosmopolitanism both identifies a range of 'imperatives' engendered by global modernity and proposes a series of 'norms' and procedures by which these imperatives might best be addressed.[4] It is, however, the insights of the 'analytical-empirical' preoccupations of cosmopolitan sociology which add most to the current concern with establishing a balanced conceptualisation of modernity's socio-cultural variegation. In respect of its 'analytical-empirical' treatment of modernity, cosmopolitan sociology includes two elements which speak directly to the topic at hand. First, it articulates an approach to modernity as 'entangled' which steers between the two extremes identified above as uncritical universalism and granular provincialism. Second, it operationalises the notion of cosmopolitan entanglement in a way which preserves the hermeneutical resilience of modernity as an analytical concept while allowing due appreciation of socio-cultural variegation as it plays out across the macro-structural, mid-range institutional and micro-social dimensions of any given society.

Regarding the first contribution, cosmopolitan sociology echoes aforementioned critiques of classical modernisation theory by rejecting its 'naive universalism' and the resulting 'diffusion or transfer of European theories' of modernity to other parts of the world. 'Implicitly applying conclusions drawn from *one* society to society (in general)', it is argued, classical theories of modernity have consequently drawn on a very narrow range of national experiences (e.g. England/Britain in the economic realm, France in the political domain and Prussia/Germany in the field of bureaucracy), which are presumed to be *universally valid* or, at the very least, a model to be replicated in other regions of the globe (Beck and Grande 2010: 411–12).

The resulting 'expectation of *convergence*' in which a homogenised 'model of (Western) modernity' is ultimately 'followed everywhere' is, the authors maintain, 'the exact opposite of our theory of cosmopolitan modernities'. Such an acknowledgement need not, though, entail the kind of granular provincialism associated above with the multiple modernities paradigm and its insufficient elaboration of the 'structural variations' of and 'relationships' between the 'respective types' of modernity conceived. While the 'cosmopolitan turn' opens up 'the possibility of a variety of different and autonomous' modernities, the 'plurality of modernities' proposed remain very much 'interlinked' or

---

[4] Beck elsewhere identifies a number of contributions which 'reflexive' (here, moderate) religion stands to make to the normative-political project of cosmopolitanism (2010).

'entangled' within the aforementioned 'cosmopolitan constellation' and its 'border-effacing', 'boundary transcending' web of 'transcontinental processes', 'global interdependencies' and 'transnational spaces ... and structures'. As a result, cosmopolitan sociology accepts the reality of difference and plurality, but does so in a manner which refuses their absolutisation and thereby avoids flipping 'over into an incommensurability of perspectives which amounts to pre-established ignorance'.

The interlinking or entanglement of modern societies within the cosmopolitan constellation of second (i.e. global) modernity, it is argued, necessitates a change of theoretical focus which moves beyond what is identified as 'methodological nationalism'. According to Beck and Sznaider, methodological nationalism equates societies with nation-state societies and sees states and their governments as the primary focus of social-scientific analysis. It assumes that humanity is naturally divided into a limited number of nations, which organize themselves internally as nation-states and externally set boundaries to distinguish themselves from other nation-states (2006: 3). In view of the historically recent formation of the aforementioned cosmopolitan constellation, the authors maintain, a new 'cosmopolitan perspective' is required to break 'the fetters of methodological nationalism' and thereby move beyond the national context as the principal 'orienting reference point for the social scientific observer'. Though necessarily entailing 'a re-examination of the fundamental concepts of "modern society"', the cosmopolitanisation of sociology does not negate the theoretical significance of 'different national traditions of law, history, politics and memory'. It does, though, involve their analytical integration within broadened conceptual horizons in which national contexts and traditions are duly acknowledged yet interpreted against the globalised hermeneutical backdrop of the 'cosmopolitan moment'.

Steering a course between the two extremes of uncritical universalism and granular provincialism, the acknowledgement and globally-informed interpretation of national contexts and traditions is effected by cosmopolitan sociology in a manner that both preserves the hermeneutical resilience of modernity as an analytical concept and permits due appreciation of localised variegation as it plays out across the macro-structural, mid-range institutional and micro-social dimensions of any given society. Accepting the need to furnish a serious theoretical account of 'how different types of modern societies' emerge, cosmopolitan sociology sets about identifying the 'patterns', 'origins' and 'consequences' of societal variation. Cosmopolitan sociology does this by drawing a theoretical distinction between the 'basic principles' and 'basic institutions' of modernity. In respect of the former, 'basic structural and organizational principles' comprise the fundamental features by which modernity, as an epochally distinct mode of social formation, can be defined. Identified as such basic principles, 'the market economy', 'individualization', 'risk' (e.g. ecological and nuclear) and 'the cosmopolitan condition' effectively function as typological characteristics of modernity. The global spread of modernity thereby occurs as basic principles such as these impact upon, manifest within and progressively interlink respective local, national and regional contexts around the world. The regional instantiation of its basic principles thereby underwrites the global diffusion of modernity as both a historically novel type of social formation and epochally distinctive mode of being in the world.

In contrast with classical modernisation theory, however, cosmopolitan sociology allows for the global diffusion of modernity engendering a 'plurality' or 'variety of modernities' across the world. The emergence of a 'variety of different types of modern society' occurs as different socio-cultural contexts actualise aforementioned basic principles through 'institutional' arrangements specific to respective national or regional domains. For example, the 'West European' context institutionalises the basic principle of individualisation through liberal-democratic and rights-based structures and processes. Within the authoritarian and collectivist context of China, however, the individualising dynamics of modernity are 'unfolding in a characteristically different, indeed reverse sequence'. Unlike the multiple modernities paradigm, though, the difference engendered by regional institutionalisation is not one of unqualified 'pluralisation' and the resulting incommensurability of granular provincialism. Rather, the plural modernities wrought by the local institutionalisation of basic principles such as individualisation are regarded as 'variants of modernity' and thereby ultimately understood against the overarching conceptual backdrop of 'cosmopolitan modernization'. Though globally diffused and regionally varied by way of their local institutionalisation, the basic principles of modernity retain their analytical resilience as typological characteristics enabling the comparing and contrasting of different forms of modern society and their respective socio-cultural variegations. A particular societal context may thereby be regarded as modern to the extent that the basic principles of modernity manifest through otherwise local institutional structures and processes; while modernity is varied as concrete institutional arrangements refract its basic principles relative to regional socio-cultural dynamics of a macro-structural, mid-range organisational and micro-social kind.

Something more, though, might be said about the dynamics of local instantiation by moving beyond cosmopolitan sociology's assertion that the same typological characteristics (here 'basic principles') of modernity may be regionally 'institutionalised' in a variety of ways relative to prevailing conditions on the ground. What the aforementioned proponents of cosmopolitan sociology do not consider, and what I wish to propose here by way further nuancing regional variegation, is the possibility that not every typological characteristic of modernity be contemporaneously instantiated within any one specific locale. Thus, not only is it possible that different locales institutionalise the same basic principles in varying ways, but it is also possible that different regions of the globe instantiate a respectively varied combination of modernity's typological characteristics. Such an assertion is feasible, I suggest, if modernity is conceptualised in a polythetic manner. Popularised among academics of religion by Alston (1967) and Southwold (1978), the polythetic (literally 'many aspects or themes') approach lends itself to defining phenomena not readily conceptualised by reference to a single characteristic or unduly narrow range of features. Arguing that the variegated character of religion makes it impossible to define relative to one or a small number of typological characteristics, Alston and Southwold independently offer polythetic definitions comprising what each respectively regards as the most commonly occurring (i.e. empirically observable) features pertaining to religious belief and practice enacted across the world (Alston 1967: 141–2; Southwold 1978: 370–371). Where a sufficient number of these characteristics are in evidence, they argue, you have religion.

Alston and Southwold do not weight the individual components of their polythetic definitions in a way which allows certain characteristics to be ranked as typologically more significant than others (e.g. necessary but not sufficient). Nor do they nuance their definitions by suggesting that each of the individual characteristics of religion may be more or less present in any one context. If qualified appropriately, however, a polythetic approach to modernity may well be weighted and nuanced in a way which permits comparisons between different regions as to the particular kind, overall number and individual aspect (i.e. how much) of the typological characteristics present. Whereas such comparisons may well involve judgements as to whether some contexts are more or less modern than others, this is not the reason I propose it here. Rather, I suggest that a polythetic conceptualisation of modernity be considered on the grounds that its employment promises to enhance appreciation of the variegated ways in which modernity plays out from one context to the next.

Putting Baby Back in the Bath

In view of preceding discussions, an understanding of modernity of sufficient analytical purchase, inclusivity and nuance to be of use to the contemporary sociology of religion must thereby meet at least three mutually complementary requirements. First, the conceptualisation of modernity must do more than reflect the de facto prevailing features of a progressively globalising modern landscape. Rather, it must capture the definitive characteristics which mark modernity as a historically novel social formation and epochally significant mode of being in the world. In keeping with established sociological method (see Weber 1949, 1968), the mode of capture involves a form of inductive abstraction in which the defining characteristics of modernity are constituted as conceptual approximations of otherwise concrete empirical phenomena identified by way of historical comparison (between then and now) and contemporary multiperspectivalism (both here and there). Modernity, then, is neither ahistorically determined nor defined relative to a normative set of socio-cultural expectations. Rather, and arising inductively through an act of theoretical abstraction, the viability of modernity as an analytical construct rests firmly upon its empirical fit with actual conditions on the grounds. Furthermore, as the empirical features by which modernity is defined undergo change, so too must their theoretical approximation.

Second, any viable understanding of modernity must be sociologically effectual. As noted above, modernity may be defined relative to a range of political processes, economic structures and philosophical approaches to the world at large. Though by no means excluding such features as inconsequential to a fuller conceptualisation of modernity, a feasible sociological definition must, at the very least, shed an immediate and thoroughgoing light upon characteristically modern enactments of the self–society, agency–structure relationship (see Archer 1996). Consequently, while previously identified notions of the 'nation-state', 'market economy' and 'autonomy of man' make valuable contributions, a sociologically efficacious conceptualisation of modernity must also include aforementioned dynamics such as rapid, widespread and ongoing societal transformation, structural differentiation, detraditionalisation, socio-cultural pluralisation, individualisation and globalisation.

Third, and likewise in respect of agency–structure relations, an understanding of modernity of use to the sociology of religion should also grasp the manner in and extent to which the defining features of the current epoch play out through regionally specific contexts and local configurations by way of mutually implicating macro-structural dynamics, mid-range institutional processes and micro-social interactions. In so doing, the socio-cultural variegation engendered by local instantiations of globalising modernity (polythetically understood) will be open to appreciation not only as actual variations on the modern theme but also as possible modifications thereof. In combination with the other two definitional requirements, the concern to identify and understand modernity as a globalising yet regionally instantiated phenomenon goes a considerable way to underwriting its conceptualisation in a manner which steers a workable *via media* between the twin extremes of uncritical universalisation and granular provincialism. Bringing these points together, and in view of preceding discussions, modernity may thereby be conceptualised as: a historically novel social formation and existential mode of being in the world constituted by the ongoing and transformative interaction of a range of epochally significant dynamics, structures and processes (e.g. nation-state, market economy, rapid, widespread and ongoing transformation, structural differentiation, detraditionalisation, socio-cultural pluralisation, individualisation and globalisation) which manifest concretely through regional/local instantiations of a macro-structural, mid-range institutional and micro-social nature.

Conclusion

My two interlocutors mentioned at the outset of this chapter are very much justified in their concerns with the unwarranted application of purportedly exogenous theories and concepts to their respective socio-cultural domains of expertise. It is certainly true that formerly dominant conceptualisations of modernity have served somewhat as theoretical Trojan horses laden with hidden evolutionary assumptions, normative projects and homogenising expectations of an implicitly Westernising bent. Buoyed by the progressive problematisation of classical modernisation theory, the regional particularism expressed by collaborator and colleague alike has been further reinforced by the academic zeitgeist and its outright rejection or qualified disavowal of 'modernity' as a viable means of articulating an overarching theorisation of societal developments of a local or regional kind. From postmodern deconstructionism, through postcolonial critiques, to the multiple modernities paradigm, the hermeneutical regionalism espoused by my interlocutors is championed by an assortment of theoretical approaches. As with much else that is fashionable, however, the worthy popularity of modernity's rejection serves only to mask the analytical shortcomings engendered by the unfortunate trade of an uncritical universalism for that of hermeneutical incommensurability. Consequently, the theoretical gains made in rejecting classical modernisation theory have been unwittingly offset by the adoption of a granular provincialism exemplified above through reference to the multiple modernities paradigm.

Preceding discussions seek to correct the overcompensation of the multiple modernities paradigm by suggesting that an understanding of modernity of use to the sociology of religion can be formulated as a *via media* charted between the twin extremes of uncritical universalism and granular provincialism. More than an exercise in intellectual moderation, however, the conceptualisation of modernity as both analytically robust and hermeneutically nuanced is, I maintain, straightforwardly good sociology if conceived and executed as a theoretical approximation of otherwise concrete historical phenomena. As such, the concept of modernity arises as: (1) an analytical abstraction from empirical processes (associated with) (2) the regionally refracted instantiation of (3) a particular set of progressively globalised structures and dynamics (which constitute) (4) an epochally novel social formation (i.e. modern society) and existentially distinct mode of being in the world (i.e. modern subjectivity). If so conceptualised, modernity functions not as an exogenous imposition upon a particular region but as an inductive abstraction from a given locale within which characteristically modern features and processes (e.g. rapid, widespread and ongoing transformation, structural differentiation, detraditionalisation, socio-cultural pluralisation and individualisation) are held to be in evidence.

It cannot be denied, however, that the dynamics and structures which serve to define modernity have historically been most closely associated with the West. In both Europe and the United States, for example, the practical-symbolic components of a modern societal constellation have been present for well over a century. Consequently, and however unpalatable my interlocutors might find the thought, any regional instantiation of modernity does, in one way or another, involve the presence of features and processes of a Western-like nature. Though by no means constituting the thoroughgoing Westernisation implicit within classical modernisation theories, and even allowing for the local variegations wrought by regional dynamics, the globalising diffusion of modernity comprises, at least in part, the *Western-like-isation* of particular socio-cultural contexts.[5] At the same time, of course, the intensified networks and exponential flows of globalising modernity are reconfiguring the West in a manner and extent previously unimagined. That chicken tikka masala and Chinese stir fry are now among the most popular meals in Britain bears a socio-cultural significance way

---

[5] The fact that the modern West was forged through relations with non-Western regions does not undermine the central thrust of this point.

beyond the culinary sphere! Such is the nature of contemporary globalisation, and such are the variegating dynamics of local instantiation, that modernity's progressive diffusion also engenders the appearance of non-Western-like features both outwith and within the traditional geographical heartlands of modern society.

In keeping with the spirit of the multiple modernities paradigm, it may justifiably be said that the local instantiation of globalising modernity includes the formation of regionally novel and socio-culturally distinct ways of being modern both within and beyond the West. The sociology of religion is thereby charged with being sensitive to and theoretically appreciative of the pluriform manner in which modernity both transforms established religion and engenders new modes of belief and practice. In contrast to the multiple modernities paradigm, however, an understanding of modernity of use to the sociology of religion need not sacrifice analytical resilience in pursuit of hermeneutical sensitivity to regional variegation. Steering a course between the twin extremes of uncritical universalism and granular provincialism, the approach delineated here suggests the possibility of an analytically robust and hermeneutically nuanced conceptualisation of modernity that allows the variations and novelties provoked by its regional instantiation to be analysed and interpreted relative to an empirically-informed set of overarching (yet revisable) key definitional features. Though both a work in progress and somewhat abstract in nature, it is hoped that preceding arguments in favour of modernity serve, at the very least, to provoke further debate as to the analytical frame and hermeneutical approach best suited to the sociological study of contemporary religious belief and ritual practice.

References

Alston, W.P. (1967). Religion, in *Encyclopedia of Philosophy*, vol. 7, ed. P. Edwards. New York: Macmillan and The Free Press, pp. 140–147.
Appadurai, A. (1996). *Modernity at Large: Cultural Dimensions of Globalization*. Minneapolis: University of Minnesota.
Archer, M.S. (1996). *Culture and Agency: The Place of Culture in Social Theory*, revised edn. Cambridge: Cambridge University Press.
Arnason, J.P. (2002). The Multiplication of Modernity, in *Identity, Culture and Globalization*, ed. E. Ben-Rafaeil and Y. Sterberg. Leiden: Brill, pp. 131–56.

Baykan, A. (1990). Women between Fundamentalism and Modernity, in *Theories of Modernity and Postmodernity*, ed. B.S. Turner. London: Sage, pp. 136–46.

Beck, U. (2010). *A God of One's Own: Religion's Capacity for Peace and Potential for Violence*. Cambridge: Polity Press.

Beck, U. and Grande, E. (2010). Varieties of Second Modernity: The Cosmopolitan Turn in Social and Political Theory and Research. *British Journal of Sociology*, 61(3), 409–43.

Beck, U. and Sznaider, N. (2006). Unpacking Cosmopolitanism for the Social Sciences: A Research Agenda. *British Journal of Sociology*, 57(1), 1–23.

Berger, P.L., Davie, G. and Fokas, E. (2008). *Religious America, Secular Europe? A Theme and Variations*. Aldershot: Ashgate.

Bhambra, G.K. (2007). *Rethinking Modernity: Postcolonialism and the Sociological Imagination*. London: Palgrave Macmillan.

Canclini, N.G. (1995). *Hybrid Cultures: Strategies for Entering and Leaving Modernity*. Minneapolis: University of Minnesota Press.

Carleheden, M. (2007). The Transformation of Our Conduct of Life: One Aspect of the Three Epochs of Western Modernity, in *Modernity at the Beginning of the 21st Century*, ed. V.H. Schmidt. Newcastle: Cambridge Scholars Publishing, pp. 62–88.

Dawson, A. (2007). *New Era – New Religions: Religious Transformation in Contemporary Brazil*. Aldershot: Ashgate.

Dawson, A. (2011). *Sociology of Religion*. London: SCM Press.

Dawson, A. (2013). *Santo Daime: A New World Religion*. London: Bloomsbury.

Eisenstadt, S.N. (2000). Multiple Modernities. *Deadalus*, 129(1), 1–29.

Featherstone, M. (2007). *Consumer Culture and Postmodernism*, 2nd edn. London: Sage.

Fourie, E. (2012). A Future for the Theory of Multiple Modernities: Insights from the New Modernization Theory. *Social Science Information*, 51(1), 52–69.

Gaonkar, D.P. (2001). On Alternative Modernities, in *Alternative Modernities*, ed. D.P. Gaonkar. London: Duke University Press, pp. 1–23.

Giddens, A. and Pierson, C. (1998). *Conversations with Anthony Giddens: Making Sense of Modernity*. Stanford: Stanford University Press.

Katzenstein, P.J. (2006). Multiple Modernities as Limits to Secular Europeanization? in *Religion in an Expanding Europe*, ed. T.A. Byrnes and P.J. Katzenstein. Cambridge: Cambridge University Press, pp. 1–33.

Kaya, I. (2004). *Social Theory and Later Modernities: The Turkish Experience*. Liverpool: Liverpool University Press.

Lyotard, J.-F. (1984). *The Postmodern Condition: A Report on Knowledge*. Manchester: Manchester University Press.

Mardin, S. (2006). *Religion, Society and Modernity in Turkey*. New York: Syracuse University Press.

Mignolo, W. (2000). *Local Histories/Global Designs: Coloniality, Subaltern Knowledges, and Border Thinking*. Princeton: Princeton University Press.

Ortiz, R. (1994). *Mundialização e Cultura*. São Paulo: Editora Brasiliense.

Possamai, A. and Lee, M. (2010). Religion and Spirituality in Science Fiction Narratives: A Case of Multiple Modernities? in *Religions of Modernity: Relocating the Sacred to the Self and the Digital*, ed. S. Aupers and D. Houtman. Leiden: Brill, pp. 205–18.

Rosati, M. (2012). The Turkish Laboratory: Local Modernity and the Postsecular in Turkey, in *Multiple Modernities and Postsecular Societies*, ed. M. Rosati and K. Stoeckl. Aldershot: Ashgate, pp. 61–78.

Rosati, M. and Stoeckl, K. (2012). Introduction, in *Multiple Modernities and Postsecular Societies*, ed. M. Rosati and K. Stoeckl. Aldershot: Ashgate, pp. 1–16.

Schmidt, V.H. (2006). Multiple Modernities or Varieties of Modernity? *Current Sociology*, 54(1), 77–97.

Schmidt, V.H. (2007a). In the Second Millenium: Modernity at the Beginning of the 21st Century, in *Modernity at the Beginning of the 21st Century*, ed. V.H. Schmidt. Newcastle: Cambridge Scholars Publishing, pp. 1–9.

Schmidt, V.H. (2007b). One World, One Modernity, in *Modernity at the Beginning of the 21st Century*, ed. V.H. Schmidt. Newcastle: Cambridge Scholars Publishing, pp. 205–28.

Smith, C. and Vaidyanathan, B. (2011). Multiple Modernities and Religion, in *The Oxford Handbook of Religious Diversity*, ed. C. Meister. Oxford: Oxford University Press, pp. 250–265.

Southwold, M. (1978). Buddhism and the Definition of Religion. *Man*, 13(3), 362–79.

Spohn, W. (2003). Multiple Modernity, Nationalism and Religion: A Global Perspective. *Current Sociology*, 51(3/4), 265–86.

Therborn, G. (1995). Routes to/through Modernity, in *Global Modernities*, ed. M. Featherstone, S. Lash and R. Robertson. London: Sage, pp. 124–39.

Wagner, P. (2012). *Modernity: Understanding the Present*. Cambridge: Polity Press.

Weber, M. (1949). 'Objectivity' in Social Science and Social Policy, in *Max Weber: The Methodology of the Social Sciences*, ed. E.A. Shils and H.A. Finch. New York: The Free Press, pp. 50–112.

Weber, M. (1968). *Economy and Society*. New York: Bedminster Press.
Yack, B. (1997). *The Fetishism of Modernities: Epochal Self-consciousness in Contemporary Social and Political Thought*. Notre Dame, IN: University of Notre Dame Press.

PART IV
Ethnographies of Listening to Churches: Aesthetics and Rationality

Chapter 8

Playing the Sensual Card in Churches: Studying the Aestheticization of Religion

Anne Margit Løvland and Pål Repstad

Introduction

'More adventure, less memorizing psalm verses', was the headline when the Norwegian newspaper *Fædrelandsvennen* interviewed confirmation leader Anne Bjørnholmen about new methods in confirmation work in the Church of Norway.[1] The point of departure for this chapter is a general hypothesis that dogmatic and cognitive dimensions of religion are giving way to more sensual, emotional, narrative – in short, aesthetic – aspects. The chapter will offer some examples of this trend based on empirical research in Norway, although we believe that this is a general shift in Western religion, perhaps even globally. We will also analyse possible tensions arising between sensual, artistic, symbolic and emotional expressions and moral, dogmatic and functional boundaries prevalent in the religious milieus.

Processes of aestheticization can be traced in many different religious contexts, ranging from changes in musical taste in congregations to a more narrative and less propositional style of preaching in churches. Our aim is to introduce aestheticization of religion as a general topic, substantially as well as methodologically. However, in order to add weightiness to the subject, we will briefly present some conclusions from a recent research project in Norway consisting of over 20 empirical subprojects. The project title is 'Religion as aestheticizing practice', and we use the acronym RESEP to refer to the project. Furthermore, we will present in more detail a phenomenon that we have studied together, namely the emergence of increasingly popular Christmas or Advent concerts in Norwegian churches. This case is well suited to identifying the relevant changes as well as tensions in question.

---

[1] *Fædrelandsvennen*, 7 May 2011. The Church of Norway is the Lutheran majority church in the country, with about 80 per cent of the population as members.

We also intend to discuss social factors lying behind the trend of aestheticization. Finally, if religion is changing its modes of expression, researchers may need to change their methodological approaches to religion. Interwoven in the chapter will be reflections on our attempt to combine sociology and contemporary social semiotics as tools of analysis and interpretation.

A Broad Perspective on the Aestheticization of Religion

The Concept

Although we will not go deeply into philosophical and conceptual discussions about aesthetics in this chapter, a working definition is needed. A commonsense definition often identifies the aesthetic with the beautiful, but according to Alexander Baumgarten, who introduced aesthetics as a core concept in modern philosophy, aesthetics is about sensory impact and configuration – and often, but not always, about beauty. Dramatic, shocking and repulsive experiences also belong in the realm of aesthetics. Baumgarten explicitly includes the experience of 'the ugly' in this realm (Baumgarten 1983 [1750]; see also Meyer 2009). It follows that aestheticization takes place when sensory impacts increase their significance compared to other perspectives like moral worth, spiritual edification or truth content.[2]

The Working Hypothesis

We claim that aestheticization is a general process, changing many forms of religion, both inside and outside religious institutions. This is a very rough hypothesis that needs to be modified and elaborated upon when confronted with empirical material. We do not claim that old time religion in the Western world was all about dogma and correct religious teachings, or that no feelings were involved among religious people, or that contemporary religion has lost all cognitive and dogmatic content. We are talking about a shift among the main dimensions in religion, not a complete transformation. We do not claim that the relation between aestheticization and dogmatic fervour is a zero-sum game, so that when aesthetics becomes significant, teachings and theology automatically become less important. Aesthetic, multimodal expressions can intensify dogmatic dimensions as well, sometimes even more than 'pure' verbal, cognitive

---

[2] This understanding of aestheticization is inspired by Herbert (2011).

communication. One can for instance think of liturgies, psalms and icons with a distinct and rather well-rehearsed and authoritative dogmatic content. But our claim is that in modern society narrative, sensual, symbolic and emotional – in short aesthetic dimensions – often start to live their own life, partly independent of the official and dogmatic framework. In the RESEP project we have found many examples that aestheticization implies less precise dogma and less importance of the cognitive, theological teachings in faith communities.

The Historical Background

An alliance of strange bedfellows, Pietism and Rationalism, has limited the positive evaluation of aesthetical creativity in religious life in Northern Europe, including Norway. Historically, the 'rage for order', to use Charles Taylor's (2007) expression, could emerge in Rationalist circles, denouncing religious aesthetic flourishing as primitive. But the strict Protestantism that regulated much public and private life in Northern Europe in the centuries after the Reformation has probably been the most forceful barrier against aestheticization. These sentiments, in Orthodox as well as in Pietist versions, implied an ascetic and restrictive attitude towards rich aesthetical expressions, for moral and religious reasons. Aesthetic richness could seduce you and tempt you to leave the narrow path, and it could distract you from concentrating on the necessary focus on salvation.

This focus on moral purity and dogmatic correctness did not mean that emotions and sensual impact had no place in the conversionist revival movement setting its mark on Norwegian Christianity in the nineteenth and early parts of the twentieth century. Seekers were to feel strongly about their own inadequacy, and feel quietly happy when they reached the status of being saved. Songs were always sung at revival meetings. But all the time the unfolding of emotions was expected to take place within a correct dogmatic framework. People found themselves under a double regime, a dogmatic as well as emotional one.[3] Today, the symbols have become ambiguous, narratives have replaced propositions in religious preaching, and verbal communication has diminished its importance. In short, the contemporary trend of aestheticization offers more space for subjective and personal interpretation. As Tord Gustavsen, a well-known jazz pianist very often heard in church concerts, expressed it in an interview with the national newspaper *Aftenposten*:

---

[3] For a presentation of the concept emotional regime, see Riis and Woodhead (2010).

Instrumental music gives all individuals in the audience a possibility to fill in their own histories ... Music at its best is sacred, but in a totally undogmatic way.[4]

Some Examples from Norway

Quite a lot of anecdotal evidence, as well as some more systematic projects, point in the direction that religion is becoming gradually more a matter of good feelings and sentiments, with less weight on existential agony. We also note that there seems to be less dogmatic pondering, especially when it comes to discussions between different confessions and creeds. A large research project on religious change in a religiously conservative region in southern Norway inspired RESEP's working hypothesis about the increasing importance of the sensual dimension in contemporary religion. This project, called 'God in Sørlandet', concluded that the region's Christianity is less concerned now with correct teachings and cognitive convictions, and that subjective, positive experience and appeal to the senses have become more important (Repstad 2009).

A survey among vicars in the Church of Norway in the region of Sørlandet showed clearly that the interest in art and aesthetics as an integral part of Sunday worship is on the increase (Olsen 2008). A national survey from 2008 showed that church buildings came second on a list of different types of buildings most frequently used for local cultural events, beaten only by community centres that are often called *samfunnshus*, and often owned by the municipality or voluntary organizations. And churches, indeed the oldest type of such local buildings, actually had the fastest increase in use for such purposes. While concerts are the most important type of such cultural events in churches, art exhibitions are also becoming more frequent (Aagedal 2009: 228).

Let us present some conclusions from a few of the projects in RESEP. Changes can be found even in the homes of active Christians. Hans Hodne (2008) has studied what kinds of art and decoration are to be found on the walls in conservative Christians' homes in Norway. He concludes that there has been a change from ascetic decorations, often embroidered scripture texts and mass-produced pictures of Jesus, to more varied and in a sense more ecumenical decorations. Confessionalism seems to be on the defensive. Icons showing Mother Mary would have been rejected as Catholic or Orthodox heresies two generations ago in the Norwegian Lutheran inner mission, but today such icons can be found in the homes of many of the low-church faithful. Hans Hodne (2013) has also studied the interior of several *bedehus*, that is fellowship halls owned by low-

---

[4] *Aftenposten*, 21 June 2011.

church movements in the Church of Norway as well as the interior of so-called 'free churches', Protestant minority churches outside the majority church. Hodne has found an increasing openness to professional art and decorations, even with a modern abstract style in some cases. Quite often the historical heritage is taken care of by moving old traditional pictures and embroidered scripture texts to smaller rooms, away from the main congregation hall.

Harald Olsen (2013) has studied discussions connected to the building of new church buildings in the Church of Norway over the last 30–40 years. He concludes that there has often been a tension between functional concerns and aesthetic expressions. The aesthetic norms are sometimes modernist, sometimes traditional ('A church should look like a church'). Olsen also finds that over the last 30 years, there is an increasingly prevalent view that new churches should have spectacular and professionally accepted artistic value. Sometimes such concerns collide with religious norms ('Can we depict Jesus like this?'), or with functional concerns, but there has been a definite movement away from the practical, functional and simple *arbeidskirker* (commonplace churches). Helje Sødal (2013) finds a similar trend in the Pentecostal movement in Norway, a movement described by her as going from tents to temples. Pentecostals have traditionally preferred the simple and functional; however, in recent decades, aesthetic ambitions have emerged.

Irene Trysnes (2013) has analysed changes in Christian songs for children, especially songs used in Sunday schools. Contemporary songs present a kinder and less strict and judgmental God than did many songs a couple of generations ago. Markers of difference are hardly presented any more. They were quite common in the old days, for instance between boys and girls ('I want to be like Daniel, and I want to be like Ruth'), between salvation and perdition, and between the Christian nation of Norway and the world of the heathens in Africa and elsewhere. The anthropology has also become more optimistic. References to sin have disappeared. Contemporary Christian songs for children are inclusive. Furthermore, they support self-confidence and self-realization, often underlined by an active body language accompanying the songs.

Hildegunn Schuff (2013) has studied how dancing has entered the Christian arena, in the free churches as well as in the Church of Norway. In a few decades, dancing has changed from being a controversial thing to being a very common and popular part of worship in churches. RESEP is not limited to studying organized Christian settings. One empirical study deals with how the style of Muslim dress codes among women in Oslo is negotiated in a process where norms of decency and puritanism meet aesthetic norms of being chic (Furseth 2014). Furthermore, some representations of religion outside organized religion are also analysed, such as references to religion in contemporary Norwegian fiction. We find less than before of the debating, critical, polemic approach to religion prevalent in many Norwegian novels and short stories in the twentieth century, where church and religion were criticized on moral or rationalist grounds for being repressive, hypocritical or naive. Today, many authors approach religion with fantasy, openness and fascination. They are curious, but have no dogmatic constraints. This corresponds to a similar development inside institutional Christianity. A new translation of the Bible has been on the Norwegian bestseller lists of fiction(!) for several months since 2011. The marketing of the new Bible has stressed its literary qualities, its aesthetic value and the fact that many famous Norwegian authors have offered advice in the translation process.[5]

Since RESEP covers religious expressions inside organized religion as well as in other parts of the culture, the breadth of empirical material has inspired a hypothesis that the differences between constructions of religion 'from inside' and 'from outside' are smaller than before. As we have seen, aestheticization from the inside can imply that religion becomes less defensive, apologetic and dogmatic, and more sensual, narrative and emotional, and is expressed more often by non-verbal symbols. Aestheticization from outside can imply that religion is constructed more as narratives about lived religion – more openly and less reductionist – for instance, less psychologizing. If both these tendencies manifest themselves, the representations of religion from inside and outside will converge.

There Are Still Tensions

Even if we claim that religion has generally grown softer and is presented in more varied and less propositional terms, the traditional Protestant cognitive and dogmatic approach to religion is still present in Norway and other European countries. Aestheticization can still be associated with superficiality and lack of real commitment, such as in this biting extract from Olav Egil Aune, editor of culture in the national Christian newspaper *Vårt Land*. Aune comments upon a multireligious Sacred Music Festival in the city of Drammen, under the heading 'Sacred Nonsense':

> If we reduce ourselves to an audience, the sacred loses its power ... Ritual acts without deep roots ... are probably wasted. Window shopping in others' culture is probably best left to Saga Sun Travels ... Serious and demanding issues in all

---

[5] For these trends in the Norwegian literary field, see Gulliksen and Justnes (2014).

religions are reduced to zero, to a pleasure-sick piety, a sensual intoxication for people who will not take a risk.[6]

Aune's comment may be seen as an insistence on existential seriousness, possibly with a Protestant religion of difference heritage somewhere in the background. We may also see the shadow of the Danish philosopher Søren Kierkegaard (1987 [1843]) somewhere back there, with his ironic description of the aesthetic young man, living completely in the empire of the senses as a slave to his desires, finally feeling empty and bored after seeking pleasure all the time, and being allergic to any serious commitment. The same heritage may have contributed to the initial scepticism towards dance as an art form in churches, as studied by Hildegunn Schuff (2013).

Other concerns than moral and dogmatic may also create tensions. We have already mentioned Olsen's study of contemporary church buildings in Norway. Several church fires have occurred over the last 25 years in Norway, a few of them started by more or less dedicated Satanists, others because of outdated electrical wiring. In many of these cases, lively discussions have followed: should the church be built just as the old church was, and on the same site? Or should one move the new church to a more central location and build a more functional church? Actually, the active congregation members have often been in favour of the functional alternative, while less regular churchgoers (although with a deep commitment to the church building) have supported the idea of copying the old and beautiful church.

From a sociological point of view, tensions over aestheticization can also be an issue between different professions. For instance, a more varied spectre of expressions in religious life may threaten the traditionally powerful position of the clergy. Ministers have usually been experts on the verbal dimensions of religion, and may lose influence when other dimensions come to the fore.

Studying Multimodal Religion

The study of Christmas concerts in churches is based on a combination of social semiotics and sociology of religion. Social semiotics is a theory of meaning-making in different social contexts; thus, the theory has both a textual and a social focus. Concepts from social semiotics remain more focused on texts than on the social context, and key researchers such as Theo van Leeuwen (2005: 1)

---

[6] *Vårt Land*, 16 September 2010.

recommend that the theory should be linked to other social theories. Sociology offers a theoretical basis for understanding the context of the texts being studied. While social semiotics and sociology partly overlap one another, they relate differently to their object of study. Sociology traditionally studies social contexts and focuses to a high degree on verbal texts, while social semiotics studies a broader set of modes, or forms of expression. The combination of disciplines can prove fruitful, as sociology has rather poor conceptual resources for analysing multimodal expressions, while social semiotics needs elements taken from sociology in order to describe the social contexts in which the cultural expressions are embedded.

Social semiotics, then, relates to a multimodal concept of text (Kress 2010). A central feature in the social semiotics tradition deals with how combinations of different modes or semiotic resources – verbal, auditory and visual – are used in different social contexts. In the following presentation of a qualitative study of Christmas concerts, we will discuss how this multimodal interaction can affect the meaning-making in the relevant texts, as well as how the use of multimodal data can influence the researcher's viewpoint and forms of interpretation.

Various modes have different ability to create meaning – in social semiotics often called 'the affordance of a mode'. A photograph, for example, may arouse strong emotions in a reader who has only cast a glance at it, while verbal language provides greater opportunity to construct an argument over time. Music is well-suited to immediately re-creating a mood through the cultural connotations and the memories it evokes. The emphasis of the different modes in the compound expressions and time the receiver invests in the meaning-making activity are important premises in the process of interpretation.

Christmas Concerts: An Evocative Ritual

In our study of Christmas concerts in Norwegian churches, we have come up with a typology of such concerts. *Local amateur concerts* can be found in different versions. They are an arena for displaying the richness and versatility of singers, musicians and choirs in the local community. As such they can be said to contribute to a kind of civil religion on the local level, intertwining a Christian heritage with local cultural patriotism. A similar version is the amateur congregation concert, where the artists have a connection to the congregation. In all such local concerts, a significant part of the audience consists of family and friends of the artists. Proud parents and grandparents often admire the efforts of their young children and adolescents.

Another type of concert is *the musically ambitious concert*, also called the classical music concert. These are usually organized in cathedrals and cathedral-like churches, often with a rich and resourceful musical life. Bach and Händel and other composers in the oratorium or cantata styles are often presented at such concerts.

Thirdly, we have *the commercial entertainment concerts* with popular music, often touring in December and visiting several churches. While the Christmas concerts using local musical resources have a much longer tradition in Norwegian churches, commercial concerts started in the late 1980s, and their popularity increased during the 1990s. We will return to some characteristics of these concerts.

Christmas concerts in churches have become an important part of church rituals for many Norwegians. In January 1912 we conducted a quantitative survey through TNS Gallup, giving a representative picture of participation in Christmas concerts in churches among Norwegians over 18 years old in December 1911. It turned out that 31 per cent – almost a third of the population – had attended at least one such concert before Christmas. Most of these visitors attend only one concert. Only 3 per cent of the population go to church for these concerts three times or more. The concerts presenting local amateur artists attract the largest audience, even though the commercial entertainers get more media attention. The survey shows that the popularity of these concerts seems to have stabilized over the past five years, after enjoying a period of increasing attendance.

Who goes to Christmas concerts in churches? Attendance increases with age (although we do not have data on concert-goers under 18). More women than men attend. People with a low level of education go more seldom. The commercial and local concerts seem to especially attract middle-class people, often in occupations within education and welfare. There is also an (admittedly weak) tendency that people with high academic education attend classical concerts more than average. Although regular churchgoers are over-represented in the audience at all types of Christmas concerts, they are joined by many others, as there are many more visitors to such concerts than to ordinary Sunday services (Løvland and Repstad 2013).

In December 2006 and 2007, we spent several evenings at Christmas concerts in churches in and around Kristiansand, which is a city in the southernmost part of Norway with a population well over 100,000, if you include nearby communities. We attended several concerts, as did a few of our colleagues and doctoral and master students, each equipped with a fairly detailed observation guide that we had prepared. We analysed field notes from nearly 30 Christmas concerts. Most of the concerts took place in the Church of Norway, but we also visited concerts in so-called free churches – Lutheran as well as Pentecostal.[7] The study has been followed up in recent years by our more sporadic visits to church concerts.

Christmas and Christmas celebration are phenomena affecting most Norwegians, although there is a big difference in how this holiday season is experienced and interpreted. For example, some people feel that the Christian interpretation of Jesus' birth is central to the holiday, while others emphasize the folk-cultural interpretation of the holiday, with Santa Claus as the main character of the festivities (or his Norwegian cousin the *nisse*). One can also find combinations of the two beliefs, including the child in the manger and Santa handing out gifts, or where the use of light – physically or metaphorically – can be interpreted both secularly and in a Christian manner. Celebrating Christmas may be about family and joy as well as the commercial pressure to spend money, or it can present a challenge for people to show Christian charity to others less fortunate than they are. Many people experience and interpret the Christmas celebration in many ways and declare their different interpretations in different contexts. We perhaps run around town busily going Christmas shopping before enjoying making gingerbread cookies with children and grandchildren while humming along with a Christmas hymn being sung on the TV in the background.

The aesthetic expression conveyed from a Christmas concert opens up for experiences that can be interpreted in many ways. The public often meets a startling puzzle of audio, verbal and visual elements which, to a greater extent than a traditional liturgy or sermon, allows for a complex aesthetic experience. While people encounter open symbols such as lighted candles and stars, first and foremost it is the music that brings back memories of past experiences. The situation encourages an immediate experience. The audience spends an hour or two of their pre-Christmas time at the concert, and the situation does not encourage repetition or clarification of ambiguities. It is this situation that must be in the researcher's focus. A thorough analysis of various parts of the concert, for example an isolated content analysis of the old hymn texts, is less interesting to us, since they do not have functional load in this situation.

We conclude that experience is more important than the doctrinal content. Puzzle pieces are put together to provide space for various forms of faith, including some Christian elements, although not necessarily expressing a clear

---

[7] For a more comprehensive report on this qualitative study of Christmas concerts, see Løvland and Repstad (2008). The only English publication from this study so far is Repstad (2008), dealing mainly with Christmas concerts in churches as a phenomenon helping to maintain vicarious religion (Davie 2007).

dogmatic standpoint. We have noted that many of the songs have ambiguous texts. Several of the songs contain words like light, darkness and stars, while others contain thoughts about love. In many cases the texts can be interpreted religiously, focusing on God who in his love for mankind brings light into the darkness of the world. But without a Christian frame of reference, the songs may be heard as referring to human conditions (love between man and woman, and so on). The star may be either the Star of Bethlehem or a completely ordinary star.

We have seen that most Christmas concerts try to build bridges between church and general culture. The religion of humanity card is played at almost all the concerts, in commercial as well as local amateur concerts. The concept religion of humanity is borrowed from Linda Woodhead and Paul Heelas (2000), where it is opposed to religion of difference. A religion of humanity in general connects God with human endeavour for a better world, while religion of difference stresses the distance between a strong and strict God and a sinful world in need of strict moral rules and grace from God. Woodhead and Heelas devote a great deal of attention to what they call experiential religions of difference, a type which combines subjective experience with a firm dogmatic framework. Pentecostal, charismatic religion is the main example of this type of religion, which carries with it quite a lot of potential inner tensions, as subjective experience may lead away from the dogmatic heritage. We have found some examples of experiential religion of difference in a few concerts in so-called free churches. However, the main tendency in the Christmas concerts seems to be in the direction of experiential religions of humanity, combining a friendly and liberal religion with an appeal to the senses. As we shall see, this is especially what we find when we include not only verbal texts, but also the whole range of semiotic resources in our analysis.

Old Christmas hymns and Norwegian folk songs are easily followed by local versions of Elvis' 'Blue Christmas' and songs in the American crooner tradition, like 'White Christmas' and 'Chestnuts Roasting on an Open Fire' (which is by no means intended as a discreet warning to stay on the narrow path). The aesthetic expression is influenced by the commercial Christmas culture. For many people Walt Disney is a more important supplier of Christmas spirit than the church, and during Christmas concerts the religious and commercial Christmas spirits tend to melt together, accompanied by 'When You Wish Upon a Star'.

Only a few decades ago, there were intense discussions among church people about what kind of music and lyrics could be played in churches and chapels; today, all kinds of musical styles seem to have access. To the extent that objections are raised, they seem to be more an expression of middle-class taste than one based on religious or theological limitations. So, we may expect rap and hard rock in churches when new generations with new tastes take over leading positions in churches. So far, however, they have not passed through the church doors in December. As for song lyrics, anything goes as long as it is not explicitly at odds with what may loosely be called a positive worldview. To name just one example, we have listened to merry Swedish summer love songs performed by Swedish pop singer Lill Lindfors in a Christmas concert at the cathedral in the city of Kristiansand.

Over the years, the audience as well has gained access to a broader menu of expressions. For instance, applause is now not only accepted in churches, but often actively encouraged. This is a clear liberalization compared to the situation found only a couple of decades ago, when God alone should be praised, not human endeavour. Still, a few elderly people hesitate to clap their hands in church; however, the ice is always broken when somebody under 14 is on stage, singing, playing or dancing.

Although practically all the concerts we attended communicated a soft and friendly Christianity, they are not without Christian content. Even if references to Hell and perdition are completely absent, references to God's power are not. In songs and what is said between songs, it is expressed and taken as a given that a small child in a manger has represented an important divine intervention in the history of mankind. However, the musical expression has the strongest functional load during concerts. The still popular Christmas hymns from eighteenth-century Danish Pietist poet and bishop H.A. Brorson often have lyrics expressing 'hard' dogma, containing a pessimistic anthropology and describing this world as a 'valley of tears'. However, the soft, warm and evocative packaging makes the whole setting quite harmless. The valley of tears become almost cosy in a context of harmonious music, nice people and small talk about childhood Christmas memories made by the performers between songs.

The American sociologist Randall Collins offers an understanding of how rituals can generate what he calls emotional energy. According to Collins, the starting point for rituals is that two or more people form a group identity. This need not be a close relationship, as physical proximity is enough. This group must also be delimited from other individuals or groups in some way. The group must have a common focus of attention on a common object. Such a situation can generate emotions that can be exacerbated by the fact that participants are part of a rhythmic, regular course (Collins 2004).

It is not difficult to place the Christmas concerts into such a model. The people attending a Christmas concert are gathered physically close to each other. Sometimes they also know each other because they belong to the same church or local community, but this is not a prerequisite. Moreover, while these concerts are usually open to all who wish to participate, the architectural style of the church makes it easy to define who actually participates and who does not. However, borders against non-participants are seldom thematized, so the 'we-feeling' is not created or strengthened by highlighting the distance from 'the others out there'. Such aspects are not the most salient at the Christmas concerts as ritual events. There may be talk about the positive value of the faith community as well as similarly positive talk about the local community. In addition to the collocation, the audience also has a common focus of attention. They are there to hear and see the musical programme. The concerts are also included in a rhythmic cycle following the calendar and the church year, and each concert features a number of repetitive similarities.

Arild Danielsen also makes use of this theory in his study of art and culture events describing the emotional energy that occurs as a mindset or a mood:

> Those who take part in a ritual will not only focus on the same concrete or abstract object, but also be elevated into a more or less clearly pre-defined mindset. (Danielsen 2006: 122)

Mood or mindset is a concept matching well the emotional energy we experienced at many concerts. Danielsen also writes that eventually a synchronization of attention and emotions occur among the participants. Such synchronization allows participants to experience a strengthening of their own emotions, and they thus experience an increased emotional intensity. The Christmas concerts we attended ended almost without exception with the audience standing up and singing the old hymn 'Deilig er jorden' [Beautiful Saviour] together. Although field observation does not give us access to people's thoughts and feelings, we often experienced a quiet, reverent and thoughtful mood among those leaving the church after singing.

Aestheticization: The Social Context

Social Factors behind the Process

Religious individualization and scepticism towards authorities are the order of the day in contemporary Western societies, although the individualization thesis can be overstated, as most people (at least most Norwegians) still develop their interpretation of life in a kind of critical dialogue with established religious traditions (Repstad 2002). But there is a marked movement from being dwellers in the direction of being seekers (Wuthnow 1998). Moreover, in Norway people have gone *From Quest of Truth to Being Oneself*, to quote the title of Inger Furseth's book (2006) on religious change in Norway through the last generations. The dynamics of change often become more intensive when conservative, Pietist Christians give up the old strategy of isolation and allow their children and youngsters to participate in common activities like sports, going to the cinema, local amateur music and so on (Hodne 2005). Furthermore, changes often come with generational shifts. This seems to be much more common than vocal discussions and quarrels. New generations move onto the scene and discreetly do things a bit differently than their parents, usually adopting a slightly more liberal lifestyle (Justvik 2007).

When taken together with weaker sanctions from leaders of organized Christianity, these changes add up to a situation where faith communities must compete more than ever before. Religious movements in contemporary pluralist societies have to increase their efforts to keep their members loyal and recruit newcomers. They may have to define their target groups better and adapt their message and profile to what consumers are believed to find attractive.

In some elaborations of rational choice theory, this implies that faith communities tend to cultivate their respective distinctive features and perhaps increase a common strictness to hold together the members who have invested in the milieu (Iannaccone 1994). However, it seems even more probable that the response to such competitive situations will be to avoid excluding or offending people and instead try to look as attractive as possible to people in general. The result will be a softer and friendlier religion. It follows as a reasonable hypothesis that a comparatively peaceful society characterized by a plurality of religions and worldviews will lead to an aestheticization of religious life in the sense that a greater variety of modes and semiotic resources will appear, and that the interplay between them also will become more varied, so that more senses and sensitivities are activated among people.

We are not saying that aestheticization automatically will soften religion. Indeed, there are several examples all over the world that political and religious conflicts can be polarized and escalate through aesthetical means. One's own heritage can be embellished through multimodal expressions, as well as the degradation of the Other. The critical thoughts of Walter Benjamin (2008 [1935]) about the aestheticization of politics in Germany and the emergence of Nazism in the 1930s still have relevance in many parts of the world. Even in Norway, the lone terrorist Anders Behring Breivik aestheticized his deeds by means of music and references to crusades. However, our claim is that in comparatively peaceful and liberal settings, religious aesteheticization will facilitate religious peaceful co-existence provided there is a will to engage in dialogue at the outset. As freedom of choice has become a kind of common supra-ideology in Norway and other liberal societies, there is a certain cultural and ideological pressure in the direction of finding less provocative and more inclusive representations of religion. In the verbal mode, narratives one may wonder about are probably increasingly replacing propositions demanding loyalty. Furthermore, non-verbal semiotic resources like drama, music and pictures are easier to relate to in a pluralist reality than verbal, cognitive claims. Aestheticization will probably imply a broader use of ambiguous symbols, and hence less precise expressions and a less essentialist cognitive content.

A situation is developing where there is increased contact across religious and worldview borders. Carriers of what was earlier called 'strange religions' have come closer, and turn out on the whole, despite media polarizations, to be human beings not radically different from ethnic Norwegians. Aestheticization of religion can also be seen as a way of handling plurality coming closer to home in a society espousing liberal, tolerant ideas. Gathering in common wondering in front of open symbols and narratives is easier and more comfortable than engaging in dogmatic conflicts.

Sometimes students of religion tend to become too near-sighted in the sense that they seek explanations of tendencies in the religious landscape in religion itself without broadening their perspective and seeing that these tendencies can be traced also in other social fields. Many historians and sociologists speak about a general visual turn in contemporary society, often in relation to mediatization and consumerism as important factors forming and framing how people act and think today. Such a broader perspective should not be ignored, and it is an interesting research topic in itself to study how such general tendencies are manifesting themselves in the religious field. The Danish media researcher Stig Hjarvard (2008, 2012) claims that media has become an important source of information about religion, and that information of religion becomes moulded in the media according to the demands of popular media genres, such as entertainment, adventure and drama. It is possible to see Christmas concerts in churches – as well as many activities in Christian youth work – as responses from organized religion to a demand for a more entertaining religion inspired by the construction of religion in the media. Mediatization in general and mediatization of religion encourage religion with appeal to the senses.

Different Situations Call for Different Methodological Sensitivities

The European academic study of religion has often focused on what is said and written through traditional analyses of verbal texts. In that sense, the intellectualist heritage from theologians has been continued. It is of course possible to study the aestheticizing process by analysing linguistic expressions. However, an expanded textual concept and a broader focus on multimodality allows for a more relevant scientific analysis in cases where there is an increasing affordance for aestheticization, such as we have seen in examples from the field of religion.

A new and stronger emphasis on multimodality in the analysis makes the interpreter more sensitive to aestheticizing than in a traditional approach. Where one previously would emphasize the verbal expression in the analysis of a religious gathering, social semiotics makes possible a more comprehensive interpretation of the interplay between language, images, music and the use of symbolic objects. So, generally speaking, social semiotics should inspire studies of the religious landscape more than it has done traditionally. Mediatization of religion and a general visual turn in contemporary culture call for such a widening of the repertoire of theoretical and methodological tools of interpretation. However, it is important to adapt the methods to the situation to be analysed. A Christmas concert is well suited for a broad analysis of multimodality. Others events or objects may still be fruitfully analysed with the main focus on verbal texts and cognitive content. A theological discussion is an example that springs to mind. But even a seemingly 'pure' intellectual discourse is probably not without its sensual, rhetorical and emotional dimensions – and should be studied with openness to such aspects as well – without falling into the trap of reductionism, emptying the expressions completely of rational content.

Brief Concluding Remarks

Using a wide brush, we have painted a picture of a society marked by plurality and competition, and with a less powerful leadership in religious organizations. We have claimed that this situation encourages a shift from dogmatic regulations to softer and more 'diffuse' emotions, and from verbal statements to more multimodal forms of religion.

We have used Christmas concerts as an example. One may object to this choice by saying that some of the concerts are not organized by the church; the church is only renting out the building to commercial artists and agencies not necessarily representing the message of the church. However, these concerts take place in the church buildings and with the approval of the local church, and thus contribute to the image that people in general have of the church in contemporary society. As we have seen, the dogmatic regime of such concerts is much weaker than only a few decades ago, and the space for expressive and aesthetic manoeuvring has increased considerably. While this does not mean that these concerts have been emptied of Christian references, the soft and kind aspects of Christianity are clearly dominant.

References

Aagedal, Olaf (2009). *Lokalt kulturliv i endring* [Changes in Local Cultural Life]. Bergen: Norsk kulturråd/Fagbokforlaget.

Baumgarten, Alexander (1983). *Texte zur Grundlegung der Ästhetik*. Hamburg: F. Meiner (originally published as *Aesthetica* in Latin, 1750).

Benjamin, Walter (2008). *The Work of Art in the Age of Its Technological Reproducibility and Other Writings on Media*. Cambridge, MA: Harvard University Press (original in German, 1935).

Collins, Randall (2004). *Interaction Ritual Chains*. Princeton: Princeton University Press.

Danielsen, Arild (2006). *Behaget i kulturen. En studie av kunst- og kulturpublikum* [Culture and its Comforts: A Study of Art and Culture Audiences]. Bergen: Norsk kulturråd/Fagbokforlaget.

Davie, Grace (2007). Vicarious Religion: A Methodological Challenge, in *Everyday Religion*, ed. Nancy Ammerman. New York: Oxford University Press, pp. 21–35.

Furseth, Inger (2006). *From Quest of Truth to Being Oneself*. Frankfurt am Main: Peter Lang.

Furseth, Inger (2014). Hijab street fashion og stil i Oslo [Hijab Street Fashion and Style in Oslo]. *Sosiologisk Tidsskrift*, 22(1), 5–27.

Gulliksen, Øyvind and Justnes, Årstein (eds) (2014). *Fra svar til undring. Kristendom i norske samtidstekster* [From answers to wondering. Christianity in Norwegian contemporary texts]. Oslo: Verbum Akademisk.

Herbert, David (2011). Mediatization, Religion and Aesthetics. Paper to a RESEP seminar, Kristiansand, 7 January.

Hjarvard, Stig (2008). The Mediatization of Religion. *Northern Lights*, 6(1), 9–26.

Hjarvard, Stig (2011). The Mediatization of Religion: Theorising Religion, Media and Social Change. *Culture and Religion*, 12(2), 119–35.

Hjarvard, Stig (2012). Three Forms of Mediatized Religion: Changing the Public Face of Religion, in *Mediatization and Religion: Nordic Perspectives*, ed. Stig Hjarvard and Mia Lövheim. Göteborg: Nordicom, pp. 21–44.

Hodne, Hans (2005). ' ... og lærer dem å holde alt det jeg har befalt dere ... ' Endringer i barneoppdragelse blant sørlandskristne [' ... and teaching them to obey everything I have commanded you'. Changes in Child Parenting among Christians at Sørlandet], in *Mykere kristendom. Sørlandsreligion i endring* [Softer Christianity: Changes in Sørlandet's Religion], ed. Pål Repstad and Jan-Olav Henriksen. Bergen: Fagbokforlaget, pp. 135–50.

Hodne, Hans (2008). Med troen på veggene [With Faith on the Walls], in *Gud På Sørlandet* [God in Sørlandet], ed. Anne Løvland, Pål Repstad and Elise Seip Tønnesen. Kristiansand: Portal forlag, pp. 66–7.

Hodne, Hans (2013). Lavkirkelighetens estetikk: Kunst og utsmykning i bedehus og frikirker [Low-Church Aesthetics: Art and Decoration in Prayer-Houses and Free Churches], in *Hellige hus: Arkitektur og utsmykning i religiøst liv* [Holy Houses: Architecture and Decoration in Religious Life], ed. Pål Repstad and Elise Seip Tønnessen. Oslo: Cappelen Damm Akademisk, pp. 111–31.

Iannaccone, Laurence (1994). Why Strict Churches are Strong. *American Journal of Sociology*, 99(3), 1180–211.

Justvik, Nils (2007). *Kristenfolkets forhold til idrett* [Relation to Sports among Christians]. PhD thesis. Oslo: Faculty of Theology, University of Oslo.

Kierkegaard, Søren (1987). *Either/Or*, vols 1 and 2. Princeton: Princeton University Press (original in Danish, 1843).

Kress, Gunther (2010). *Multimodality. A Social Semiotic Approach to Contemporary Communication*. London: Routledge.

Løvland, Anne and Repstad, Pål (2008). *Julekonserter* [Christmas Concerts]. Oslo: Universitetsforlaget.

Løvland, Anne and Repstad, Pål (2013). Vi takkker og jubler i tusinde tal ... Publikum på julekonserter [We Thank and Rejoice, Thousands of People ... Audiences at Christmas Concerts], in *Fra forsakelse til feelgood: Musikk, sang og dans i religiøst liv* [From Renunciation to Feelgood: Music, Song and Dance in Religious Life], ed. Pål Repstad and Irene Trysnes. Oslo: Cappelen Damm Akademisk, pp. 245–59.

Meyer, Birgit (2009). Introduction, in *Aesthetic Formations: Media, Religion and the Senses*, ed. Birgit Meyer. New York: Palgrave Macmillan, pp. 1–28.

Olsen, Harald (2008). Mot stillheten og skjønnheten: Endringer i sørlandske statskirkepresters spiritualitet [Towards Silence and Beauty: Changes in Spirituality among Vicars at Sørlandet]. *Halvårsskrift for praktisk teologi*, 25(2), 37–48.

Olsen, Harald (2013). Fra 'kaffedraler' til monumentalbygg: Estetikk og funksjonalitet i nyere norsk kirkearkitektur [From 'Coffee-House Churches' to Monumental Buildings: Aesthetics and Functionality in Recent Norwegian Church Architecture], in *Hellige hus: Arkitektur og utsmykning i religiøst liv* [Holy Houses: Architecture and Decoration in Religious Life], ed. Pål Repstad and Elise Seip Tønnessen. Oslo: Cappelen Damm Akademisk, pp. 58–92.

Repstad, Pål (2002). Has the Pendulum Swung too Far? The Construction of Religious Individualism in Today's Sociology of Religion. *Temenos*, 37–8, 181–90.

Repstad, Pål (2008). Christmas Concerts – Maintaining Vicarious Religion, in *Sosial samhörighet och religion* [Social Solidarity and Religion] Festschrift for Susan Sundback, ed. Lise Kanckos and Ralf Kauranen. Åbo: Åbo Akademi University Press, pp. 101–10.

Repstad, Pål (2009). A Softer God and a More Positive Anthropology: Changes in a Religiously Strict Region in Norway. *Religion*, 39(2), 126–31.

Riis, Ole and Woodhead, Linda (2010). *A Sociology of Religious Emotion*. Oxford: Oxford University Press.

Schuff, Hildegunn (2013). Kristi kropp i bevegelse: Endringer i dansens plass i kirken [The Body of Christ Moving: Changing in the Role of Dance in the Church], in *Fra forsakelse til feelgood. Musikk, sang og dans i religiøst liv* [From Renunciation to Feelgood: Music, Song and Dance in Religious Life], ed. Pål Repstad and Irene Trysnes. Oslo: Cappelen Damm Akademisk, pp. 81–97.

Sødal, Helje K. (2013). Telt og tempel: Forsamlingslokaler i pinsebevegelsen [Tent and Temple: Assembly Halls in the Pentecostal Movement], in *Hellige hus: Arkitektur og utsmykning i religiøst liv* [Holy Houses: Architecture and Decoration in Religious Life], ed. Pål Repstad and Elise Seip Tønnessen. Oslo: Cappelen Damm Akademisk, pp. 132–71.

Taylor, Charles (2007). *A Secular Age*. Cambridge, MA: The Belknap Press.

Trysnes, Irene (2013). Fra 'Vær forsiktig lille øye' til 'Takk, min Gud, for hele meg'. Endringer i kristne barnesanger [From 'Be Careful Little Eye' to 'Thank You, My God, For All of Me'. Changes in Christian Songs for Children], in *Fra forsakelse til feelgood: Musikk, sang og dans i religiøst liv* [From Renunciation to Feelgood: Music, Song and Dance in Religious Life], ed. Pål Repstad and Irene Trysnes. Oslo: Cappelen Damm Akademisk, pp. 41–65.

van Leeuwen, Theo (2005). *Introducing Social Semiotics*. New York: Routledge.
Woodhead, Linda and Heelas, Paul (2000). *Religion in Modern Times*. Oxford: Blackwell.
Wuthnow, Robert (1998). *After Heaven: Spirituality in America Since the 1950s*. Berkeley: University of California Press.

Chapter 9
Listening Subjects, Rationality and Modernity

Anna Strhan

On a sunny September Sunday, I arrived early before the morning service at St John's, a large conservative evangelical church in London. David,[1] the rector, was up in the large, wooden carved pulpit at the front of the church, speaking through a wireless headset microphone to test the sound system that had recently been installed. 'That's too loud', he said to the sound technician, 'a bit quieter, more conversational. Most of the time, I'll be speaking like *this*', he said, 'but sometimes, I might be a bit louder', increasing his volume as he spoke, whilst the technician adjusted the volume to achieve the required 'conversational' tone.

Studies of Protestant practices have often focused on their asceticism, the ways in which the invisible soul has been elevated above the visible body. Yet, as Fenella Cannell notes, 'Christian doctrine in fact always also has this other aspect, in which the flesh is an essential part of redemption ... [T]his ambivalence exists not just in theory, but as part of the lived practice and experience of Christians' (2006: 7). When I began fieldwork at St John's, the critique church leaders expressed of forms of Christianity they described as 'ritualistic', 'sacramentalist' or 'emotional' led me at first to interpret this culture as marked by a pronounced dematerializing impulse. Over time however, I became more sensitive to the pragmatic concerns of members of the church about their own material practices and how changes in broader cultures of embodiment and media technologies impacted on their desire to be formed as 'listening' subjects who hear God speak. David's sensitivity to the precise volume of his voice amplified by the sound system indicates this pragmatic engagement with an acoustic 'aesthetics',[2] central to the formation of conservative evangelical subjectivities.

---

[1] The names of all informants, and of the church, have been changed.
[2] I follow Birgit Meyer in my use of the term 'aesthetics' here to refer to 'our total sensorial experience of the world and to our sensuous knowledge of it' (Meyer and Verrips 2008: 21).

In this chapter, I engage with the question of what it means to 'listen' in modernity, drawing on sociological and anthropological theories of embodiment and ethnographic fieldwork at St John's. British conservative evangelicals have garnered increased public visibility in recent years due to their arguments that Christians are being marginalized and campaigns against gay marriage, abortion and the ordination of women and gay clergy, yet studies of their everyday religious lives are rare. I conducted fieldwork at St John's – a large conservative evangelical Anglican church considered by other evangelicals to be an influential representative of conservative evangelicalism – from February 2010 to August 2011.[3] Some members of this church were involved in these broader campaigns, and spoke of themselves as increasingly marginalized in British society, for example when David spoke of Britain as being increasingly shaped by an 'illiberal, intolerant, secularist fundamentalism' inhospitable to the public expression of faith. However more central to most members' self-identifications was their sense of themselves as 'distinctive' from those around them, as 'aliens and strangers in the world', and they related this to their sense of relationship with God. My analysis therefore focused on how this sense of relationship with God and related self-identification as distinctive were practically formed; central to this was their desire to become, in David's words, 'people who give ourselves to *listen* to Him'.[4]

Theorists of modernity have often argued that at least since the Enlightenment, vision has been the privileged means of knowing the world, with listening subordinated to seeing.[5] Although historians are wary of accounts that trace a generalized shift from aurality to ocularcentrism, it is now, as anthropologist Charles Hirschkind notes, 'widely recognized that the politics, ethics, and epistemologies that defined the Enlightenment project were deeply entwined with a set of assumptions regarding the relative value of the senses' (2006: 13). Whilst vision is predicated on a distance between the eye and the object of perception, listening bridges the gap between interior and exterior worlds, involving the self's 'immersion within a sound from without,

---

[3] During this time, I attended two of the three weekly Sunday services. I also participated in two weekly Bible study groups, one for students and one for more established members of the congregation, and attended other church and social events with members of the church. I conducted more formal, open-ended interviews with 32 members of the church towards the end of the fieldwork.

[4] I use the gendered 'Him', 'He', 'His', etc. when referring to God throughout, as this was how members of St John's referred to God.

[5] See, for example, discussions in Buck-Morss (1991) and Levin (1993).

an engulfment that threatens the independence and integrity that grounds the masculine spectatorial consciousness' (13).

The associations of listening with an understanding of religion that was suspect to enthusiasts of human autonomy can be seen, for example, in Ludwig Feuerbach's writing:

> If man had only eyes, hands, and the senses of taste and smell, he would have no religion, for all these senses are organs of critique and scepticism. The only sense which, losing itself in the labyrinth of the ear, strays into the spirit or spook realm of the past and future, the only fearful, mystical, and pious sense, is that of hearing. (1967: 27–8, cited in Schmidt 2000: 250)

The very phenomenology of listening, implying receptivity and passivity, presented a danger to the rational autonomy of the modern subject. Yet modernity is, as Mellor and Shilling argue (1997), 'Janus-faced' in its cultures of embodiment, characterized not only by Enlightenment ideals of rationality and a Cartesian dualism privileging mind over matter, but also by 'another modernity: that of Schopenhauer's "senseless will", Nietzsche's "will to power", Baudelaire's *flâneur*, and the reassertion of sensuality in baroque culture' (131), a sensuality in which the ear is calibrated to modes of consumption and distraction afforded by new media forms. Focusing on what it means to listen within evangelicalism therefore opens up questions about how religious modes of embodiment are shaped by broader sensory hierarchies and the modes of sociality these afford. I begin by considering the place of 'listening' in modernity, drawing on the work of Michel de Certeau and Charles Hirschkind. I then describe the means through which conservative evangelicals seek to become 'listeners', and discuss the significance of rationality within this. I conclude by suggesting that focusing on techniques of listening connects the sociology of the body to analysis of piety and, following Turner (2011: 285), allows a way of drawing the approaches opened up by the sociology of the body into the concerns of mainstream sociology.

Listening, Meaning and Modernity

In *The Practice of Everyday Life*, Michel de Certeau describes modernity as characterized by a loss of the ability to hear God's Word: the 'disenchantment' of the world was 'fundamentally a predicament of hearing, a fracturing of words and revealer, a loss of God's living voice' (Schmidt 2000: 29). De Certeau outlines a shift from what he terms a 'listening' to a 'scriptural economy', arguing that prior to the modern period, the Bible speaks: it 'is a voice, it teaches (the original sense of *documentum*), it is the advent of a "meaning" (*un "vouloir-dire"*) on the part of a God who expects the reader (in reality, the listener) to have a "desire to hear and understand" (*un "vouloir-entendre"*) on which access to truth depends' (1984: 137). The 'modern age', he argues, is 'formed by discovering little by little that this Spoken Word is no longer heard, that it has been altered by textual corruptions and the avatars of history. One can no longer hear it. "Truth" no longer depends on the attention of a receiver who assimilates himself to the great identifying message' (137). Within the listening economy, the identity of the Speaker had been certain, and 'attention was directed toward the deciphering of his statements' (138). But the authority of the institutions that guaranteed the credibility of that voice were progressively weakened in Western societies, so that 'the voice that today we consider altered or extinguished is above all that great cosmological Spoken Word that we notice no longer reaches us: it does not cross the centuries separating us from it' (137).

De Certeau argues that when people heard the Spoken Word, their identities had been established in relation to the social institutions that projected the divine voice. With that voice's disappearance, there was 'a loss of the identities that people believed they received from a spoken word. A work of mourning. Henceforth, identity depends on production, on the endless moving on (or detachment and cutting loose) that this loss makes necessary. Being is measured by doing' (137). New substitutes for the unique speaker had to be found, and modern societies worked to redefine themselves without that voice, for example, in revolutions and new nationalist identities.

The task of 'writing' in this 'scriptural' economy symbolizes a change in relationship with language and meaning. As people no longer believed their identities were received with reference to the Spoken Word, human subjectivity and society were redefined without that voice: humans sought to understand *themselves* as the authors of meaning. As language in the modern age had to be '*made* and not just *heard* and understood', there emerged a 'vast sea of progressively disseminated language, in a world without closure or anchorage' (138). The individual's place in society could no longer be assigned as a 'vocation and a placement in the order of the world', but became a 'void, which drives the subject to make himself the master of a space and to set himself up as a producer of writing' (138). This 'new writing' is formed through 'a moving on (*une marche*) that always depends on something else to provide available space for its advance' (137).

This depiction of a shift from a 'listening' to a 'scriptural' economy is, de Certeau admits, an artefact, constructed to depict a shift in modernity from divine to human agency, and a fracturing and deferral of meaning accompanying this. Taking 'writing' as symbolic of the activity of different modes of cultural production, de Certeau's account is consonant with theories positing modern and postmodern culture as characterized by the circulation of products and information taking place at ever greater speed, threatening the possibility of meaning and coherence. With the ever-faster production and circulation of the stuff of consumer capitalism, this multiplicity of objects, images and sounds produces 'many more cultural artefacts or signs ("signifiers") than people can cope with. People are bombarded with signifiers and increasingly become incapable of attaching "signifieds" or meanings to them' (Lash and Urry 1994: 3). Schmidt cites the composer R. Murray Schafer expressing anguish over this 'polluted "soundscape"' of modernity by invoking Meister Eckhart: 'Still the noise in the mind: that is the first task – then everything else will follow in time' (2000: 29).

This story of the loss of the ability to 'listen' is, as Schmidt writes, mostly, 'finally, a story of religious absence' (2000: 29). Whilst de Certeau tells this through depicting a move from a listening to a writing economy, narratives detailing a move from 'hearing' to vision as the prominent means of knowing the world likewise suggest that modernity has been marked by a move away from valuing attentive receptiveness towards an Other. Walter Benjamin explored this theme in his essay *The Storyteller* (1969) which, as Hirschkind outlines, describes storytelling as one of the principal means of transmitting wisdom from one generation to the next in pre-modern Europe, a process depending on dispositions formed through slow rhythms of artisanal labour (2006: 26). This required a 'naïve relationship to the storyteller' (Benjamin 1969: 91) and a form of passivity that would allow the story to sink into the listener's perception. Benjamin, like de Certeau, depicts a loss of the ability to listen as related to changes in the conditions of knowledge associated with a rise of 'information', a form of knowledge that is understandable in itself rather than grounded in the authority of tradition or a speaker. 'Information', in Benjamin's depiction, is a way of knowing that is rootless, which 'has the effect of undermining the forms of knowledge and practice that depended on processes of gradual sedimentation and embodiment' (Hirschkind 2006: 26–7).

Has the time of listening then passed? The contemporary appeal of different forms of evangelicalism *is* often explained in terms of a longing for an ultimately authoritative revelatory voice that speaks outside of time and anchors truth, so that the act of listening establishes a referential unity that 'stems [the] semiotic drift' arising with the fragmentation of modernity (Comaroff 2010: 29). We will see that there is still a longing for a 'holy listening' in the lives of conservative evangelicals, and that as Schmidt and Hirschkind argue, 'narratives about rupture, silence, and devocalization remain narrow and inadequate stories' (Schmidt 2000: 31).

Hirschkind's (2006) evocative ethnography of cassette listening within the Islamic Revival in Cairo demonstrates how focusing on contemporary forms of religious aurality raises questions about the nature of conventional binaries such as public/private and reason/affect. He addresses liberal modernist suspicions about Muslim listening practices and the ear's vulnerability to being affected by nonrational means, citing an American researcher's discomfort as not uncommon: "'It's scary walking past a mosque on Friday when the preacher is raging away, filling the minds of those people with wild fears about the tortures of hell, or the perversity of sex-obsessed Westerners. All of these bearded men crying and shouting 'Allah' – I'm always half-expecting them to jump up and come running after me'" (18). Hirschkind argues that such visceral discomfort indicates that 'reasonableness' is not something decided abstractly at the level of 'content', as implied in normative political conceptions of rationality, but has its own habitus: 'reason has a feel to it, a tone and volume, a social and structural architecture of reception, and particular modes of response' (18). Hirschkind describes sermon listening as a technique of attempting to shape the self according to pious Muslim virtues. This is achieved through habituated modes of affective receptivity, in which the individual learns to feel emotions appropriate to particular verses of the Quran, functioning as a means of disciplining the self. One of his informants, for example, a taxi driver, stated that through listening, 'one is reminded what Islam really entails ... See, I am not very Islamic [pointing to his cigarette], I smoke, but when I hear those things on tape, I am encouraged, steered towards correct practice' (71). Hirschkind argues that listening constructs here a 'counter-public' that 'exhibits a conceptual architecture that cuts across the modern distinctions between state and society and between public and private that are central to the public sphere as a normative institution of modern democratic politics' (107). The sermons render 'public' issues that the liberal state locates within the sphere of 'private' choice, for example, the danger of gossip, gestures in prayer, or modesty of dress, and therefore 'constitutes an obstacle to the state's attempt to secure a social domain where national citizens are free to make modern choices, as it *repoliticizes* those choices, subject them to public scrutiny' (112). Moreover the interpretive norms shaping individuals' responses to these sermons are not based solely in logics of deliberative rationality, as in some liberal understandings of a public sphere, but also in the affective, poetic and sensory power of language to move people to particular modes of being and acting (113).

Hirschkind's work offers a point of departure for considering other forms of religious listening and the understandings of public, political and ethical life these imply. Conservative evangelical cultures of listening *do* seem to imply a liberal, secular separation between 'public' and 'private' and a privileging of discursive rationality over emotions, whilst at the same time expressing a desire for coherence across all spheres of life that transcends such binaries. Thus examining the means by which conservative evangelicals listen provides insight into the affective embodiment of 'rational' sensibilities and public/private distinctions.

To analyse how conservative evangelicals seek to become listeners, 'body pedagogics' (Mellor and Shilling 2010) and 'technologies of the self' (Foucault 1988) are useful concepts. Mellor and Shilling propose that the study of body pedagogics involves 'an investigation of the central institutional *means* through which a religious culture seeks to transmit its main embodied techniques, dispositions and beliefs, the *experiences* typically associated with acquiring these attributes, and the embodied *outcomes* resulting from these processes' (2010: 28). This helps examine how religious practices, techniques and experiences have significant consequences for forming '*embodied orientations* to the self and world, characterized by a *transcendent* configuration of *immanent* social realities' (28) and enables us to analyse the directional logic towards the world formed through these means. This can be drawn together with Foucault's 'technologies of the self', developed in his later work describing practices constituted in Greco-Roman philosophy and Christian spirituality and monasticism as forms of 'care of the self'. Foucault defines 'technologies of the self' as:

> permit[ting] individuals to effect by their own means or with the help of others a certain number of operations on their own bodies and souls, thoughts, conduct, and way of being, so as to transform themselves in order to attain a certain state of happiness, purity, wisdom, perfection, or immortality ... [This] implies certain modes of training and modification of individuals, not only in the obvious sense of acquiring certain skills but also in the sense of acquiring certain attitudes. (1988: 18)

This process of subject formation is inseparable from morality, but is about more than just learning to follow moral rules: it is also to do with 'the way in which the individual establishes his relation to the rule and recognizes himself as obliged to put it into practice' (27). Examining contemporary forms of listening as religious 'technologies of the self' thus opens up how individuals experience the intersection of dominant moral codes shaping everyday practice and how their subjectivities are formed through establishing relations to these. Let us consider then how evangelicals learn to listen.

Learning to Listen

The privileging of listening at St John's is not surprising for a church that locates its identity within the Reformed tradition. Being in relationship with God is understood in terms of having heard Jesus, believing in him, and choosing to internalize and obey his words. David Morgan describes how within Protestantism, the sacred is regarded as 'information, as content-laden delivery of proper knowledge. God is in the information, the knowledge of salvation and divine intention for one's life' (2012: 177). Within the history of Protestantism, there was an emphasis on forming subjects who located their agency to believe and interpret the Word within themselves rather than in the authority of a mediating priest, creating the conditions for the emergence of the autonomous subject of the Enlightenment (Keane 2007: 219). This orientation to words and cognitive belief meant that information given through sensations and emotions was understood as 'knowledge' only after processes of categorization and filtering through the mind (Mellor and Shilling 1997: 23–4). Belief – in terms of an internal assent to propositions, mediated through *hearing*, accepting and then *knowing* Jesus as saviour – became separated from and privileged over experiences of the sacred gained through 'carnal knowing' (23).

This understanding of a relationship with God shaped by words and knowledge is still central within conservative evangelicalism. As Freddie, a curate at St John's stated, 'The life of faith is the life of the Word. "Abide in me", says Jesus, "abide in my words"'. Listening is described at St John's as *the* most important practice of the Christian life. David preached in one sermon:

> There is only one priority that counts: listening to Jesus. There is only one thing that really matters: listening to Jesus. There is one item that trumps all others on the list of things that you need to do today, tomorrow, this week, next week, next month, the month after, until the day we die. Put *this* in place as *the* priority above all others.

David stated that listening must be 'personal and public', explaining that by 'personal' he meant a programme of daily Bible reading, study and listening to audio-recordings of sermons, and by 'public' he meant listening within church services and Bible study groups.

In Sunday services, listening to the Word was positioned as central, indexed spatially through the positioning of musicians on the floor, the Bible reading given from the stage above that, and the sermon preached from the elaborately carved pulpit above that. The sacrality of the Bible was emphasized in every service, for example when David said to the congregation, before the Bible reading: 'we come now to the heart of our meeting, the reason why we're here, to hear God speak to us. It is, you might say, the high point, to hear God's Word as it is read to us and explained'. He usually asked the congregation to 'please take hold of any electronic device and switch it off so that no one is disturbed while we're listening to God's Word', reinforcing the sense that *this* is the moment people have come for, and almost everyone I interviewed described the sermon as their favourite part of the service.

The leaders aimed to encourage techniques through which individuals could become 'better' listeners. In one Sunday service, one of the curates interviewed a member of the church staff about what being a good listener involves. She gave the congregation tips from her own practice about 'how to listen well', such as finding out the passage in advance from the church website and reading it before the service, listening for 'three or four key themes' to remember later in the week and writing notes during the sermon to return to during individual 'quiet times'. During the Bible reading and sermon, the congregation follow the text in Bibles and take notes on handouts or in notebooks. Whilst other conservative and charismatic evangelical churches often use PowerPoint slides during sermons, these are not used at St John's, a conscious decision to encourage people to focus on the ministers, who – all skilled orators – scarcely look at their notes while preaching, instead making eye contact with the congregation. Thus whilst listening is discursively privileged, this is bound up with a visual aesthetics, as the congregation look up to follow the expressive faces of the male preachers, look down at the words on the page, and jot notes on handouts.

The spatial arrangement of the congregation sitting to listen also functions as a visual marker, conveying shared dispositions of 'solemnity, respect, and submission to authority' (Morgan 2012: 176). The church interior is brightly lit, with white walls and utilitarian seating, and these visual forms together emphasize the centrality of 'listening', performing in their plainness as 'sounding boards' to return the words to the hearer more effectively. Thus the 'iconicity of the text' is underlined, as Morgan describes: 'bodies are disciplined to attune the ears to the prevailing soundscape and to predispose feelings to arise as if separate from the body; and spaces host sound and allow light to lift the eyes from objects and to illuminate the spaces and plain walls that reverberate with sound' (167). Visuality and other forms of embodiment are at work, but they perform unobtrusively, 'all the better to turn words into pure content, delivered in an unadultered, immaterial form' (167).

This constructs an aesthetic boundary distinguishing 'authentic' Christianity as Word-based from other Christian traditions placing greater emphasis on ritual or emotion. David, for example, said in one sermon:

> Reformed Christianity is always challenged by Deformed Christianity ... If somebody backslides from the Christian faith, they've been in a church like this, they very, very rarely completely throw over the whole boat. Normally what happens is you go into a deformed form of Christianity that isn't so focused on a final word and a finished work. And you start saying ... 'I need something extra to give me assurance, I need a worship leader to lead me into the presence of God, or I need a priest, charismatic catholic' ... That's not to say that there aren't real, genuine, lovely Christians in those movements. But actually, a Christianity that starts to rely on the visual and the tangible, and to add to the final word and the finished work, I need something extra, a fresh word, an extra experience to assure me that I'm in the presence of God, that's deformed Christianity.

Such discourse, distinguishing 'authentic' Christianity as Word-based from other forms of Christianity that 'rely on the visual and tangible' was frequently articulated. Yet despite this, members of the church were nevertheless conscious that their formation as listeners depends on specific modes of embodiment, for example, their engagement with music.

As many members of St John's have previously attended or have friends who attend charismatic evangelical churches, they are conscious of their distinctiveness from this lifeworld, and this affects their understanding of music in church. Members of St John's describe songs as functioning pedagogically, reinforcing the main listening event as the sermon, rather than providing an opportunity to 'receive' the Holy Spirit as in charismatic churches. Rebecca, a 22-year-old graduate, said singing is 'a medium by which the Word of God can dwell in you richly'. While 'the sermon should be expositing the Word of God', the next day, 'when I wake up, what I'll be remembering in the shower is the song; so the song should be so full of the words of God that actually it's almost like helping it to dwell richly in me'. She said singing is not about the individual before God, but is 'horizontal: we sing to each other so that the word of Christ dwells in us richly ... so that it's really embedded in my thoughts'.

Through this metaphor of Christ 'dwelling' in them as they draw his words into themselves, belief and body are connected by their discursive practices and they understand their listening bodies as vessels for the divine. The metaphors of 'chewing' and 'hunger' that were frequently used – for example, in song lyrics such as: 'Speak, O Lord, as we come to you / to receive the food of your holy Word' (Getty and Townend 2005) – can be connected with this. De Certeau describes belief as knotting individuals into relations with others, functioning like sacrifice in the Durkheimian sense of establishing a society: 'by what it takes from individual self-sufficiency, it marks on what is proper to each (on the body or on goods) the existence of the other' (1985: 194). As listening to sermons is experienced as the most sacred moment in services, so this metaphor of 'eating' to describe listening can be compared with the sacrament of the Eucharist: as they 'chew' on these sacred words, their bodies are marked with the existence of the other through receiving the 'food' of the Word and this marks their social collectivity (cf. Coleman 2000: 127–8).

As Hirschkind described listening as a means of ethical self-formation, so sermons at St John's function to 'address the listener's conscience' (Keane 2007: 219). Ministers pose questions throughout the sermons, asking the congregation to consider their actions and attitudes in response to the ideals being outlined, and pose questions for them to ask each other afterwards. In one sermon, for example, Pete, one of the curates, stated that 'Our God [is] the God of heaven and earth, the one who knows all and sees all and hears all ... a God who chose to reveal himself in words. He's a God who cannot lie', and challenged the congregation 'Christian: be a man or woman of your word'. Members of the congregation then discussed at length over coffee whether they ever ended up telling 'white lies'. Through listening to such sermons, individuals learn to align their moral norms with the congregation's shared expectations and seek to fashion themselves as receptive to the words addressed to them by a God who, in Pete's words, 'knows all and sees all and hears all', a kind of transcendent panopticon (Foucault 1979). This means of governing the self is achieved through orienting attention to a temporal framework that transcends mundane urban life in the act of listening. As David stated in another sermon, 'As we come to Jesus then and sit at his feet and listen, we find salvation, light, life, wisdom, insight, eternity, peace, reconciliation'.

The church leaders suggest a variety of techniques for individuals to shape their bodies as vessels for the words they hear in addition to listening to sermons in church. These include writing out verses from the Bible reading and displaying them around the home, talking to and praying with others about the sermon, 'praying through' the Bible reading from the service later in the week, and writing out the notes taken during the sermon into a diary. Individuals are encouraged to download MP3s of sermons and play and discuss them with others in workplace or university Christian unions. During my fieldwork, the church launched an iPhone application and many subscribe to its podcast channel. Pre-dating these technologies, sermons were recorded on CDs and cassettes and individuals often had favourite sermons they listened to repeatedly. Jenny, an insurance worker, told me there was a talk on the Psalms she listened to whilst ironing that 'just hits the spot and encourages you to keep going', and said now she has an iPhone, she 'put[s] the earphones on and listen[s] to a talk in the middle of the night'.

The busy-ness of urban life means finding time to listen can feel pressured. Jenny said she would like to spend 15 minutes on 'quiet times' of prayer and listening on an average morning, but: 'It depends on how panicky I am about work, whether I can actually get my act together to realize that this is more important'. Thus although members of the church develop a *desire* to listen and sense that this *should* be their priority, this can feel an ongoing struggle. Thus David prayed for the congregation:

> Thank you our loving Lord that you know everything about us. You know how busy we've made ourselves, you know the long lists of things we think we have to do, and we pray that it would become a joy to us to listen to the Lord Jesus day by day. Please put this discipline at the centre of our beings and as we listen, please enable us ... to act on what you say.

In these words, we see an understanding of the evangelical subject as divided within himself, aware he is divided in his attention, and labouring to come closer to the ideal of the attentive, undistracted listener. Whilst listening can thus be seen as a means of directing attention to a transcendent beyond busy urban rhythms and spaces, it also introduces a tension into individuals as they become conscious that they do not necessarily always put listening as 'the priority before all others' in their lives.

The other space of 'public' listening at St John's is Bible study groups, each with around 10–15 members, meeting at church once a week. There was an informal atmosphere at meetings, which began as members arrived and chatted over supper. At 8 p.m., one of the ministers would address everyone from the stage and pray a short prayer, asking 'that we would listen as you speak to us through your Word'. Appointed group leaders would then lead the group's conversation, beginning by asking someone to open in prayer, then asking another member to read the Bible passage aloud. The style of discussions in many ways resembled academic seminars, and individuals prepared for meetings using set preparation questions. Leaders encouraged group members to focus on the text in front of them as the means of forming a disposition of attentiveness to the *words* of the text as the means of hearing God. Through their discussions, individuals learn to develop a particular temporal engagement with the text: they were asked to consider what the author of the text was trying to achieve at that particular point in history and what God was saying to them individually and as a church today through that passage. Although there has been a shift away from focusing on 'meanings' in rituals, these practices of listening to the words of the Bible read together in the group become dense with meaning as individuals learn to interpret this as the means by which God speaks to them. As one woman said to me, 'the longer you are a Christian, the more you realize how amazing it is that the Creator God has revealed himself to us in this book'. She picked up a Bible from the seat next to her and hugged it: 'it's the way God *speaks* to us, the way we get to know him'.

This listening might appear to threaten the independence of the autonomous modern subject. As David said in one sermon, 'the trouble is, listening to his Word in the Bible like this can seem so un-experiential. I mean, you're just sitting there, and ... it seems kind of just rather a passive thing'. Yet this listening is *also* interwoven with norms of autonomy and rationality.

Listening as the Practice of Rationality

The centrality of rationality at St John's was brought home to me in my first meeting with David, when he recommended I read Stark and Finke's *Acts of Faith* (2000) which, in his words, posits faith as 'entirely rational'. This emphasis on rationality meant listening was understood as a process through which the listener is able to evaluate the preacher's interpretation of the Bible and look for 'evidence' in the text of the Bible to support their views. Freddie told me that the ministers 'try and show our working [in sermons] enough to enable someone to evaluate whether they agree with what's said in the pulpit, but also to enable them to think, "I can apply that working method myself"'. As many members of St John's work in highly rationalized professions, it is not surprising that this shapes interactions in church. In the Bible study group I observed, members' professions were in law, financial services, teaching and medicine. When I asked Alistair, one of the group's leaders and himself a lawyer, why there were so many lawyers at St John's, he said he thought there was a homology between law and Protestantism, pointing out that Martin Luther had studied law before becoming a monk, and that Calvin had been a lawyer. 'So what do you think the similarities are?' I asked. 'Words', he replied, 'words, structure, analysis ... And also evidence'. He said he liked evidence, the tradition of British empiricism, and for things to be rational.

This privileging of rationality is a prominent marker of not only St John's, but also other large conservative evangelical churches, bound up with the social class background of this movement in Britain. As David said in one sermon, 'many of us are Stoics by upbringing ... stiff upper-lipped'. The formation of this culture is bound up with the male, public-school habitus of twentieth-century British evangelical leaders and the historical privileging of evangelism at public schools, leading to a privileging of reason over emotion (Ward 1997: 40), and some members of St John's linked this culture with the church's male leadership. A retired man I interviewed said he'd left his previous church because a new minister had taken the church in a direction with 'too much emphasis on the charismatic, and other social nonsense'. I asked what he meant. He replied that there used to be children allowed in throughout the service, because the mothers complained they would miss the sermon if they took them out, 'but of course, they couldn't hear it anyway, and neither could anyone else'. He said that at St John's, 'there is a tight male grip', which means that 'there is much more *discipline* in these areas'.

The intellectualized culture of listening at St John's requires high levels of literacy to participate, and this shapes how individuals characterize the church's culture. Alistair asked the Bible study group one evening how they'd describe St John's to their friends. Philip, another group leader, replied, 'We might talk about the excellent, intellectual preaching'.

'The witty illustrations', Alan, a group member added.

'The intellectual, clear rational and witty sermons', Alistair summarized. 'Anything else?'

'The smoked salmon sandwiches?' Lorna, another member, added, partly joking – she'd brought smoked salmon sandwiches to celebrate the end of term.

This emphasis St John's places on rationality is also linked with wider perceptions of evangelicalism as irrational and anti-intellectual (Noll 1994). Yet the roots of this emphasis on rational listening run deeper than this and are interrelated with a desire for a certain kind of 'public' culture. David expressed a sense of connection between rational listening and public life in a sermon in which he discussed how the church staff had read Neil Postman's *Amusing Ourselves to Death* (1985) over the summer:

> Postman's thesis was that with the arrival of television, methods of communication have changed radically. He suggests that we have entered a world – this is 1985,

remember – where instant rather than permanent, impression rather than reason, entertainment rather than serious discourse are the norm. As you read the book ... surely we have to say that Postman's thesis was right, that ... we've entered a world of soundbite and spin, where politicians appear to be elected at least in part on looks and media appeal, newscasters are employed on the basis of their ability to look good in front of the camera, and where celebrity culture has taken over from an age of carefully reasoned, sustained logic in our public discourse.

David argued that this has led to evangelical celebrity preachers whose 'teaching style is anecdotal, short on substance, light on logic, full of self-referencing stories that puff up the preacher, that do little to instruct the listener'.

David argued that as the Corinthian church St Paul was addressing had been open to 'false teaching' by being impressed by 'worldly preachers', so Christians today are also 'wide open to false teaching' because of the cult of the 'celebrity preacher'. He described 'authentic Christian ministry' as characterized by 'failure', 'weakness' and 'frailty', and said:

> It's never nice to look around at other ministries, but Paul does ... Some of you will have come across, for example, Joel Osteen, *Your Best Life Now*, that has sold millions of copies around the world. Or here in London, Hillsong. There's no doubt that their message is different to the authentic message of the New Testament. You will not hear cross-shaped living: 'if any man would come after me, let him ... deny self'. You will hear: 'your best life now'. But because this is presented in a style that is so deeply attractive and deliberately apes the celebrity culture of our age, hundreds, thousands of people have been taken in by it.

David's idealization of a rational public culture does not, however, straightforwardly reflect a 'modern' norm of autonomy. It is bound up in a conviction in *both* God's authoritative speaking in scripture *and* people's ability to use reason as they listen to discern 'authentic' Christian teaching.

Postman's book idealizes nineteenth-century public culture in the United States, in which audiences had the capacity to concentrate on political speeches lasting a couple of hours. David's desire for 'reasoned' public listening and discourse similarly expresses dissatisfaction with the perceived triviality of contemporary public discourse and suggests a desire for forms of 'rational' public debate on 'non-trivial' issues in which religious voices resonate. In a sermon on secularism, David described the British public sphere as shaped by 'secularist fundamentalists' who 'ban[ned] from the public sphere the possibility of discussing and openly criticizing and weighing and condemning the relative value and truth claims and moral values as to what is good and bad in the different religions and no religion'.

David's words, like Postman's, describe individuals' modes of listening as themselves affected by broader cultural shifts and new technologies. When I interviewed Mark, the church's head of media, he said it was important to be aware of how the media affects people's ability to listen. He said the church needs 'to reverse the trend of short attention spans. We need to educate people to listen, because the Christian message is a coherent message ... The Bible – particularly the letters of Paul – is full of arguments, and you've got to learn to be able to follow an argument, and to *think*, and that is increasingly countercultural ... [T]he core business of what we're doing is getting people to *listen* very carefully'. He gave me a paper he'd written for church leaders addressing how modern media 'affect our culture and particularly how they impact/should shape our preaching'. He wrote:

> Ease and speed of communication means recipients are potentially bombarded at all times of day and night by incoming information, mostly trivial. In the absence of sufficient self-discipline, recipients are easily and frequently distracted by incoming data ... The tendency towards shorter attention spans, caused by the 24/7 bombardment, undermines people's capacity to think critically and coherently and to follow reasoned argument.

Mark argued that whilst new media should be used to 'maximize scale of distribution through social networking sites etc.', the church should help train attentiveness:

> If people have difficulty concentrating during a sermon, they need to *develop* the discipline and faculty of listening. Talk outlines (and notetaking) can help, but the sermon should still be able to function without these aids ... If people cannot concentrate on a sermon, how will they be able to concentrate on reading the Bible for themselves? It is important to *develop* these skills rather than find a substitute genre ... It is the duty of the Church to encourage concentration and the appreciation of sustained argument, so that believers can benefit from sermons and personal Bible study. Just as the Reformation caused a huge growth in literacy in the past in the places they touched ... so too today's Church needs to counteract the short attention spans of the Internet age and foster an abiding appreciation of the written and spoken word of God.

Some individuals at St John's were however critical of this privileging of rationality. Hannah, who'd been at St John's for over 20 years, expressed a sense that through her time there, she had lost an emotional intimacy in her relationship with God. She said, 'I think sometimes we are *too* rational, and not emotional enough ... I wouldn't ever want to take away from the rational side of [St John's], but sometimes I think we perhaps don't allow ourselves to love God enough', and John, who'd previously attended a charismatic church said he found services at St John's 'quite dry ... it's all stand up, sit down, hands in pockets'. In Bible study groups, individuals sometimes opened meetings by praying that the study 'would not just be intellectual, but Lord, that you would change our hearts and lives by your Word'. Thus despite the focus on rationality, individuals *desire* an experience of God that is both intellectual/rational *and* emotional/intimate.

A complex picture of evangelical subjectivity emerges from these practices of internalizing sacred language, rational listening, and desire for intimate relationship with God. Although this emphasis on reason might appear in line with modern autonomy, this is bound together with the impulse to 'deny the self' in attending to God as other. Members of St John's form themselves as listeners through techniques of making the Bible's words their own. Although this is presented in terms of a self-discipline, this is bound up with the ideal of subjection to the Word whom members of the church hold, as one of the ministers, described, as 'total wisdom and total authority', anchoring meaning and identity. Although human agency is implied in the valuing of rationality, this is held together with a critique of autonomy, for example when David said that 'what stops people accepting God is that they don't want to submit to Him. When it comes down to it, they don't want someone else deciding how they should live, their autonomy is too important to them ... This is what we call sin'.

Members of St John's are therefore 'un-modern' in the sense of being marked by their relation to the spoken Word they strive to heed. Although there is a sense of individual agency implied in their work to form themselves as listeners, this listening also reveals a desire to direct attention towards something that transcends the self, whose address, asking for their response, simultaneously individuates them. Jonathan, a young graduate I interviewed, criticized charismatic evangelical songs because they 'make the focus the individual much more than God and who *He* is, what He's done for us, who we are in the light of Him'. The body pedagogic means of incorporation into the church is thus both a form of communion with others whilst also sowing the 'seeds of individualism' as their individual bodies become vessels of redemption through receiving and internalizing Jesus's words (Mellor and Shilling 2010: 32). This creates a sense of separation from those outside the church and connection with others in the church, whilst indexing the inter- and intrasubjectivity of the evangelical in relation to God, who is felt as both Other and experienced within the self, shaping a notion of agency in which the Christian is always understood as participating in what transcends any notion of self. As Robert Orsi describes religions as practices of 'concretizing the order of the universe, the nature of human life and its destiny, and the various dimensions and possibilities of human interiority itself' (2005: 73), so the concerns articulated at St John's about the agency of God, objects, society and themselves in relation to listening can be seen as a means of expressing irreducible interconnections between self and other, agency and subjection, and experiences of power and powerlessness, drawing into question modern ideas of self-sufficiency.

Conclusion

Bryan Turner argues that American fundamentalism can be seen as 'a sustained struggle against the expressive revolution, a struggle between two conceptions of the self – the Kantian ascetic and disciplined self, and the expressive-affective mobile self. The first is the direct descendent of Protestant asceticism and the second is a distortion of the expressive self of the conversionist sects of the eighteenth and nineteenth centuries' (2011: 81). The culture of listening at St John's discursively privileges the ascetic, disciplined self, but this is held together with expressive-affective dispositions, as individuals seek to have their 'hearts and lives' changed by their listening. This aesthetics of listening functions to construct a boundary of separation from 'others' who do not hear God or who place emphasis on other means of connecting with the divine, most prominently, charismatic evangelicals, shaping a distinctive institutional identity for St John's in comparison with other evangelical churches people might choose in London.

The idealization of 'public' listening David articulates on one level corresponds with norms of rationality in broader understandings of a modern 'public sphere' (Habermas 1989).[6] Yet, on another level, it might *also* to a certain extent be conceptualized in terms of a 'counterpublic', cutting across public/private distinctions. Hirschkind argues that the temporal frame of the Islamic *umma* mediated through listening to sermons encourages not only towards

---

[6] Space here precludes discussion of the historical interrelations of evangelical Christianity and the norms of a public sphere, themes extensively debated in relation to the formative era of American politics and religion (see Hatch 1989; Butler 1990; Porterfield 2012).

ethical self-formation but also critique of contemporary politics and calls for moral renewal in Egypt (118). At St John's, listening mediates a temporal frame orientated towards a past history of Christianity and towards future promises expressed in biblical narratives. This likewise encourages individuals to examine their own practices *and* broader moral and political norms in the light of these, shaping, for example, their critique of a broader culture of individualism. However, in contrast with the Islamic traditions Hirschkind describes, members of the church's willingness to express such critiques 'publicly' outside the church is inhibited by British middle-class norms of privacy and reserve (cf. Strhan 2013).

Whilst this 'public' listening shapes members of the church's orientations towards their own moral formation and wider public life, this 'counterpublic' does not undercut notions of public and private to the extent Hirschkind outlines in Egypt. Furthermore, whilst Hirschkind's informants were 'critical of rationalist, academic approaches … [that] succeeded in neither grabbing the attention of an audience nor stirring the pious passions' (2001: 630), at St John's, 'reason' is understood as a virtuous means of relating to God. Yet although rationality is discursively privileged above emotion at St John's in a way that is distinctive from Hirschkind's informants' listening, individuals seek likewise to form themselves and all their everyday practices in obedience to a Spoken Word, orienting themselves towards a transcendent beyond the fragmentation of the city.

Turner argues that the study of piety enables insights from the emerging sociology of the body to be brought into mainstream sociology. Piety, he argues, is about constructing

> definite and distinctive lifestyles involving new religious tastes and preferences. In short, piety or the pietisation of the everyday world, has these … characteristics of combining new elements to create a religious habitus that stands in competition with other possible combinations in a competitive religious context. These new combinations are then defined as the orthodox standard by which the worth of a good Christian or a good Muslim or a good Jew could be measured. (2011: 285)

Evangelical listening practices offer one means of exploring the 'pietisation of everyday life', opening up questions about the interrelations between subjectivity, agency and rationality in modern urban contexts. This focus reveals how conservative evangelicals' soundscapes are fragmented by sounds, voices and other modes of practice that affect their longing for a holy listening, whilst simultaneously leading individuals to work to form themselves as more attentive, binding them in their sense of connection with each other and separation from 'secular' and other religious 'others'. Exploring listening as a technique of the self therefore allows analysis of the practical means by which a religious culture introduces temporal and moral orientations that rub against the grain of broader norms of self-determination and encourages the development of particular virtues and the lived effects of these tensions, providing resources for investigating the complex textures of moral and religious landscapes individuals negotiate in everyday life.

Acknowledgements

I am very grateful to all members of 'St John's' who participated in my study. This research was made possible through funding from a University of Kent doctoral studentship and from a Leverhulme Trust Early Career Fellowship. I would like to thank Gordon Lynch, Chris Shilling, Simon Coleman, Linda Woodhead and Jeremy Carrette for comments on an earlier version of this chapter.

References

Benjamin, W. (1969). *Illuminations*, ed. Hannah Arendt, trans. Harry Zohn. New York: Schocken Books.
Buck-Morss, S. (1991). *The Dialectics of Seeing*. Cambridge, MA: MIT Press.
Butler, J. (1990). *Awash in a Sea of Faith: Christianizing the American People*. Cambridge, MA: Harvard University Press.
Cannell, F. (2006). Introduction: The Anthropology of Christianity, in *The Anthropology of Christianity*, ed. F. Cannell. Durham, NC: Duke University Press, pp. 1–50.
Coleman, S. (2000). *The Globalisation of Charismatic Christianity: Spreading the Gospel of Prosperity*. Cambridge: Cambridge University Press.
Comaroff, J. (2010). The Politics of Conviction: Faith on the Neo-Liberal Frontier, in *Contemporary Religiosities: Emergent Socialities and the Post-Nation-State*, ed. B. Kapferer, K. Telle and A. Eriksen. New York: Berghahn, pp. 17–38.
De Certeau, M. (1984). *The Practice of Everyday Life*. Berkeley: University of California Press.
De Certeau, M. (1985). What We Do When We Believe, in *On Signs*, ed. Marshall Bronsky. Oxford: Basil Blackwell, pp. 192–202.

Feuerbach, L. (1967). *Lectures on the Essence of Religion*, trans. Ralph Manheim. New York: Harper & Row.

Foucault, M. (1979). *Discipline and Punish: The Birth of the Prison*, trans. Alan Sheridan. New York: Vintage Books.

Foucault, M. (1988). Technologies of the Self, in *Technologies of the Self: A Seminar with Michel Foucault*, ed. L.H. Martin, H. Gutman and P.H. Hutton. Amherst: University of Massachusetts Press, pp. 16–49.

Getty, K. and Townend, S. (2005). Speak, O Lord. *Thank You Music: Hymn Collection* [Online]. Available at http://gettymusic.com/hymns-speakolord.aspx [accessed: 17 August 2012].

Habermas, J. (1989). *The Structural Transformation of the Public Sphere: An Inquiry into a Category of Bourgeois Society*, trans. T. Burger. Cambridge: Polity Press.

Hatch, N. (1989). *The Democratization of American Christianity*. New Haven: Yale University Press.

Hirschkind, C. (2001). The Ethics of Listening: Cassette-Sermon Audition in Contemporary Egypt. *American Ethnologist*, 28(3), 623–49.

Hirschkind, C. (2006). *The Ethical Soundscape: Cassette Sermons and Islamic Counterpublics*. New York: Columbia University Press.

Keane, W. (2007). *Christian Moderns: Freedom and Fetish in the Mission Encounter*. Berkeley: University of California Press.

Lash, S. and Urry, J. (1994). *Economies of Signs and Space*. London: Sage.

Levin, D.M. (ed.) (1993). *Modernity and the Hegemony of Vision*. Berkeley: University of California Press.

Mellor, P.A. and Shilling, C. (1997). *Re-forming the Body: Religion, Community and Modernity*. London: Sage.

Mellor, P.A. and Shilling, C. (2010). Body Pedagogics and the Religious Habitus: A New Direction for the Sociological Study of Religion. *Religion*, 40, 27–38.

Meyer, B. and Verrips, J. (2008). Aesthetics, in *Key Words in Religion, Media and Culture*, ed. D. Morgan. New York: Routledge, pp. 20–30.

Morgan, D. (2012). *The Embodied Eye: Religious Visual Culture and the Social Life of Feeling*. Berkeley and Los Angeles: University of California Press.

Noll, M. (1994). *The Scandal of the Evangelical Mind*. Michigan: William B. Eerdmans.

Orsi, R. (2005). *Between Heaven and Earth: The Religious Worlds People Make and the Scholars who Study Them*. Princeton: Princeton University Press.

Porterfield, A. (2012). *Conceived in Doubt: Religion and Politics in the New American Nation*. Chicago: University of Chicago Press.

Postman, N. (1985). *Amusing Ourselves to Death*. London: Methuen.
Schmidt L.E. (2000). *Hearing Things: Religion, Illusion and the American Enlightenment*. Cambridge, MA: Harvard University Press.
Stark, R. and Finke, R. (2000). *Acts of Faith: Exploring the Human Side of Religion*. Berkeley: University of California Press.
Strhan, A. (2013). The Metropolis and Evangelical Life: Coherence and Fragmentation in the 'Lost City of London'. *Religion*, 43, 331–52.
Turner, B.S. (2011). *Religion and Modern Society: Citizenship, Secularisation and the State*. Cambridge: Cambridge University Press.
Ward, P. (1997). *Growing Up Evangelical: Youthwork and the Making of a Subculture*. London: SPCK.

PART V
Power, Gender and Discourse

Chapter 10
Critical Discourse Analysis and Critical Sociology of Religion[1]

Titus Hjelm

If recent English-language textbooks are the measure, *critical* sociology of religion does not currently exist (see Aldridge 2007; Davie 2007; Furseth and Repstad 2006; Hamilton 2001; McGuire 2002; Possamai 2009; Roberts and Yamane 2011; cf. Lundskow 2008; Goldstein 2006). There is critical and emancipatory work on religion vis-à-vis ethnicity, gender and sexuality – very much less on religion and class – of course, but this does not constitute anything resembling a coherent critical approach. One reason for this, I think, is that looking at paradigmatic textbook wisdom, 'living' sociology of religion seems to descend almost exclusively from Durkheim and Weber. Sociology's third foundational figure, Marx, is often glossed over by trotting out his 150-year-old critique of religion as 'the opium of the people', reducing critique to an historical curiosity. This 'reductionist or illusionist tradition' does not seem to have room alongside the 'great comparative sociologists', Durkheim and Weber (Collins 2007: 20–23). Unfortunately, this attitude also reflects much recent scholarship.

In this chapter I want to suggest critical discourse analysis (CDA) as a framework for a critical agenda in the sociology of religion. By combining discourse theory and critical, Marxist theory – both underrepresented in current sociology of religion – CDA provides an approach to examining the legitimacy of religion and religions, and the ways in which religion contributes to the construction, reproduction and transformation of inequality.

---

[1] A different version of this chapter was published originally in *Critical Sociology* (published online 4 March 2013, DOI: 10.1177/0896920513477664). Used with permission.

Critical Sociology of Religion and the Importance of Discourse

The starting point for a critical sociology of religion that takes discourse seriously is in two relatively recent developments in the modern world. First, although yet insufficiently studied, there are indications that the much-discussed global resurgence of religion is connected with the likewise global expansion of deregulated capitalist markets. So far research has been mostly interested in the individualising aspects of consumer societies and the consequent interest in 'spirituality' (as opposed to more institutionalised 'religion', e.g. Heelas and Woodhead 2005). But there are other ways of looking at the relationship in the context of the twenty-first century: on the one hand, globalisation and deregulation threaten tradition in general and religion in particular, which creates religious opposition movements such as the Taliban and American conservative evangelicalism, to name two of the most visible examples. On the other hand, increasing global inequalities can be seen to create a 'market' for religions that provide a 'promise of salvation' (Riesebrodt 2010) for the global underclass, in a similar (if not the same) sense as Marx envisioned when talking about the 'sigh of the oppressed creature' (Marx 1844: 175; see McLellan 1987). Despite a period when social class fell out of fashion in the social sciences, ever more obvious and increasing inequalities in the developed countries reproduce these developments on the regional, national and local levels. If ever there was a time for a critical, engaged sociology of religion, this would be it. Yet, the paradigmatic discussions (as represented by textbook knowledge) still revolve around the question of disappearance versus resurgence of religion, with little or no attention paid to religious inequality and religions' role in reproducing and transforming inequality. In the last section of the chapter, I will discuss three ways in which a critical discourse analytical approach could address this imbalance. As is clear from the above, my justification for a critical sociology of religion is a pragmatic – there are significant gaps in research – rather than a methodological one. The debate around positivist and normative sociology of religion is well covered by Goldstein (2006), for example.

The second development, the 'mediatization' of culture – the process through which our everyday knowledge becomes increasingly mediated by forms of mass communication – is a ubiquitous aspect of modern societies. Writing in 1990, John B. Thompson, who coined the term, was prescient in his analysis (Thompson 1990). While in 1990 the media explosion was already apparent, Thompson's (and others') main concern at the time was the one-sidedness of media communication. Unlike the face-to-face situation, a response to a newspaper article only rarely becomes public. In the twenty-first century, however, previously unforeseen forms of mediated social interaction have emerged: blogs and social media abound with commentary of news from around the world, for example. Words and symbols have ceased to be the exclusive property of elites. Even if Internet access is not equal globally, the '21st-century citizen will work in media-, text-, and symbol-saturated environments. For the unemployed, underemployed, and employed alike, a great deal of service and information-based work, consumption, and leisure depends on their capacities to construct, control, and manipulate texts and symbols' (Luke 1995–6: 5–6). It is therefore not an exaggeration to say that we live in an age of discourse.

The above provides a backdrop or a *Zeitdiagnose* – a 'diagnosis of our time' (Hjelm 2009; Mannheim 1944) – of the context in which sociology of religion finds itself in the twenty-first century. Against this backdrop it seems that (1) there is a distinct lacuna in the field regarding critical (Marxist) approaches to religion in the modern world that take issues of domination and inequality seriously, and (2) that it is premature to claim – somewhat fashionably – that the study of discourse is outdated. There have been calls for abandoning the study of discourse in favour of the study of practice. While I agree that ritual and non-propositional forms of practice are central to understanding religion, text and practice are not incompatible: studying discourse is not only about studying what things *mean* to people, but what people *do* when they talk about things. A discursive approach does not, therefore, contrast saying and doing; both are included. In other words, discourse analysis in the sociology of religion means looking at the ways in which religion, spirituality, belief, etc. are constructed in discourse.

This is not exactly a novel idea in some respects. James A. Beckford, perhaps most explicitly, has talked about his approach to sociology of religion as 'social constructionist' (Beckford 2003). Approaches that explicitly employ discourse analysis are, however, far and few between. Although this might sound odd to people familiar with the work of, for example, von Stuckrad (2003, 2010), Brown (2009) or Wuthnow (2011), I would like to make a distinction between *discursive* and *discourse analytical* approaches in the sociology of religion. In my proposed terminology, *discursive* approaches include what Moberg (2013) calls first- and second-level approaches that discuss meta-theoretical and theoretical issues, but provide little practical advice on doing analysis – the approach that all of the above-mentioned *discursive* studies take. *Discourse analytical* approaches focus instead on 'conducting *actual discourse analyses*' using empirical materials (Moberg 2013, emphasis in the original). As I will show below (and as Moberg notes) even 'practical' discourse analysis always includes substantial epistemological and theoretical thinking, so the boundaries are blurred. I do, however, think that the above distinction is useful in mapping previous and future approaches to discourse analysis in the sociology of religion.

The focus of a *critical* approach is to examine the role of religion in creating and sustaining inequalities. Although Marx's analysis of nineteenth-century social transformations cannot be applied mechanistically to the twenty-first century, the Marxist focus on economic power and inequality is central to CDA, both in terms of analysing discourses of class and the impact of class on discourse in capitalist society. This focus on class and the close interaction of discourse, power and material conditions shares some concerns with Goldstein's (2006) worthwhile attempt at a neo-Marxist 'new paradigm' of critical sociology of religion (see also McCloud 2007). It has, however, little to do with the 'critical theory of religion' inspired by the Frankfurt School that is at the heart of this 'new paradigm'.

In many ways my project is restitutive rather than revolutionary in tone (despite the obvious irony!). I think that the purpose of a genuinely critical sociology of religion is not to be in awe of, say, the effects of consumerism on religion – putatively leading to a whole new understanding of religion (and sociology of religion) – but to go 'back to the basics' and critically analyse how these effects perpetuate or potentially transform inequality. Also, a 'critical agenda' does not mean abandoning the secularisation thesis in favour of a 'post-secular' approach (Davie 2007), but instead encourages the examination of how constructions of secularity and 'post-secularity' affect the social position of individuals, communities and religious traditions. CDA provides an excellent tool for this kind of analysis.

Because of the scarcity of studies employing CDA (for an excellent overview, see Moberg 2013), my approach is suggestive rather than evaluative, that is, the focus is on how CDA could be used, rather than how it has been used. The chapter is divided into four main sections: firstly, I will discuss the concept of discourse and its different meanings. Secondly, I will discuss what being 'critical' means in the context of discourse analysis. Thirdly, I will explore the embeddedness of discourse and how that makes CDA different from other discursive approaches. Finally, I will discuss themes in critical sociology of religion where CDA can provide a powerful tool for analysis and theorisation.

Understanding Discourse

There are as many definitions of 'discourse' as there are of 'religion', ranging from the historical 'act of conversation' to postmodern theorisations about ontology. In one of the few analytical reviews of the use of 'discourse' in the study of religion, Engler (2006) makes a distinction between cultural studies and linguistic approaches to discourse. In Engler's schema (echoed by Moberg 2013) cultural studies approaches focus on how 'discourse shapes or constitutes the subject, in opposition to the view that language is simply a tool used by autonomous subjects' (2006: 517). Engler uses McCutcheon's (2003) discussion on 'Sui Generis religion' as a prime example of a Foucault-inspired cultural studies approach in the study of religion. Linguistic approaches in turn – with considerably less impact on the field – focus instead on empirical study of texts both on micro and macro levels (Engler 2006).

The aim of CDA is to bridge these two approaches. Norman Fairclough, the main proponent of CDA (whom I will draw upon most in my own discussion), combines Foucault's ideas with what is referred to as 'functional linguistics', creating a powerful tool for the close analysis of texts (Fairclough 1992). The theoretical underpinnings and methodological implications of CDA are crystallised in two properties that discourse is said to have: it is both *constitutive* and *functional*.

Discourse is *constitutive*, because it does not simply reflect or represent things 'out there', but 'constructs' or 'constitutes' them (Fairclough 1992: 3). According to Fairclough (1992), the three things that are constituted in discourse are (1) social identities or 'subject positions'; (2) social relationships; and (3) systems of knowledge and belief. These, of course, are continuously overlapping, but the distinction provides a useful analytical focus. In the sociology of religion, the 'cult controversies' provide a good example of the constitutive nature of discourse: how can it be that the same religious beliefs and practices are to some the way to salvation and to others deviant, harmful and evil? The answer is in the different discourses that the adherents, on the one hand, and the anti-cult movement, on the other, employ. It is not that either side is consciously telling lies (although sometimes that happens as well), but rather that 'while people may tell the truth, and nothing but the truth, it is impossible for anyone to tell the *whole* truth. Everyone (more or less consciously) selects what is to be included or excluded from their picture of reality according to a number of criteria – one criterion being what is relevant to their interests' (Barker 2011: 200, emphasis in original). Although not explicitly using a discourse analytical framework, the sociology of new religious movements has been a forerunner in analysing religion (in this case 'cults') as a discursive construction (e.g. Beckford 1985; Richardson 1997).

Discourse has a second characteristic closely connected to Barker's observation about the interests of social actors. In addition to being constitutive, discourse is also *functional* (Fairclough 1992; Potter and Wetherell 1987: 32–3). It is important to note that this use of the term *function* does not refer to *functionalist* ideas about society – ideas which in many ways inspired constructionist critiques, which in turn have been an inspiration for discourse analysis (see Hjelm 2014). Instead, discourse is seen as a form of social *practice*, contributing both to the reproduction of society and to social change (Fairclough 1992; Potter 1996: 105). Edwards and Potter (1992) talk about the 'action orientation' of discourse, that is, how things are *done* with discourse – closely echoing the perhaps better known idea of 'performativity' as discussed by Butler (1990) and others. Again, the discourse of the anti-cult movement is thick with not only constructions of cults, but also descriptions of the ways cult members can be 'cured' and practical policy recommendations on how the influence of cults can be prevented. This 'cult discourse' both constructs cults as a social problem and also offers practical avenues of action to dealing with the problem (see Hjelm 2011a).

Being Critical

As mentioned above, Foucault and functional linguistics are two important sources of CDA. The third is Marx, or rather ideas developed by prominent Marxists such as Antonio Gramsci and Louis Althusser (although the latter features less in Fairclough's later work; Fairclough 1989, 1992, 2003; Fairclough and Graham 2010). Drawing from this critical tradition of social science, CDA focuses on 'the dynamics of power, knowledge, and ideology that surround discursive processes' (Phillips and Hardy 2002: 20). The key terms for CDA are *ideology* and *hegemony*.

In everyday talk *ideology* is often understood as something akin to a worldview and has sometimes been explicitly contrasted with religion. John B. Thompson summarises this 'grand narrative of cultural transformation' that has its sources in Marx and Weber: 'The decline of religion and magic prepared the ground for the emergence of secular belief systems or "ideologies", which serve to mobilise political action without reference to other-worldly values or beings' (Thompson 1990: 77). While this sense of 'ideology' is rooted in the history of the concept, CDA uses it in a different sense. The critical conception of ideology can be concisely defined as 'meaning in the service of power' (Thompson 1990: 8; cf. Beckford 1983). Speaking in the plural, Fairclough defines ideologies as 'constructions of reality (the physical world, social relations, social identities), which are built into various dimensions of the forms/meanings of discursive practices, and which contribute to the production, reproduction or transformation of relations of domination' (Fairclough 1992: 87).

The contemporary discursive conception of ideology sees power as increasingly exercised through the use of persuasive language instead of coercion. When 'proper' ways of thinking about and doing things give a one-sided account that ignores the variety of practices, discourse is said to function ideologically (Chouliaraki and Fairclough 1999: 26). For example, when the characteristics of a group of people are represented as derivable from their ethnic or religious background (e.g. 'Muslim terrorists'), the discourse 'irons out' the variety of beliefs, practices and ways of thinking in the group. Although the historical use of the term has broader connotations (Gramsci 1971; Bocock 1986), in the CDA context *hegemony* ('hegemonic discourse') denotes the peak of ideology, the point when all alternative constructions are suppressed in favour of one dominating view.

The methodological implications of the critical conception of ideology are twofold: first, the focus is on how different aspects (e.g. grammar, rhetoric) of language use contribute to one-sided constructions of things or events that serve the interests of particular social groups. This is 'meaning in the service of power' in action. Furthermore, it is equally important for CDA to study what is *not* said, that is, what we take for granted. According to Fairclough, any reference to 'common sense' is 'substantially, though not entirely, *ideological*' (Fairclough 1989: 84, emphasis in original). Because common sense *naturalises* our conceptions of everyday life, it is the most effective way of sustaining hegemony, that is, an exclusive interpretation of reality. The aim of CDA is to 'unmask' the ways in which power imbalances are sustained through discourse – indeed, getting rid of 'false consciousness' (Fairclough 1995: 17) – by drawing attention to the suppression of alternative constructions of the world. Put this way, the unmasking function of CDA could be characterised as a theory of alienation with a constructionist twist (Berger 1973: 92, see below).

Being 'critical' implies a normative stance. CDA aims at the transformation of social practice: 'CDA is unabashedly normative: any critique by definition presupposes an applied ethics' (van Dijk 1993: 253). Normativity is, however, understood in different ways within CDA. For Fairclough, unmasking reified constructions of social reality and drawing attention to inequality are certainly at the heart of a critical approach, but CDA 'must not go beyond providing a resource for people to use in making their own decisions – it must scrupulously avoid setting out blueprints for emancipatory practice' (Fairclough 1995: 218). From this perspective, Fairclough and other critical discourse analysts might in practice be critical of the prevailing system of capitalist hegemony, but this does not mean that CDA as such can provide the signposts for change – revolutionary or otherwise: 'CDA can contribute to the social imaginary, to the stock of feasible Utopias which can inform choices which people make individually and collectively, but the choices must be made by the people concerned and affected on the own behalf' (Fairclough 1995: 232). Considering the social power of academics, this seems like an obvious thing: our social impact is largely defined by the reach and effectiveness of our discourse. However, this can also imply a disinterested stance towards practical politics. Not surprisingly, other critical discourse analysts take a firmer stand on things. Richardson (2007: 43), for example, argues that analysis is truly critical only when it is subjected to ethical and political critique, 'challenging the features that contribute to the perpetuation of structural inequalities'. Indeed:

> We should recognise that all scholarly discourse is produced in social interaction, is part of social structure and context, and hence is socio-politically situated whether we like it or not: research which takes a neutral or impartial approach to social injustice does not solve the problem, indeed it could be argued that academic neutrality contributes to the perpetuation of such injustice. (Richardson 2007: 2; cf. Knapp and Spector 2011: 287)

While proponents of CDA do not shy away from normative claims, there are, as the above examples show, different takes on how far normativity extends in academic practice.

The Embeddedness of Discourse

Although the ideas of constitution and function are shared by most discourse analytical approaches, the epistemological and ontological background assumptions and, consequently, the methodological and interpretive implications vary. A crude difference could be made between approaches that see discourse as interacting with an extra-discursive social structure ('materialists') and those that deny or at least are indifferent towards any claims of ontological reality outside of discourse ('idealists'; Richardson 2007: 27). Although discourse analysis – and the underlying epistemology of social constructionism more broadly – has often been identified only with the latter view, CDA is decidedly 'materialist' and sees discourse in dialectical interaction with the material world and other social formations that on the one hand constrain discourse but on the other are also changed by discourse (Fairclough and Wodak 1997). Chouliaraki and Fairclough (1999: 1) call this approach – following Bourdieu – alternatively 'constructivist structuralism' or 'structuralist constructivism'.

This has important methodological implications: if – as the more 'postmodern' approaches claim – the social context of discourse is continually constructed and thus cannot be independent of discourse itself, the focus is usually on smaller units of analysis, such as sequences of talk (see Wooffitt 2006). However, if the context of discourse is seen as something independent – and stable forms of discourse practice, such as genre, suggest that this is indeed a useful view – the unit of analysis is often larger and contrasted with the broader social and cultural framework (see Fairclough 1992; Silverman 2007). In other words, CDA always considers discourse to be embedded in particular contexts which are partly discursive, but partly beyond discourse.

Methodologically CDA aims to ensure an embedded approach by dividing analysis into three different aspects that feed into each other: (1) textual analysis; (2) analysis of discourse practice; and (3) analysis if social practice (for a diagrammatical representation of the three aspects, see Fairclough 1992: 73). I discuss these aspects in detail elsewhere (Hjelm 2011b, 2013a), whereas a short outline will have to suffice here. Firstly, CDA obviously focuses on *textual analysis*. 'Text' in CDA is broadly conceived and can include printed, 'found' (i.e. created independently of the researcher, see Silverman 2007) material such as newspaper text, or 'manufactured' data such as interview transcripts. There are myriad ways of conducting text analysis (see e.g. Fairclough 2003) ranging from the linguistic to the interpretive. On the linguistic level a focus on words, as one aspect among many, helps us understand how topics of discussion are contextualised. So, for example, boundary maintenance in religious movements is often done by reframing competing belief systems as evil, as in the case of the neo-Pentecostal Universal Church of the Kingdom of God, which depicts the 'spiritual entities that play central, positive, healing roles in Umbanda and Candomble [syncretistic Afro-Brazilian religions] ... as "demons"' (Engler 2011: 211). Another example is naming. In a report in the *Independent*, a British daily newspaper, about the defeat of the government's Terror Bill in the House of Lords, the Conservative Earl of Hounslow is quoted asking: 'Why, if the home secretary thinks Mohammad el-Smith wants to do something and is planning to do something and has talked to others about doing something nasty, that is not conspiracy?' (quoted in Richardson 2007: 50). The point the earl is making is that existing conspiracy laws would be sufficient enough to cover acts of terrorism, but it is the use of 'Mohammad el-Smith' that is interesting from a CDA perspective. The name is a combination of 'Smith', arguably the most common family name in Britain, thus the 'average man' (i.e. 'Joe Bloggs', 'John

Doe'), and 'Mohammad', arguably the most common Muslim male name. The implication here is that the speaker 'believes the average terrorist suspect to be Muslim' (Richardson 2007: 51).

Secondly, CDA involves what Fairclough (1992) calls *analysis of discourse practice*. As noted above, analysing discourse is always analysing language use in a particular social context. This is the domain of interpreting texts in light of broader 'social practice' (discussed below). Between text and social context is the field of production and consumption of texts. As Phillips and Jørgensen (2002: 69) explain, to study discursive practices is to study 'how authors of texts draw on already existing discourses and genres to create a text and … how receivers of texts also apply available discourses and genres in the consumption and interpretation of the texts'. Ideally, then, a full-scale study of discourse is not only textual, but also takes into account the immediate contexts of production and consumption. In the field of religion and media, for example, Hoover's earlier work (1998) has been important in examining how the routines and conventions of the daily 'beat' affect the production of religion news. At the other end are studies such as Clark (2003), which explore the effects of popular media on religious identity-building. Although neither is an example of CDA, a full analysis would delve into the production and consumption dynamics of a particular discourse.

Thirdly, although discourse is capable of both reproducing and transforming society, it would be naive to think that all discourse is equal. We can all have an opinion, but who gets to speak in public and who is listened to depend on one's structural positioning. In the case of Islam in Britain, for example, there has been a rather glaring imbalance between bureaucratic sources and Muslim respondents in newspaper discourse (Richardson 2006). Similarly, during the early stages of the Satanism Scare in Finland, the hegemonic discourse was based almost exclusively on evangelical Christian 'expertise' on the topic (Hjelm 2008). The point is even clearer in everyday practice: in Western societies, most people prefer to take medical advice from qualified professionals rather than religious leaders (although there are important exceptions to this, such as Christian Science). Taking these structural factors into account is referred to as *analysis of social practice* in CDA. Locke (2004: 42) summarises the analysis of social practice as 'a focus on such things as the immediate situation that has given rise to its production and the various sociocultural practices and discursive conditions at both institutional and societal levels that provide a wider contextual relevance'. The question then is whether texts support particular types of social practice by reproducing a hegemonic agenda, or if there are 'transformative impulses' (Locke 2004: 43) in the text. An example of this is a law proposal presented in the Finnish parliament in 2006 by two members of the Green League. The aim of the proposal was to change laws privileging the Lutheran state church (and to a lesser degree the Orthodox Church) in order to make religious communities in Finland more equal. The interesting part is not necessarily the staunch opposition to the proposal by the leader of the conservative Christian Democratic Party, or by MPs with a Christian (in some cases priestly) background. More telling was the fact that out of 200 MPs, only eight took part in the discussion in the first place. The obvious opponents of the proposal did speak, but MPs from the left, for example – conventionally depicted as secular – were as silent as the mainstream. The privileged position of the Lutheran Church in Finland is a deeply hegemonic social practice that is reflected in the discourse and the *lack* of discussion – the 'taken-for-grantedness' of the social situation (Hjelm 2013b).

The above examples show that texts alone are not sufficient in analysing discourse. Discourse – or the absence of discourse – makes sense only within a broader social framework. The social context is analysed empirically, by looking at actors, groups and relationships within groups and between actors in society. In the framework of CDA, the context is also analysed theoretically, by looking at the structuration of power in a field of ideology and hegemony. It is this analysis of social practice that makes CDA distinctively different from some other approaches to discourse analysis. It is also analysis of social practice that gives CDA explanatory power: where discourse analysis has traditionally been more suitable for answering *how* questions (see Silverman and Gubrium 1994), a focus on the social context enable us to argue that a line of action was one among a choice of actions that the discursive framework enabled – or alternatively, how the choice of action was constrained by the social and cultural framework. In Max Weber's terms this would be something akin to a 'causally adequate' explanation (Buss 1999; Ringer 2002).

Critical Discourse Analysis in the Sociology of Religion

Finally, I would like to discuss the relevance of CDA to several current issues in the sociology of religion and discuss topics for which a CDA approach would be especially conducive to. While reflecting on broad themes instead of a detailed case study using CDA might seem like an odd strategy in light of the discursive versus discourse analytical distinction made above, I think it is justified by the fact that whereas analysing constructions of religion with discourse analysis is possible from a multitude of perspectives, *critical* DA (and sociology of religion) has specific emphases, three of which I explore here: (1) the religious legitimation of social inequality, (2) the legitimacy of religions as a discursive construction, and (3) a CDA perspective on (de-)secularisation.

Opium of the People – and More

This is no place to enter the exegetical debate on the correct interpretation of Marx's famous 'opium of the people' phrase (see Hamilton 2001: 93; McKinnon 2006). When Cadge et al. (2011: 442) refer to the 'excesses of old-fashioned Marxist portraits of religion as an opiate of the masses', they don't seem to have analytical sociology of religion in mind. Suffice it to say here that for Marx, religion is more than a numbing drug; it is 'a force which legitimates' the social order (Hamilton 2001: 93–4). Although rarely considered a proponent of 'critical' sociology, and despite his ardent personal dislike of Marx*ism*,[2] Peter Berger – arguably the most influential sociologist of religion of his generation – picked up this idea (minus the class emphasis) in his widely read *The Sacred Canopy* (published in the UK as *The Social Reality of Religion*):

> [R]eligion has been the historically most widespread and effective instrumentality of legitimation. All legitimation maintains socially defined reality. Religion legitimates so effectively because it relates the precarious reality constructions of empirical societies with ultimate reality. The tenuous realities of the social world are grounded in the sacred *realissimum*, which by definition is beyond the contingencies of human meanings and human activity. (Berger 1973: 41)

Especially for the later Berger, legitimation is a matter of social cohesion (Turner 2008: 496), but from a critical perspective, legitimation is a struggle for hegemony. In this sense religion, as expressed by Berger, is an example of ideology, or 'meaning in the service of power', as discussed above: alternative constructions of reality are suppressed by reference to an ultimate, unquestionable source – the sacred. This of course ties in with what many consider Marx's most important *sociological* (qua economic) contribution: the theory of alienation (Marx 1961: 175–85, 250; see Ollman 1976; Swain 2012). The question for CDA is: how are these legitimations accomplished discursively? How is religious alienation reproduced and/or challenged in discourse? In this sense CDA provides a methodological source that has been rarely tapped in the sociology of religion – Marxist or otherwise.

---

[2] Berger's move from essentially Marxist dialectics to conservatism has been discussed in Goldstein (2009). See also Berger (2002).

Despite processes of secularisation, religious legitimations remain important in the modern world, and not just in the developing world. The obvious ones are often related to gender roles, sexuality and reproduction. Thus we have the Catholic Church's continuing opposition to contraception, fundamentalist 'pro-life' campaigners against abortion, and completely separated spheres of life for men and women in Orthodox Jewish communities in Israel and under the Taliban rule in Afghanistan, for example. Even research that otherwise celebrates what it sees as the continuing relevance of (relatively liberal) mainstream European Christian churches (see Bäckström et al. 2011) acknowledges that the very same churches are the source of notions that have enabled the reproduction of unequal gender relationships in society (Edgardh 2011: 63). The aim of CDA is to look at how these practices are discursively reproduced and transformed.

Religion as Legitimate Identity

One of the reasons why Fairclough has distanced himself from his earlier work is the sole emphasis on class as a difference marker. Even if Marx set the scene for analysing religion's contribution to class domination, the same domination applies to other areas of social life as well. Race, ethnicity, gender and sexuality have all emerged as central topics of analysis during the previous couple of decades. As long as secularisation was accepted as the hegemonic narrative about the fate of religion in the modern world, less attention was paid to the role of religion as a difference marker. Historically, of course, religion has been *the* dividing issue in many contexts, but relegated to the margins of modern identity formation. That is, until at least the post-Cold War awakening to a globalised world where religion still mattered. Now, of course, eminent sociologists write books about religion – without any reference to the sociology of religion – because reality seems to defy the indifference of the past 40 years or so. Secularisation certainly still happens, but there is no denying that religion has re-emerged as an identity marker in the modern world.

A less-discussed aspect of this re-emergence is that religion seems to be increasingly represented as a social problem (Hjelm 2011a). While there is grand talk about 'post-secularity', and the need to acknowledge religion in the public sphere, what is at stake is the legitimacy of religion and religions in modern society. Thus, instead of looking at how religion legitimates inequality, the other side of the coin is to look at how the legitimacy of religion and religions is constructed discursively. Again, the obvious example would be Islam, but other minority and alternative religions are also struggling to define themselves as legitimate all around the world (see e.g. Hjelm 2006, 2011a, 2012a; Poole and Richardson 2006).

The Discursive Dialectics of Secularisation

If there is one major 'paradigmatic' change in recent sociology of religion, it is the near-complete abandonment of the secularisation thesis in favour of 'desecularisation', or even more fashionably 'post-secularity'. While initially sceptical of 'desecularisation' (Hjelm 2012b), I have come to think that – from a CDA perspective at least – it is a preferable term to the now-hegemonic 'post-secularity' and its variants. Goldstein (2009) has usefully pointed out that the 'common-sense' vision of 'old paradigm' theories of secularisation as linear and inevitable is not fully justified, but that many contain dialectical elements. My aim is to complement this idea of secularisation as a dialectical process with a focus on discourse.

On the one hand, a CDA approach to secularisation challenges vulgar interpretations of the 'diminution in the social significance of religion' (Wilson 1982: 149) – 'vulgar' in the sense that they assume a rigid linear progress (Bruce 2011: 3–4). Recent years have shown that public discourse – surely part of the 'social significance' of religion – can be desecularised in the sense that religion is back on the agenda. On the other hand, the discursive dialectics of secularisation challenges 'post-secularism' when that is presented as a 'state of things': firstly, desecularisation implies a *process* that is dialectical and reversible. There is nothing inevitable about the current prominence of religion in public discourse and prominence as such tells us little. Secondly, a CDA of the public discourse on religion in Western societies can reveal that the fact that religion is back on the agenda quantitatively is not a sufficient measure for abandoning the secularization thesis as such. Quite contrary, it might reveal that, yes, religious communities are reasserting themselves as public actors, but that their discourse is increasingly secular – a point that Bruce (2011: 171) makes in reference to the 'culture wars' in the United States. I think he is absolutely right in saying that '[S]ince Jürgen Habermas popularized talk of a "post-secular Europe", there has been much confusion between religion becoming more troublesome and people becoming more religious' (Bruce 2011: 203; see Beckford 2012).

In addition, studies such as Wohlrab-Sahr et al. (2008) suggest that discursive conflict can also explain the subjective appropriation of a (in their case) secularised habitus. Their argument (in a nutshell) is that communicating a conflict between a scientific worldview and religion, and the incompatibility of politics and religion, had a secularising effect on individuals in their case study of the GDR. What CDA could offer to this theory is, firstly, a methodological toolkit enabling a close analysis of *how* the conflict was communicated, defined and interpreted, key terms that almost beg for methodological refinement. Secondly, conflict alone is not sufficient to explain why people appropriate particular beliefs; a theory of hegemony (see above) is needed to answer the question why people choose one of the conflicting options, not the other.

The CDA approach to secularisation is, therefore, a modest approach. It provides refined tools for analysing the dynamics of public discourse on religion. However, when understood to include both text analysis the study of production and reception of texts, it offers a powerful complement to more demographic and quantitative analyses.

Conclusion

There is justified debate about whether the world is as 'furiously religious' as ever, as Berger (1999: 2) and others have claimed, but the fact that *discourse about religion* is as ubiquitous as ever demonstrates that religion still matters. So, sociologists of religion still have a job to do. What has been missing (or at least very much underrepresented) in the field so far, however, has been a genuinely critical sociology of religion that looks at the role of religion in the reproduction and transformation of social inequality and domination, the ways in which religion and religions are legitimated, and the dialectical processes of public discourse and constructions of religion. Critical discourse analysis that draws from the Marxist tradition provides a powerful and yet mostly untapped source for analysing how this legitimation, reproduction or transformation is achieved. The spectre of communism may have been laid to rest for most of the world, but I am convinced that the spectre of Marx still has a lot to offer – not least for the sociology of religion.

References

Aldrige, A. (2007). *Religion in the Contemporary World: A Sociological Introduction*, 2nd edn. Cambridge: Polity Press.

Bäckström A., Davie, G., Edgardh, N. and Petterson, P. (2011). *Welfare and Religion in 21st Century Europe: Volume 2*. Aldershot: Ashgate.

Barker, E. (2011). The Cult as a Social Problem, in *Religion and Social Problems*, ed. T. Hjelm. New York: Routledge, pp. 198–212.

Beckford, J.A. (1983). The Restoration of 'Power' to the Sociology of Religion. *Sociological Analysis*, 44(1), 11–32.

Beckford, J.A. (1985). *Cult Controversies: The Societal Response to the New Religious Movements*. London: Tavistock.

Beckford, J.A. (2003). *Social Theory and Religion*. Cambridge: Cambridge University Press.

Beckford, J.A. (2012). SSSR Presidential Address: Public Religions and the Postsecular: Critical Reflections. *Journal for the Scientific Study of Religion*, 51(1), 1–19.

Berger, P.L. (1973). *The Social Reality of Religion*. London: Penguin.

Berger, P.L. (1999). The Desecularization of the World: A Global Overview, in *The Desecularization of the World: Resurgent Religion and World Politics*, ed. P.L. Berger. Grand Rapids: Eerdmans, pp. 1–18.

Berger, P.L. (2002). Whatever Happened to Sociology? *First Things*, 126, 27–9.

Bocock, R. (1986). *Hegemony*. Chichester: Ellis Horwood.

Brown, C.G. (2009). *The Death of Christian Britain*, 2nd edn. London: Routledge.

Bruce, S. (2011). *Secularization: In Defence of an Unfashionable Theory*. Oxford: Oxford University Press.

Buss, A. (1999). The Concept of Adequate Causation and Max Weber's Comparative Sociology of Religion. *British Journal of Sociology*, 50(2), 317–29.

Butler, J. (1990). *Gender Trouble*. London: Routledge.

Cadge, W., Levitt, P. and Smilde, D. (2011). De-centering and Re-centering: Rethinking Concepts and Methods in the Sociological Study of Religion. *Journal for the Scientific Study of Religion*, 50(3), 437–49.

Chouliaraki, L. and Fairclough, N. (1999). *Discourse in Late Modernity*. Edinburgh: Edinburgh University Press.

Clark, L.S. (2003). *From Angels to Aliens: Teenagers, the Media, and the Supernatural*. Oxford: Oxford University Press.

Collins, R. (2007). The Classical Tradition in Sociology of Religion, in *The Sage Handbook of the Sociology of Religion*, ed. J.A. Beckford and N.J. Demerath III. London: Sage, pp. 19–38.

Davie, G. (2007). *The Sociology of Religion*. London: Sage.

Edgardh, N. (2011). A Gendered Perspective on Religion and Welfare in Europe, in *Welfare and Religion in 21st Century Europe: Volume 2*, ed. A. Bäckström, G. Davie and N. Edgardh. Aldershot: Ashgate, pp. 61–106.

Edwards, D. and Potter, J. (1992). *Discursive Psychology*. London: Sage.

Engler, S. (2006). Discourse, in *The Brill Dictionary of Religion*, ed. K. von Stuckrad. Leiden: Brill, pp. 516–19.

Engler, S. (2011). Other Religions as Social Problem: The Universal Church of the Kingdom of God and Afro-Brazilian traditions, in *Religion and Social Problems*, ed. T. Hjelm. New York: Routledge, pp. 211–28.

Fairclough, N. (1989). *Language and Power*. London: Longman.

Fairclough, N. (1992). *Discourse and Social Change*. Cambridge: Polity Press.

Fairclough, N. (1995). *Critical Discourse Analysis*. London: Longman.

Fairclough, N. (2003). *Analysing Discourse*. London: Routledge.

Fairclough, N. and Graham, P. (2010). Marx as Critical Discourse Analyst: The Genesis of a Critical Method and its Relevance to the Critique of Global Capital, in *Critical Discourse Analysis*, 2nd edn, ed. N. Fairclough. London: Longman, pp. 301–46.

Fairclough, N. and Wodak, R. (1997). Critical Discourse Analysis: An Overview, in *Discourse Studies: A Multidisciplinary Introduction*, vol. 2, ed. T.A. van Dijk. London: Sage, pp. 67–97.

Furseth, I. and Repstad, P. (2006). *An Introduction to the Sociology of Religion*. Aldershot: Ashgate.

Goldstein, W.S. (2006). Introduction: Marx, Critical Theory, and Religion: A Critique of Rational Choice, in *Marx, Critical Theory, and Religion*, ed. W.S. Goldstein. Chicago: Haymarket Books, pp. 1–7.

Goldstein, W.S. (2009). Secularization Patterns in the Old Paradigm. *Sociology of Religion*, 70(2), 157–78.

Gramsci, A. (1971). *Selections from the Prison Notebooks*. New York: International Publishers.

Hamilton, M. (2001). *The Sociology of Religion*, 2nd edn. London: Routledge.

Heelas, P. and Woodhead, L. with Seel, B., Szerszynski, B. and Tusting, K. (2005). *The Spiritual Revolution: Why Religion is Giving Away to Spirituality*. Oxford: Blackwell.

Hjelm, T. (2006). Between Satan and Harry Potter: Legitimating Wicca in Finland. *Journal of Contemporary Religion*, 21(1), 39–58.

Hjelm, T. (2008). Driven by the Devil: Popular Constructions of Youth Satanist Careers, in *The Encyclopedic Sourcebook of Satanism*, ed. J.R. Lewis and J. Petersen. Amherst: Prometheus Books, pp. 361–80.

Hjelm, T. (2009). Religion in Our Times: *Zeitdiagnose* as a Sociological Genre. Paper presented at the Biennial Meeting of the International Society for the Sociology of Religion, 28 July, Santiago de la Compostela, Spain.

Hjelm, T. (2011a). Religion and Social Problems: Three Perspectives, in *Religion and Social Problems*, ed. T. Hjelm. New York: Routledge, pp. 1–11.

Hjelm, T. (2011b). Discourse Analysis, in *The Routledge Handbook of Research Methods in the Study of Religion*, ed. S. Engler and M. Stausberg. London: Routledge, pp. 134–50.

Hjelm, T. (2012a). Introduction: Islam and Muslims in European News Media. *Journal of Religion in Europe*, 5(2), 137–9.

Hjelm, T. (2012b). Desecularization, in *Encyclopedia of Global Religion*, ed. M. Juergensmeyer and W.C. Roof. Thousand Oaks: Sage, pp. 292–4.

Hjelm, T. (2013a). Religion, Discourse and Power: Outline of a Critical Agenda for the Sociology of Religion. *Critical Sociology*. Published online 4 March 2013. (DOI: 10.1177/0896920513477664).

Hjelm, T. (2013b). National Piety: Religious Equality, Freedom of Religion and National Identity in Finnish Political Discourse. *Religion*, 44(1), 28–45.

Hjelm, T. (2014). *Social Constructionisms: Approaches to the Study of the Human World*. Basingstoke: Palgrave.

Hoover, S. (1998). *Religion in the News: Faith and Journalism in American Public Discourse*. Thousand Oaks: Sage.

Knapp, P. and Spector, A.J. (2011). *Crisis and Change: Basic Questions of Marxist Sociology*. Lanham: Rowman & Littlefield.

Locke, T. (2004). *Critical Discourse Analysis*. London: Continuum.

Luke, A. (1995–6). Text and Discourse in Education: An Introduction to Critical Discourse Analysis. *Review of Research in Education*, 21, 3–48.

Lundskow, G. (2008). *The Sociology of Religion: A Substantive and Transdisciplinary Approach*. Thousand Oaks: Pine Forge Press.

Mannheim, K. (1944). *Diagnosis of Our Time*. New York: Oxford University Press.

Marx, K. (1844). Contribution to the Critique of Hegel's Philosophy of Law: An Introduction, in *Marx/Engels Collected Works, volume 3*. London: Lawrence & Wishart, pp. 175–87.

Marx, K. (1961). *Selected Writings in Sociology and Social Philosophy*, ed. T.B. Bottomore and M. Rubel. Harmondsworth: Penguin.

McCloud, S. (2007). *Divine Hierarchies: Class in American Religion and Religious Studies*. Chapel Hill: University of North Carolina Press.

McCutcheon, R.T. (2003). *Manufacturing Religion: The Discourse on Sui Generis Religion and the Politics of Nostalgia*. Oxford: Oxford University Press.

McGuire, M. (2002). *Religion: The Social Context*, 5th edn. Long Grove: Waveland Press.

McKinnon, A.M. (2006). Opium as Dialectics of Religion: Metaphor, Expression and Protest, in *Marx, Critical Theory, and Religion*, ed. W.S. Goldstein. Chicago: Haymarket Books, pp. 11–29.

McLellan, D. (1987). *Marxism and Religion*. Basingstoke: Macmillan.

Moberg, M. (2013). First-, Second-, and Third-level Discourse Analytic Approaches in the Study of Religion: Moving from Meta-theoretical Reflection to Implementation in Practice. *Religion*, 43(1), 1–22.

Ollman, B. (1976). *Alienation: Marx's Conception of Man in Capitalist Society*, 2nd edn. Cambridge: Cambridge University Press.

Phillips, L. and Jørgensen, M.W. (2002). *Discourse Analysis as Theory and Method*. London: Sage.

Phillips, N. and Hardy, C. (2002). *Discourse Analysis: Investigating Processes of Social Construction*. Thousand Oaks: Sage.

Poole, E. and Richardson, J. (eds) (2006). *Muslims and the News Media*. London: I.B. Tauris.

Possamai, A. (2009). *Sociology of Religion for Generations X and Y*. London: Equinox.

Potter, J. (1996). *Representing Reality: Discourse, Rhetoric, and Social Construction*. London: Sage.

Potter, J. and Wetherell, M. (1987). *Discourse and Social Psychology: Beyond Attitudes and Behaviour*. London: Sage.

Richardson, J.E. (2006). Who Gets to Speak? A Study of Sources in the Broadsheet Press, in *Muslims and the News Media*, ed. E. Poole E and J.E. Richardson. London: I.B. Tauris, pp. 103–15.

Richardson, J.E. (2007). *Analysing Newspapers: An Approach from Critical Discourse Analysis*. Basingstoke: Palgrave.

Richardson, J.T. (1997). The Social Construction of Satanism: Understanding an International Social Problem. *Australian Journal of Social Issues*, 32(1), 61–85.

Riesebrodt, M. (2010). *The Promise of Salvation: A Theory of Religion*. Chicago: Chicago University Press.

Ringer, F. (2002). Max Weber and Causal Analysis, Interpretation and Comparison. *History and Theory*, 41(2), 163–78.

Roberts, K.A. and Yamane, D. (2011). *Religion in Sociological Perspective*, 5th edn. Thousand Oaks: Pine Forge Press.

Silverman, D. (2007). *A Very Short, Fairly Interesting and Reasonably Cheap Book about Qualitative Research*. London: Sage.

Silverman, D. and Gubrium, J.F. (1994). Competing Strategies for Analyzing the Contexts of Social Interaction. *Sociological Inquiry*, 64(2), 179–98.

Swain, D. (2012). *Alienation: An Introduction to Marx's Theory*. London: Bookmarks.

Thompson, J.B. (1990). *Ideology and Modern Culture*. Stanford: Stanford University Press.
Turner, B.S. (2008). The Constructed Body, in *The Handbook of Constructionist Research*, ed. J.A. Holstein and J.F. Gubrium. New York: The Guilford Press, pp. 493–510.
van Dijk, T.A. (1993). Principles of Critical Discourse Analysis. *Discourse & Society*, 4(2), 249–83.
von Stuckrad, K. (2003). Discursive Study of Religion: From States of the Mind to Communication and Action. *Method and Theory in the Study of Religion*, 15(3), 255–71.
von Stuckrad, K. (2010). Reflections on the Limits of Reflection: An Invitation to the Discursive Study of Religion. *Method and Theory in the Study of Religion*, 22(2–3), 156–69.
Wilson, B. (1982). *Religion in Sociological Perspective*. Oxford: Oxford University Press.
Wohlrab-Sahr, M., Schmidt-Lux, T. and Karstein, U. (2008). Secularization as Conflict. *Social Compass*, 55(2), 127–39.
Wooffitt, R. (2006). *The Language of Mediums and Psychics: The Social Organization of Everyday Miracles*. Aldershot: Ashgate.
Wuthnow, R. (2011). Taking Talk Seriously: Religious Discourse as Social Practice. *Journal for the Scientific Study of Religion*, 50(1), 1–21.

Chapter 11
Beyond Habitus: Researching Gender and Religion through the Ontology of Social Relations

Marta Trzebiatowska

Bourdieu and Gender

Pierre Bourdieu needs no introduction. Since the 1990s his work has influenced social scientists in his native France and internationally (Silva and Warde 2010) and he has become a patron of collective intellectual endeavour 'which disregards borders between disciplines and countries' (Wacquant in Truong and Weill 2012). He is mostly known for his writings on education, class, consumption and art (see Bourdieu and Wacquant (1992) for an excellent overview) but in 1991 he wrote *Masculine Domination*, an essay later amended and turned into a book (1998), and subsequently translated into English in 2001. The book was largely ignored by feminists and had seemingly little impact on the 'cottage industry' that had grown around Bourdieu's work (King 2000: 417). The overall argument broadly reflects Bourdieu's preoccupation with the role of power relations in maintaining the symbolic order, but in this instance he zooms in on the question of the possibility of permanence and change in the gender order in particular. The central question of *Masculine Domination* concerns the historical mechanisms behind the relative universality and tenacity of the structures of gender (Bourdieu 2001: viii). Although his analysis is by no means novel in the eyes of feminist scholars, the manner in which he arrives at his conclusions helps to understand the operation of the gender order in greater depth than if we simply stated that gender difference and inequality are socially created and reproduced. In the course of building his argument Bourdieu places particular emphasis on the amount of hard work that goes into presenting the relationship between men and women as natural and ahistorical.[1] Social institutions – the family, the church, the state, the educational system, the media – all contribute to creating the illusion that the gender order is eternal, ahistorical and natural, therefore commonsensical and 'just-so'. Bourdieu terms this commonsensical view of the world 'doxa' (2000: 15). What we think is common sense, however, amounts to the outcome of our particular habitus – the collection of experiences, beliefs and norms internalised throughout our lives, hence both internal and external to us. Our habitus operates to match individual expectations to the objective reality that surrounds us. The two are interconnected and difficult to disentangle. Herein lies the paradox of the commonsensical view of gender too. It is surprising, remarks Bourdieu, that most individuals do not question the order of gender and there are relatively few transgressions and subversions, which is exactly how the order reproduces itself effortlessly. Part of the reason for such a lack of subversion is the operation of symbolic violence in its reproduction.[2] Bourdieu uses the concept of 'symbolic violence' to describe an invisible, subtle coercion exerted over the dominated group. Masculine domination over women operates successfully thanks to the 'paradox of doxa' – the surprising ease with which the order of the world as we know it reproduces itself without any significant difficulty (Bourdieu 1998). The trouble with challenging masculine domination is that even when explicitly trying to do so women end up drawing on the very 'modes of thought that are the product of domination' (Bourdieu 2001: 5). The only way of breaking the cycle of reproduction is to treat masculine domination as 'at once familiar and exotic' (Bourdieu 2001: 5).

Bourdieu uses his early ethnography of the Kabyle society in Algeria to demonstrate the operation of the symbolic gender order (1979). Amongst the Kabyles male and female characteristics are organised as a set of oppositions that define one another (up/down, straight/curved, dry/wet) (2001: 6). The distinction between the sexes is present not only in the bodies and behaviour of men and women but also in the objective social world because mundane everyday objects are accorded masculine or feminine characteristics. For example, every part of the house is labelled as either masculine or feminine. Thus, the masculine,

---

[1] This work has been described by gender scholars as 'doing gender' (West and Zimmerman 1987) and 'performativity' (Butler 1990), but Bourdieu's analysis goes beyond interactionism and micro-level explanation because he positions gender scripts in the wider field of objective social relations.

[2] Bourdieu has been heavily criticised for presenting gender divisions as fixed and simplistic and ignoring the challenges to the status quo from several generations of feminist activists and academics (see Lovell 2002).

androcentric order is presented as neutral and in no need of justification. As women mobilise these dominant schemes of perception, they also internalise their submission and form a view of feminine sexuality that is negative and inferior to its masculine counterpart. Consequently, the symbolic gender order is constructed and legitimated through both: the objective division and subjective cognitive schemes. But gender does not exist in a vacuum. Femininity and masculinity necessarily operate relationally because the feminine and the masculine cannot be understood without reference to each other. The formative process of gendering bodies, Bourdieu stresses, is not entirely conscious but rather achieved through everyday division of labour and rituals all aimed at encouraging the development of appearance and behaviour deemed appropriate for one's gender. Repetition brings the gender order into being (Butler 1990). And so this gender apprenticeship 'is all the more effective because it remains essentially tacit: femininity is imposed for the most part through an unremitting discipline that concerns every part of the body and is continuously recalled through the constraints of clothing and style' (Bourdieu 2001: 27). As a result of this tacit operation of the gender order, neither men nor women fully realise the degree to which they reproduce the relationship of domination through their everyday actions. Even when women draw on strategies to undermine this relationship, they usually end up further reinforcing the androcentric view. Their own tools of resistance are rooted in the very symbols and myths that they try to undermine and consequently: 'because their dispositions are the product of embodiment of the negative prejudice against the female that is instituted in the order of things, women cannot but constantly confirm this prejudice' (Bourdieu 2001: 32). Bourdieu further illustrates this point through an example of French women's preference with regard to future husbands. Surveys demonstrate that a high percentage of French women express a desire for a man taller and older than they are (two-thirds explicitly reject shorter men) (2001: 36). In this case the objective schemes of perception and the subjective preferences coalesce and become difficult, if not impossible, to disentangle. Love, in this scenario, 'is often partly amor fati, love of one's social destiny' (Bourdieu 2001: 37). Interestingly, the desired age gap between a woman and a man decreases as the woman's independence increases and marriage ceases to be a means of achieving a higher social status, which shows that there is no inevitability about the gender order. Once women have gained access to professional avenues of mobility in the public sphere, 'erotic capital' (Hakim 2011) quickly becomes redundant. Therefore, according to Bourdieu, the only way to understand symbolic violence as exercised by men over women is to move beyond constraint and consent (between mechanical coercion and voluntary submission) and focus on understanding symbolic domination as exerted through the schemes of perception and action that are constitutive of habitus and which operate below the level of conscious decisions and thus 'set up a cognitive relationship that is profoundly obscure to itself' (Bourdieu 2001: 37). The interaction between masculine domination and feminine submissiveness can only be understood by examining the 'durable effects that the social order exerts on women (and men), that is to say, the dispositions spontaneously attuned to that order which it imposes on them' (Bourdieu 2001: 38). In order to operate successfully symbolic violence needs to be met halfway by the individuals involved and this is only possible if they have performed the (embodied) efforts necessary for the production of these 'durable dispositions' (Bourdieu 2001: 38).

The dominated co-produce their own domination by acting in accordance with the expectations of the dominant. Bourdieu gives examples of embodied emotions and sentiments, such as shame or respect, to illustrate this point (2001: 39). Simply being aware of the expectations and the manner in which they are met does nothing to displace the mechanism of submission because it is so deeply embedded into the individual's consciousness and bodily actions. The body, and the gendered and sexual body, is a container and a vessel for the habitus (internalised dispositions and experiences) (Krais 2006). To put it simply, the excluded exclude themselves naturally and effortlessly as a result of the 'somatization of the relation of power' (Bourdieu 2001: 56).[3]

Bourdieu is very conscious of the dangers inherent in suggesting that women participate in reinforcing their own submission (2001: 114). This not only victimises women further but also can serve as an excuse for men's actions. Of course, Bourdieu does not mean to suggest that women actively choose to be submissive, are their worst enemies, or enjoy the domination. The durability and relative strength of the structures of domination lies in the subtle operation of symbolic power which can only be exercised with the contribution from those at the receiving end, and they are only at the receiving end because they are complicit in the construction of the relationship. In a sense, Bourdieu's analysis of the gender order is a version of the Hegelian master-and-slave dialectic, also famously mobilised by Simone de Beauvoir in her seminal writings on gender relations (1949). The cognitive structures drawn on by both the dominant and

---

[3] Interestingly, women's own contribution to their objective subordination has received a lot of public attention and coverage due to the publication of books such as *Lean In: Women, Work and the Will to Lead* (Sandberg 2013) and *Honey Money: The Power of Erotic Capital* (Hakim 2011). While these books are highly controversial in their claims about gender inequalities, they indicate a shift in both, the place of women in public sphere and their perception of it.

the dominated are socially constructed but even the act of construction is the effect of power (Bourdieu 2001: 40). Symbolic efforts to raise consciousness among the dominated is not sufficient because the conditions in place are too strongly inscribed in bodies, so the only way to alter the effects of symbolic violence is to change the conditions of its production (Bourdieu 2001: 41). As Bourdieu describes it:

> a relation of domination that functions only through the complicity of dispositions depends profoundly, for its perpetuation or transformation, on the perpetuation of transformation of the structures of which those dispositions are the product. (2001: 42)

There is no danger of women defying the collective expectations and thus challenging the gender order because their dispositions are so perfectly attuned to the objective expectations. The very position of the dominant makes it possible to render their view of reality universal and therefore very difficult to challenge (Bourdieu 2001: 62).[4] This explains why in some religions women would not attempt to gain access to the positions of power. The positions in question 'are tailor-made for men' and so the mismatch between dispositions and objective conditions 'naturally' prevents transgression (Bourdieu 2001: 63). The harsh reality of this gender order then is that women are simultaneously tools and assets in the production of symbolic and social capital in male power struggles (Bourdieu 2001: 44). This is evidenced most clearly in social norms with regard to honour and nowhere is this more obvious than in traditionally religious groups where women perform morality on behalf of men and preserve the collective honour of the community through monitoring their behaviour and reputation. Women's honour becomes perceived as 'a fetishized measure of masculine reputation' (Bourdieu 2001: 45). This is achieved partly, if not fully, through the construction, representation and experience of the female body as 'body-for-others' (Bourdieu 2001: 63). Bourdieu points out that being interpellated to partake in the masculine 'games of honour' and to assert masculinity constantly is also a burdensome duty and a 'trap' (2001: 50). He gives the impression that the demands imposed on men by their particular habitus produce their own version of insecurities, especially that manliness is always judged against femininity and has to be legitimated by other men in the community. Femininity, therefore, symbolises a threat to the successful achievement of the masculine status, which

---

[4] Some commentators found Bourdieu's argument patronising towards women (see, for example, Wallace 2003).

necessarily makes the accomplishment of masculinity relational – fashioned in direct opposition to what it is not.

Feminist Critique of *Masculine Domination*

To say that *Masculine Domination* met with a cool reception on the part of feminists and gender studies scholars would be a gross understatement. Initially, the essay was ignored altogether and subsequently a number of criticisms were levelled at Bourdieu, most of which could be subsumed under the general label of 'the collective androcentric unconscious' (Witz 2004: 212). I will now turn to these criticisms and then make a case for the particular usefulness of *Masculine Domination* for the study of religion and gender.

First, Bourdieu defines gender as a set of mutually exclusive characteristics rooted in sexual difference. This is problematic because it overlooks the fundamental distinction between sex and gender which is at the root of feminist understanding of gendered identities as socially constructed (Mottier 2002: 351). Focusing on difference obscures the role of power in the production of gendered individuals. Combining gender difference with a conceptualisation of power relations would provide a much more convincing basis for Bourdieu's theory of symbolic violence and misrecognition (Mottier 2002: 351). Second, mobilising a pre-modern, agrarian society, such as Kabylia, as a template to extrapolate from, is not helpful because it implies that modernisation is a uniform process that can only unfold in one way, and that this model of the gender order itself is internally stable and reproducible in other contexts (Mottier 2002). The gender order appears unrealistic because it is so neatly laid out (Krais 2006). Third, Bourdieu insists on the importance of public institutions as the key engines of enactment and reproduction of masculine domination, while the private sphere of the home acts only as a site of manifestation of gendered power relations. This flies in the face of the feminist claim that 'the personal is political' and thus shuts off a whole segment of social life where gender inequalities are played out and experienced in mundane lived realities of women and men' (Mottier 2002: 352). Fourth, Bourdieu's account of structure and agency 'lacks a strong concept of subjectivity' (Mottier 2002: 354). Subjectivity is central to feminist theory and research because it opens the door to the formation of critical agency which, in turn, leads to structural transformations in the gender order. Bourdieu places too much emphasis on the permanence and inflexibility of masculine domination and gives too little credit to the potential for change in the gender order. Although he does pay heed to developments, such as women's entry into the labour market, or alternative models of family and sexualities, he insists on the traditional structures' continuing influence over these changes (Mottier 2002: 353). Fifth, Bourdieu constructs the gender order as a binary of the dominant versus the dominated, which presents both domination and power as homogenous, internally uniform states. By extension, such a reading also sees political interests as undifferentiated (Mottier 2002: 355). Moreover, he sees femininity and masculinity as clear-cut and neatly defined categories, rather than internally contradictory and pluralistic social scripts on a continuum of genders (Paechter 2006). In other words, Bourdieu's conceptualisation of masculine domination and potential for generative agency is marred by the absence of nuance and complexity and he appears oblivious to the work of his feminist colleagues, which in itself may suggest to some that he is indeed the product of his own masculine habitus, and not as 'epistemologically vigilant' as he aspires to being (Fowler 2003; Lovell 2002; Witz 2004; Krais 2006: 124).

Probably the most consistent criticism of Bourdieu's work in general, and his theory of masculine domination in particular, is concerned with determinism (e.g. Jenkins 1982; Alexander 1995; Schatzki 1997). Habitus determines individual agency and thus precludes any challenge to the status quo. As a consequence, masculine domination is portrayed as rigid and implacable, despite the significant gains of the feminist movement and the subsequent shifts in the gender order. The remainder of this chapter examines Bourdieu's 'practical theory' as the antidote for this determinism and gives concrete examples from research on religion, gender and sexuality where the ontology of social relations rooted in collective practices (and not the idea of a lone individual facing her or his habitus) is the key tool for sociological analysis (King 2004).

Even those feminist critics who find some merit in and offer a sympathetic reading of *Masculine Domination* tend to focus on the concept of the habitus at the expense of Bourdieu's theory of action (see Dillabough 2010; Fowler 2003; Krais 2006; Mottier 2002), which creates an incomplete and somewhat misleading representation of his ideas. Obviously, Bourdieu's conceptualisation of agency is inseparable from habitus as the two are mutually susceptible but following King (2000, 2004) I will argue that instead of separating habitus and practice, one can see the former as simply a reification of 'particular moments in the social process which consists ... of individuals interacting meaningfully with other individuals' (King 2000: 431). Social action is intersubjective but not individualistic because it relies on shared understandings and, as such, it is never an isolated act performed by a lone Sartrean individual. This line of thought is developed in the next section.

Beyond Structure and Agency: Critical Hermeneutics in the Study of Religion and Gender

Contemporary social theorists can be seen as divided into two camps which foster two distinct approaches to society (King 2004). Both are dualistic in nature, i.e. social reality is understood as a combination of structure and agency. Whether structure is defined as a set of rules, or as objective institutions, society is always explained as the interaction between structure and agency. However, this social ontology is untenable: structure is nothing more than social relations based on shared understandings and to assume its epiphenomenal status is to commit an error because 'in every case, structure can be reduced to social relations' (King 2004: 84).

According to Krais (2006), the reason why Bourdieu's writings on gender have been misconstrued is that they are understood in the context of a very particular theory of socialisation and social roles. If social roles are seen as imposed externally and simply acted out, they become normative restrictions, leaving no room for reflexivity and agency (Krais 2006: 125). When an individual takes on a role, she becomes involved in a set of structural conditions, not just 'other people's subjective expectations' (Archer 2000: 468). Thus, the act of marriage implies compliance to legal rules, which agents are aware of, yet their awareness does not create those rules. The legal system pre-exists the individuals who decide to marry, thus it is autonomous and independent of them. However, one could argue that for those individuals to marry, everyone else needs to be in agreement on what marriage entails! Marriage as a legal institution might have been created in the past, yet it does not make it autonomous of social actors in the present. Catholics may well be aware of the difficulties of obtaining an annulment and thus be forced to make a choice between remaining a legitimate member of the church or re-marrying, but the reason why it is so is not some superior and autonomous force. It is purely other people who have a common understanding of the laws within the Catholic Church. Those laws have been created, reproduced and modified through human interaction. Thus, whilst they might be autonomous with respect to one particular agent, they can be reduced to series of interactions between groups of individuals. Similarly, an Orthodox Jewish woman can choose to divorce her husband but in the eyes of the Jewish law, if her husband does not agree to the divorce, she is still legally married to him.[5] A Catholic nun's symbolic marriage to Jesus may be regarded as ludicrous

---

[5] The state of limbo referred to as 'agunah' – a 'chained woman'. If an 'agunah' re-marries and has children, they are not considered legitimate and the marriage regarded as

by unsympathetic lay observers because they do not share the understanding of its validity. However, it makes perfect sense to her fellow sisters. Similarly, a Buddhist nun's renunciation of marriage may be equated with social failure because of the collective understanding of what it means to be a woman in Taiwanese society (see Crane 2004).

It is a 'solipsistic error' to reduce the explanation of the social structure to the commonsensical perspective of a single individual, i.e. the individual experience (King 1999: 217). Undeniably, individual experience matters. Nevertheless, it is only through interaction with other people that we learn how to meet those social expectations and this is the vital condition for the individual to develop his or her self. Humans draw on available stocks of knowledge in order to make sense of their own (religious and gendered) experience. If we view the individual as facing external, autonomous reality instead of social context which is nothing more than 'interacting networks of individuals' (King 1999: 219), we end up with the notion of society and the (single) individual, not society and a plurality of individuals. One person's action is only made meaningful through their interactions with other members of the group. To render action meaningful, an individual must assign it a meaning by referring to the collectively shared understandings, not their individual perspective.[6] The danger of prioritising habitus over practice and positing it as autonomous of social relations is that it leads to excusing social inequalities like poverty by presenting them as objective, therefore nobody's responsibility (King 1999: 222). Similarly, if we argue that an individual faces God and his choices in every stage of their life, we can easily slip into assuming a fatalistic account of agency that very much resembles Bourdieu's 'love of destiny'. Things are so and not otherwise because the habitus is so and not otherwise and there is nothing we can do about it except embrace it and make the most of it. This is not to deny the existence of 'background conditions which cannot be reduced to their micro dimensions' (King 1999: 223). We may

---

invalid in the eyes of the Jewish law (Glicksman 2006: 300–302).

[6]   Opponents of this view would argue that interpretive sociologists commit the 'epistemic fallacy' – confusing the knowledge of reality with the way reality is (see Archer 2000: 469). The interpretive tradition is solipsistic in its account of the social world because it somehow grants individuals permission to make whatever they wish of social reality as long as their understanding can be somehow coordinated with that of other people. Nonetheless, such a critique fails to acknowledge the fact that this common understanding constitutes the constraint the interpretive theory points to and that it is produced during interaction, not coordinated prior to it. The world is not disallowed any role as a regulator of the assertions that can be made about it, however the major constraint and regulator of what can and cannot be asserted about the world is the social context, which is the sum of interactions between individuals (King 1999: 220).

well use the term 'structure' to describe these conditions but only if by structure we mean the interactions of a variety of people in different historical times and locations, and not a god-like metaphysical entity which hovers above individuals 'or is more than the sum of all individuals and their interactions' (King 1999: 223). This understanding of structure, as exhibited in the concept of habitus, is beneficial for the study of religion and gender because it allows us to see both as embedded in mutually sustained social relations and understandings of particular social groups. Such an interpretive approach to social reality makes it possible to understand God as a relational concept, contained within society, rather than beyond it. This does not entail ignoring people's beliefs in abstract powers but it does point to a sociologically valid account of the divine. As belief is central to the study of religious groups and individuals, it cannot be dismissed, but the emphasis should be on how the divine is drawn upon by individuals in the context of their groups, communities and in relation to non-religious fields.

Studying Religion and Gender with (and against) Bourdieu

Gender and sexuality are two of the most obvious social divisions and social markers of division. Gender is omnipresent and dictates the rule of identity and engagement in all social situations to a large extent. The difficulty of studying gender lies in its simultaneous rigidity and fluidity, which are both contextual. In the manner of a chemical substance that changes when coming into contact with other substances, gender manifests itself differently depending on the social situation but, unlike many social roles, it never entirely disappears from view, or loses its relevance. Therefore, the act of 'doing gender' can be best described as 'extending an analogy', not as acting out a gender rule as an isolated individual (Barnes 1995: 55). Gender order is a self-fulfilling prophecy on a large scale: ordered and yet open to a wide variety of interpretations within the constraints of 'regulated liberties' (Bourdieu 1991: 102). Religion is a social structure which both affects and is affected by gender. The relationship is this of mutual susceptibility, which makes it particularly difficult to analyse because we are dealing with two social properties that are both relatively stable and yet in the state of constant flux.

There are several possibilities for the interaction between gender and religion: religions remain overwhelmingly male-dominated, with women leaving at a fast pace; women gain access to positions of power and authority but religious institutions become feminised at all levels; new forms of spirituality are set up by women and for women (for example, the overwhelming majority of women in holistic spiritualities as shown by Heelas and Woodhead (2005)). The potential for wide structural changes comes from the internal inconsistencies and contradictions in the individuals' own biographies and in the system they inhabit. Mere awareness of gender divisions and inequalities in religion will not suffice to effect transformation, however. Collective efforts, not individual action, lead to gradual transformation of seemingly monolithic structures. The women who engage in subversive practices in private make a difference to their personal lives but their actions only count if they have tangible social consequences.

Paradoxically, the sociological critique of heteronormativity means that sexual identities and experiences that fall into the realm of the socially normative are presented as relatively unproblematic and thus remain unexplored (Smart 1996; Jackson 1999; van Hooff 2011). Sonya Sharma's work fills this gap to a certain extent. Her elegantly written and data-rich book *Good Girls, Good Sex* (2011) explores the constant negotiation between oppression and liberation which young Protestant women engage in on a daily basis. Her study is notable for its focus on (predominantly) heterosexual Christian women and shows the struggle between religious values and personal lives. Sharma's research participants highlighted the power of accountability to their religious tradition, as well as to their fellow Christians, that can provide a comfortable buffer against the oversexualised and secular mainstream society. At the same time this accountability restricts their individual sexual freedom and choices. Perhaps the most striking aspect of this study is the evident difficulty of separating religious and sexual identities – the two are locked together and mutually susceptible against the wider background of the church community. This is where Bourdieu's concept of 'split habitus' (*habitus clivé*) becomes a useful tool of analysis. As social identities are fashioned out of a whole range of, often contradictory, experiences, so the habitus is made up of conflicting elements (Bennett 2007). The young Christian women described in Sharma's study are acutely aware of the inequalities and injustices of some religious structures and institutions, and yet constituted by them at the same time. All the ingredients necessary for the persistence of the androcentric order are in place: the idea of being a good Christian girl is deeply internalised in the bodily hexis and safeguarded by feelings of shame and guilt; symbolic violence is exercised by the women themselves as they monitor their thoughts during sexual encounters and punish their bodies afterwards (one of Sharma's interviewees self-harmed after sexual encounters as a means of purification); and masculine domination is preserved and reinforced by the women in the church community (Sharma 2011: 52–67). A particularly poignant example of the power of communal accountability is the way in which young women police their own behaviour in anticipation of being scrutinised by others. 'A Christian leader said that she could tell if a girl had had sex, just by the way she carried herself. Whether or not this was true, it caused me to monitor my behaviour lest it be questioned otherwise', confessed one of Sharma's young participants (2011: 53). Others recall feelings of guilt accompanying sexual encounters, even those within marriage, and having to 'unlearn the shame' associated with sex (Sharma 2011: 69). It is clear from Sharma's study that the interaction between religion and gender in this case is not driven by an overarching social structure but by collective norms that are drawn upon and enacted by real individuals in everyday life scenarios. In particular, the concepts of shame and 'good versus bad Christian girl' operate in exactly the same way as honour games among the Kabyles. Shame is not something the individual woman experiences independently of the community she is part of. But neither is this shame unchallenged in light of changing circumstances. Sharma cites an amusing and revealing anecdote of an attempt to combine Christianity and female expression of sexuality in a religiously acceptable manner where a husband buys his wife a Bible and a vibrator for her birthday (2011: 86). The combination of these two seemingly incompatible items created consternation for the 'good Christian girl' but also demonstrates how the rules dictated by her habitus can be manipulated and interpreted to accommodate the social changes in women's view of their own sexuality. If masculine domination was as rigid as the concept of the habitus implies and women 'imbibed androcentric values' unreflexively (Grenfell 2004: 181), this scenario would be impossible. In a way, Bourdieu understates the role of reflexivity in the structuring of the habitus, except for allowing it in rare instances of crisis when the synchronicity between the habitus and the field is disturbed (1977: 83, 1990: 108). However, if we see the constraint not in habitus as a structure but rather in the shared communal agreement that is necessarily open to renegotiation and subtle alteration, change in the religious shaping of the gender order becomes a possibility.

Shereen El Feki's exploration of sexual lives in Egypt provides even more instructive examples of the centrality of social relations to the study of religion and gender (2013). El Feki offers a complex and multi-faceted account of the negotiations and changing values in a society that continues to be governed by strict, in comparison to western standards, religious rules and regulations. While premarital sex is strictly forbidden by the Qur'an, Egyptian men and women find ingenious ways of circumventing the obstacles by, amongst other things, using the Internet for 'virtual cruising' (El Feki 2013: 101), or entering pleasure marriages (*zawaj mut'a*) which have a time-limit and serve the purpose of legitimising sexual practices outside of official marriage (El Feki 2013:

43). However, the power of masculine domination exercised through strong communal understandings of female honour and respectability produces different consequences of such negotiations for men and women. Unsurprisingly, it is the women who pay the heaviest price for departing from the gender order because their honour is 'like a match; it only lights once' (El Feki 2013: 93). Thus, while for men such deviations from the rule remain acceptable on the whole and rarely influence their life in the long run, women have to resort to behind-the-scenes practices that re-light the match of honour in public. Hymen repair is considered shameful and costly in Egypt but at the same time gynaecologists who perform the surgeries are sympathetic towards young women looking for help because they are aware of the social consequences for 'unrepaired' brides (El Feki 2013: 117). The point I am trying to make here is that the sheer complexity of the relationship between religion and the gender order in a place like modern-day Egypt clearly demonstrates that it is the virtuoso agency of those involved in shaping the social order that is the key to understanding the nature of social reality. If we wished to explain the manipulations of these rules by referring to the habitus as mechanically imposing itself on individuals, no such manipulation would be possible in the first place because habitus 'insists on a complete fit between the individual's practices and his objective circumstances' (King 2000: 430). The case of sexual negotiation in Egypt shows that we are dealing with skilful social actors who have at their disposal a wide array of courses of action but they are guided by their sense of what is appropriate in light of their group membership. For example, the decision of whether to perform hymen repair on a young female patient is not determined by the religious, or even cultural, habitus. The practitioner improvises on the spot because her knowledge of her own social context is so profound that she can easily accommodate unforeseen contingencies.

Towards an Ontology of Social Relations in the Study of Gender and Religion

Pierre Bourdieu's work on gender does not suggest itself automatically as a useful framework for studying the intersection of religion, gender and sexuality. Indeed, there is a wealth of theoretical approaches by gender scholars who may be better suited to the task. However, I believe that Bourdieu's theory of masculine domination and his general approach to analysing power relations can help us understand the possibility of change in the gender order, as well as the reasons for its relative durability and rigidity. For this to happen, however, every historical period needs to be examined separately to establish 'the system of agents, and institutions – family, church, state, educational system, etc., which, with different weights and different means at different times, have helped to remove the relations of masculine domination more or less completely from history' (Bourdieu 2001: 83).

The late modern world is complex and women are both objects and subjects who participate in the political struggle. This is why Bourdieu's theory of practice constitutes a fruitful approach to studying gender relations in religious fields. Moving away from the habitus to collectively created practices and agency of female, male (and other) virtuosi goes some way to produce a more convincing and all-encompassing account of gender and religion in late modernity. Habitus can be understood as transcending the individual/structure dualism but only in the sense that individuals are active in the world where structure refers to nothing more than the historically positioned interactions between groups of individuals in possession of various amounts of capital, competing in fields of social life where symbolic violence is exercised but also resisted and challenged. Curiously, Bourdieu finishes *Masculine Domination* with a utopian postscript on love as a liberating force from oppression and extreme individualism. He posits love as the exception 'to the law of masculine domination' (Bourdieu 2001: 109) and a salvation of sorts for both the dominant and the dominated. Engaging in the act of loving requires both individuals to eschew the relationship of domination and come together in 'an act of free alienation that is definitely asserted' through uttering 'I love you' (Bourdieu 2001: 112). This postscript could be read as patronising and utopian because Bourdieu ignores the fact that 'being in love' itself is never a neutral act that happens outside dominant discourses and scripts on intimate relationships. On the other hand, the passage also points to the universal human potential for collective creation of the Durkheimian 'soul' and subsequent re-definition of situations individuals find themselves in. The task of researching the intersection of gender, sexuality and religion poses a number of difficulties because all elements continuously shift internally and in relation to one another in a manner of images in a kaleidoscope. In order to produce a most complete and balanced account of such shifts, we must pay attention to the sum of historical interactions between the parts, instead of assuming a reified structure that rules over and determines all of them.

References

Alexander, J. (1995). The Reality of Reduction: The Failed Synthesis of Pierre Bourdieu, in *Fin de Siècle Social Theory*, ed. J.C. Alexander. London: Verso, pp. 128–217.

Archer, M. (2000). For Structure: its Reality, Properties and Powers: A Reply to Anthony King. *Sociological Review*, 48(3), 464–72.

Barnes, B. (1995). *The Elements of Social Theory*. London: UCL Press.

Beauvoir, S. de (1997 [1949]). *The Second Sex*. London: Verso.

Bennett, T. (2007). *Habitus Clivé*: Aesthetics and Politics in the Work of Pierre Bourdieu. *New Literary History*, 38(1), 201–28.

Bourdieu, P. (1977). *Outline of a Theory of Practice*. Cambridge: Cambridge University Press.

Bourdieu, P. (1979). *Algeria 1960: The Disenchantment of the World: The Sense of Honour: The Kabyle House or the World Reversed: Essays*. Cambridge: Cambridge University Press.

Bourdieu, P. (1990). *The Logic of Practice*. Cambridge: Polity Press.

Bourdieu, P. (1991). *Language and Symbolic Power*. Cambridge: Polity Press.

Bourdieu, P. (1998). *La Domination Masculine*. Paris: Seuil.

Bourdieu, P. (2000). *Pascalian Meditations*. Cambridge: Polity Press.

Bourdieu, P. (2001). *Masculine Domination*. Cambridge: Polity Press.

Bourdieu, P. and Wacquant, L. (1992). *An Invitation to Reflexive Sociology*. Cambridge: Polity Press.

Butler, J. (1990). *Gender Trouble: Feminism and the Subversion of Identity*. London: Routledge.

Crane, H. (2004). Resisting Marriage and Renouncing Womanhood: The Choice of Taiwanese Buddhist Nuns. *Critical Asian Studies*, 36(4), 265–84.

Crane, H. (2007). Becoming a Nun, Becoming a Man: Taiwanese Buddhist Nuns' Gender Transformation. *Religion*, 37(2), 117–32.

Dillabough, J. (2010). Class, Culture and the 'Predicaments of Masculine Domination': Encountering Pierre Bourdieu. *British Journal of Sociology of Education*, 25(4), 409–506.

El Feki, S. (2013). *Sex and the Citadel: Intimate Life in a Changing Arab World*. London: Random House.

Fowler, B. (2003). Reading Pierre Bourdieu's *Masculine Domination*: Notes Towards an Intersectional Analysis of Gender, Culture and Class. *Cultural Studies*, 17(3/4), 468–94.

Glicksman, J. (2006). Almost, But Not Quite: The Failure of the New York's Get Statute. *Family Court Review*, 44(2), 300–315.

Grenfell, M. (2004). *Pierre Bourdieu: Agent Provocateur*. London: Continuum.
Hakim, C. (2011). *Honey Money: The Power of Erotic Capital*. London: Allen Lane.
Heelas, P. and Woodhead, L. (2005). *The Spiritual Revolution: Why Religion is Giving Way to Spirituality*. Oxford: Blackwell.
Jackson, S. (1999). *Heterosexuality in Question*. London: Sage.
Jenkins, R. (1982). Pierre Bourdieu and the Reproduction of Determinism. *Sociology*, 16(2), 270–281.
King, A. (1999). Against Structure: A Critique of Morphogenetic Social Theory. *The Sociological Review*, 47(2), 199–277.
King, A. (2000). Thinking with Bourdieu Against Bourdieu: A 'Practical' Critique of the Habitus. *Sociological Theory*, 18(3), 417–33.
King, A. (2004). *The Structure of Social Theory*. London: Routledge.
Krais, B. (2006). Gender, Sociological Theory and Bourdieu's Sociology of Practice. *Theory, Culture & Society*, 23(6), 119–34.
Lovell, T. (2002). Thinking Feminism with and against Bourdieu. *Feminist Theory*, 1(1), 11–32.
Mottier, V. (2002). Masculine Domination: Gender and Power in Bourdieu's Writings. *Feminist Theory*, 3(3), 345–59.
Paechter, C.F. (2006). Power, Knowledge and Embodiment in Communities of Sex/Gender Practice. *Women's Studies International Forum*, 29(1), 13–26.
Sandberg, L. (2013). *Lean In: Women, Work and the Will to Lead*. New York: WH Allen.
Schatzki, T. (1997). Practices and Actions: A Wittgensteinian Critique of Bourdieu and Giddens. *Philosophy of the Social Sciences*, 27(3), 283–308.
Sharma, S. (2011). *Good Girls, Good Sex: Women Talk about Church and Sexuality*. Winnipeg: Fernwood Publishing.
Silva, E. and Warde, A. (eds) (2010). *Cultural Analysis and Bourdieu's Legacy: Settling Accounts and Developing Alternatives*. London: Routledge.
Smart, C. (1996). Collusion, Collaboration and Confession: Moving beyond the Heterosexuality Debate, in *Theorising Heterosexuality: Telling it Straight*, ed. D. Richardson. Buckingham and Philadelphia: Open University Press, pp. 161–77.
Truong, N. and Weill, N. (2012). A Decade After His Death Pierre Bourdieu Stands Tall. *Guardian*, 21 February [Online]. Available at www.theguardian.com/world/2012/feb/21/pierre-bourdieu-philosophy-most-quoted [accessed: 10 September 2013].
Van Hooff, J. (2011). Rationalising Inequality: Heterosexual Couples' Explanations and Justifications for the Continuing Division of Domestic

Labour along Traditionally Gendered Lines. *Journal of Gender Studies*, 20(1), 19–30.

Wallace, M. (2003). A Disconcerting Brevity: Pierre Bourdieu's *Masculine Domination*. *Postmodern Culture*, 13(3). Available at http://pmc.iath.virginia.edu/issue.503/13.3wallace.html [accessed: 12 September 2013].

West, C. and Zimmerman, D. (1987). Doing Gender. *Gender and Society*, 1, 125–51.

Witz, A. (2004). Anamnesis and Amnesis in Bourdieu's Work: The Case for a Feminist Anamnesis, in *Feminism after Bourdieu*, ed. L. Adkins and B. Skeggs. Oxford: Blackwell, pp. 211–23.

Index

Aborigines, Australia 5, 6–7, 51
Abrahamic religions 75, 79–80, 87
action 246, 249, 251
aestheticization of religion 12–13, 179–80, 181–5, 191–3, 194; *see also* Christmas concerts
aesthetics 180–181, 199, 207, 216
agency 76–7, 169–70, 215, 216, 248, 249, 250, 251
agenda-setting theory 35, 41–3
Alston, W.P. 168
Altglas, V. 90, 92
American fundamentalism 216
attitude surveys 34
Axial Age 11, 53, 55, 58–9, 60, 61–3, 66, 67

Bax, M. 83, 106
Beck, U. 9–10, 165n4
Becket, T. 120
Beckford, J.A. 11, 41, 225
Bellah, R.N. 52, 53, 55, 60, 63, 66, 67
    Confucianism 55, 59, 61
    religion 59, 68
Benjamin, W. 3, 39, 144–6, 192, 203
Berger, P.L. 22, 37, 234, 237
Bhambra, G.K. 154
Bloch, E. 145
body pedagogics 205, 215–16
Bourdieu, P. 13, 37, 243–6, 247, 248–9, 250, 253, 254, 255–6
Brazil 94, 95–6, 99, 100–101, 231
Buddhism 4–5, 60, 62, 63, 251

Capetian dynasty 112–13, 114
capitalism 3, 52, 64, 67, 112, 144–6, 224
Carolingian Empire 112, 113–14

Carranza, B. 89
castellans 109, 113
cathedrals 120, 122
Catholicism 81, 82–3, 84–5, 88–90, 92, 98, 99, 235, 250–251
CDA (critical discourse analysis) 13, 223, 224, 225, 226, 227, 228–30, 231–3, 234–7
charismatic movements 60, 76, 88–9, 90, 189
Charismatic Renewal 88–9
China 53, 56–7, 60, 63–5, 67, 167
    Confucianism 4, 53, 55, 57, 59, 60, 61, 62, 63, 64–5
Chinese religions 53–4, 56, 57, 61, 62
Christianity 4–5, 12–13, 20, 54, 57, 60, 61–2, 79–80, 81–2, 101
    Norway 181, 182–4, 190, 192, 195
    St John's 199, 206, 208, 213, 217
Christmas concerts 12, 179, 185, 186, 187–9, 190–191, 193, 194–5
Church of Norway 179, 182–3, 185
civilizing process 106–9, 110–113, 118, 122–3
Collins, R. 190
Confucianism 4, 53, 55, 57, 59, 60, 61, 62, 63, 64–5
critical discourse analysis, *see* CDA
critical sociology of religion 223, 224, 225, 226, 233–7
Crusades 109–10, 116–18
cults 79, 99, 227, 228

Danielsen, A. 191
Dawson, A. 12
de Certeau, M. 201–3, 209
discourse 225–8, 230–231, 233, 237

Duby, G. 113, 116
Durkheim, É. 4, 37, 54, 56, 58, 59, 67, 68, 119–20, 131, 138
  religion 5–7, 8, 33, 51, 55–6, 62, 66, 223

Egypt 204, 216–17, 254–5
Eisenstadt, S.N. 53, 55, 60, 154–5, 161–2
El Feki, S. 254
Elias, N. 12, 54, 105, 106, 107, 109–10, 113, 116, 123
  civilizing process 107–8, 110–113, 118, 122–3
Engler, S. 227
ethnomethodology 41–2
evangelical churches
  St John's, London 199–200, 211–16
    Christianity 199, 206, 208, 213, 217
    listening 200, 206–11, 212–14, 216, 217
  see also Latin America

Fairclough, N. 227, 228–30, 232, 235
faith communities 28, 181, 190–191, 192
femininity 244, 245, 246, 247–8, 249; *see also* gender order
Finland 232–3
Foucault, M. 37, 41, 205, 228
Fourie, E. 153, 157, 160
Frisby, D. 131, 132, 133
fundamentalism 21–2, 216
Fundamentalism Project 21–2

Gaonkar, D.P. 158, 159–60, 164
gender 13, 42, 43, 235, 243–5, 248, 250–251, 252–3, 256
gender order 243–7, 248–9, 252, 254–5
Giddens, A. 37, 51, 162
Gorski, P. 11
Granet, M. 56, 66
Gutierrez, G. 91

Habermas, J. 31, 41

habitus 244, 245–6, 247, 249, 251–2, 253, 254, 255, 256
  medieval 107, 108, 110, 118, 122, 123
Heelas, P. and Woodhead, L. 43
hegemony 228, 229–30, 232, 233, 237
Hinduism 61, 62, 63
Hirschkind, C. 203, 204–5, 209, 216–17
Hjelm, T. 13
Hodne, H. 182–3

ICLARS (International Consortium for Law and Religion Studies) 26
immigration 22
institutionalized religions 68, 75, 76, 79–81, 83, 87
Islam 4–5, 20, 22, 60, 61–2, 68, 79–80, 232, 235, 254–5
Islamic Revival 204–5, 216–17

Jaspers, K. 53, 58, 66
  Axial Age 58–9, 60, 61, 62–3, 67
John Paul II (Pope) 83, 88
Judaism 4–5, 59, 60, 75, 79–81, 85–7, 99, 250

Kabyle society, Algeria 244, 254
Kepel, G. 21

Latin America
  Pentecostalism 11–12, 88, 92–5, 96–7, 98
  Theology of Liberation 76, 90–92
Lazarsfeld, P. 44–5
Leck, R.M. 143
Lehmann, D. 11–12
listening 12, 199, 200–201, 202–6, 216–18
  St John's 200, 206–11, 212–14, 216, 217
Lourdes, France 82, 84, 90
Løvland, M. and Repstad, P. 12
Luther, M. 141
Lynch, G. 11
Lyotard, J.-F. 153

Macedo, E. 97, 100

marriage 245, 250–251, 254–5
Martin, D. 10, 29, 37, 54
Marx, K. 39, 141, 226, 228, 234, 237
　　religion 2–3, 8, 33, 223, 234, 235
masculine domination 244–5, 246, 248–9, 253, 254, 255, 256
masculinity 245, 247–8, 249; *see also* gender order
McKinnon, A.M. 12
mediatization 193, 194, 214, 224–5, 232
medieval habitus 107, 108, 110, 118, 122, 123
Medjugorje, Croatia 83–4
Mellor, P.A. and Shilling, C. 201, 205
Merton, R.K. 44, 45, 47
Mignolo, W. 153–4
modernity 10, 151–2, 153–4, 158–68, 169–70, 171–2, 200, 201
money 130–131, 132–3, 140–143
monopoly mechanism 108, 109, 111, 112, 119, 123
Motak, D. 12
multimodality 186, 194
multiple modernities theory 12, 60, 152, 154–8, 159–60, 161–2, 165–6, 167, 171, 172
music 186, 187, 188, 189–90, 208, 214
mysticism 5, 65, 85

neo-Pentecostal churches 79, 94–5, 98, 100–101
neo-Pentecostalism 76, 92, 93, 98–9, 101
New Age spirituality 43
Nielsen, D.A. 138
normative social theory 35, 38–40, 41
normativity 229, 230
Norway 12, 179, 185, 192–3
　　Christianity 181, 182–4, 190, 192, 195
　　Christmas concerts 12, 179, 186, 187–9, 190–191, 194–5

Occidental religions 65
Olsen, H. 183
Oriental religions 65, 66

Padre Pio, Italy 82–3, 84, 90
pax Dei movement 12, 109, 113, 114–16, 117–18, 119, 121, 122, 123
Peace Councils 109, 114–16, 117–18, 121, 122
Peace of God movement 12, 109, 113, 114–16, 117–18, 119, 121, 122, 123
peasantry 109, 113–14, 115, 121
Pentecostal churches 92–3, 95–8, 99
Pentecostalism 76, 93–4, 95, 183, 189
　　Latin America 11–12, 88, 92–5, 96–7, 98
Pietism 181
piety 56–7, 118, 121, 217
pilgrimage sites 82–4, 90, 120
popular religion 11–12, 75, 76–7, 81–2, 84–6, 87–8, 89–90, 92
Protestantism 5, 41, 66–7, 181, 184, 199, 206

rationalism 5, 181
rationality 38, 43, 44, 201, 204–5, 211–15, 216, 217
religion 1–7, 8, 9–10, 20–23, 24–8, 30–31, 34–5, 45–7, 77
　　Bellah 59, 68
　　Durkheim 5–7, 8, 33, 51, 55–6, 62, 66, 223
　　institutionalized 68, 75, 76, 79–81, 83, 87
　　Marx 2–3, 8, 33, 223, 234, 235
　　popular 11–12, 75, 76–7, 81–2, 84–6, 87–8, 89–90, 92
　　Simmel 130–131, 133–5, 136–8, 139, 140–142
　　Weber 3–5, 8, 33, 51, 52–3, 55, 57, 60, 61, 65–6, 68, 223
religious elite 106, 107, 108, 113, 123–4
RESEP (Religion as aestheticizing practice) 179, 181, 182–4
rituals 4, 5–6, 7, 51, 59, 75, 77–8, 79, 81–2, 92–3, 190
Roetz, H. 60–61, 67
Rosati, M. and Stoeckl, K. 156

Rosenwein, B. 107–8
royal mechanism 108, 109, 111, 112–13, 119, 123

sacramental mechanism 108–9, 119, 120, 122
Schmidt, V.H. 157, 159, 160, 164
secular elite 107, 113
secularisation 10–11, 19, 20–21, 23–4, 28–30, 42, 46, 76, 90, 92, 236–7
Sharma, S. 253–4
Shilling, C. 139
Simmel, G. 12, 51, 129, 131–2, 138–9, 145
    money 130–131, 132–3, 140–143
    religion 130–131, 133–5, 136–8, 139, 140–142
social semiotics 185–6, 194
social theory 33, 34, 35–6, 37–8, 39–40, 41, 44, 45, 47
society, theory of 129, 131–2
sociology of religion 1, 2–6, 7–11, 19–20, 28–30, 33–5, 51, 58, 67–8, 152, 169–70
    critical 223, 224, 225–6, 233–7
Socrel 7–8, 11
South Africa 95, 97
Southwold, M. 168
Strhan, A. 12, 13
structure 169–70, 248–9, 250–252, 256
supernatural 75, 76, 77, 78–9, 80–81, 83, 84, 87
symbolic violence 244, 245–6, 247, 248, 253, 256

tactical religion 89–90
'technologies of the self' 205–6
Theology of Liberation 76, 90–92
Thiery, D. 109, 121
Torah study 85–6
totemism 5, 6–7, 51

Truce of God 115–16, 118, 119, 122
Trzebiatowska, M. 13
Turner, B.S. 11, 36n5, 40, 104, 133, 216, 217

United States (US) 2, 19, 28, 54, 68, 92, 171, 213
Universal Church of the Kingdom of God
    Brazil 94, 95–6, 99, 100–101, 231
    South Africa 95, 97
Urapmin, Papua New Guinea 79, 100
Urban II (Pope) 117–18

van Krieken, R. 106–7
van Wyck, I. 97
violence 53, 54, 59–60, 63, 67, 105, 106, 109–11, 116–19, 120–122, 123–4
    symbolic 244, 245–6, 247, 248, 253, 256

Wagner, F. 146
Wagner, P. 157, 162
WCC (World Council of Churches) 23
Weber, M. 37, 43, 51, 58, 59, 65, 67, 144, 146, 233
    China 53, 63–5
    Chinese religions 53–4, 56–7
    Confucianism 53, 55, 57, 61, 62, 63, 64–5
    religion 3–5, 8, 33, 51, 52–3, 55, 57, 60, 61, 65–6, 68, 223
welfare 26, 28
Woodhead, L. 11, 87–8, 89–90
Woodhead, L. and Heelas, P. 189
World Council of Churches, *see* WCC

Yack, B. 160–161

Zande 79
zeitgeist metaphors 35, 40, 41